LOGISTICS SYSTEMS ANALYSIS, REVISED EDITION

Frank H. Mossman
Paul Bankit
Omar Keith Helferich

University Press of America™

BADADUQ

PREFACE

The purpose of this book is to provide students and practitioners in the discipline of logistics with an overview of the analytical methods which are used in the planning for total logistics systems. The book is aimed primarily at graduate students desirous of having an understanding of the tools necessary for logistics planning and control.

The book is divided into two parts. The first part establishes the basic framework of logistic systems. The second part presents methods for total logistic systems analysis.

The basic framework of logistic systems is developed in the first four chapters. In Chapter 1 the evolution of the logistics concept is related to systems theory; the use of models of varying complexities is discussed as a means of controlling and regulating logistic systems. The combination of logistics systems components into the concentration and dispersion systems is analyzed in Chapter 2 with a discussion of the resulting cost characteristics. Since an important part of any logistics system is the location of the physical facilities, the theory of retail store location and warehouse terminal locations is discussed in Chapter 3. The information system necessary for logistic systems planning and control is presented in an operational form in Chapter 4. Thus, the student and/or practitioner is presented with the basic framework for receiving information on market change, combining the component parts of the logistic system required to meet this external change, and the required accounting information necessary for planning and controlling the system on an on-line real time basis.

Part two, the major portion of the book, is devoted to an analysis and application of the analytical methods for total logistic systems. Graph methodologies and applications are discussed in Chapter 5. The specific methods discussed are PERT, critical path, dynamic programming, and linear programming. Specific examples are given to illustrate the uses of each of these tools in logistic systems planning. Systems network theory, a relatively new concept in the logistics systems field, is presented in Chapter 6 with an application of the methodology. Although systems network theory is not yet used on a wide scale by logistic systems planners, its potential is such that it is included in this book because of its great possible uses in the near future.

The use of simulation in the modeling of logistic systems is analyzed at length in Chapter 7. Strategic planning through static simulation is presented through the following models: Kuehn and Hamburger, Shycon and Maffei, and the Systems Research Incorporated distribution planning model. Tactical/operational planning for the firm through the use of dynamic simulation is developed through the use of several dynamic simulation models. The specific dynamic simulation models which are analyzed include the industrial dynamics model, the distribution system simulator, and the LREPS operational planning model.

In Chapter 8 the emphasis is on the application of selected methodologies to logistic systems analysis. A managerial guide for systems design is presented in the earlier part of the chapter. Within this framework an application is presented for dynamic programming, mixed integer linear programming, static simulation, dynamic simulation, and a simulation utilizing both static and dynamic models. Some suggestions and considerations regarding modeling techniques and future utilization of models are used to conclude the chapter.

TABLE OF CONTENTS

LIST OF FIGURES

CHAPTER I

GENERAL SYSTEMS

Evolution of the Logistics Concept

A logistics system is the logical conceptual arrangement of
the functional areas of an operation which moves goods and persons
from one location to another. It is designed to provide managers
with better means for planning and controlling the adaptability of
their respective systems. The adaptation process consists essentially of changes in the number of relationships important to the
firm, and the managerial skill to devise profitable responses.

During the first half of the Twentieth Century, the three
Rs of intercity common carrier transportation--rates, rules,
regulation--covered adequately the field of logistics. By the
late 1950s and early 1960s, however, this sphere had come to en-
compass other subject matter areas, particularly plant and warehouse location, packaging and containerization, and inventory size
and location, all items of expense directly related to, and/or a
part of, the system for the movement of goods.

This concern with the total costs of moving the product
through raw material accumulation, manufacture, and distribution
came to be known as the total cost approach to logistics systems.
As logistics broadened in scope, quantitative measurement was
applied increasingly to each of the component parts, in order to
arrive at uniquely determined goals. While some attempts at cost
trade-offs between component parts of the system have been made,
these should be viewed as crude, initial attempts to arrive at
total systems goals.

The technological change of the 1950s and early 1960s was
traumatic for those who failed to acquire the new knowledge. For

those who did, personal opportunities to advance in corporate management levels were enhanced.

New techniques continue to evolve in the specialized areas of logistics, but the interrelationship of these areas has not kept pace. We have specialists developing new knowledge, but we need to step up our efforts to get these specialists into communication with each other.

This problem is not unique to the field of logistics. It is true of most disciplines which grow in knowledge, subdivide, regroup, and become concerned with problems of communication among their component parts.

General Systems Theory

Many feel this problem transcends any one discipline. Solutions have been sought through a search for a general systems theory capable of handling interdisciplinary problems. Kenneth Boulding sees the problem thus:

> If the interdisciplinary movement is not . . . to lose that sense of form and structure which is the 'discipline' involved in the various separate disciplines, it should develop a structure of its own. . . .
>
> The first approach is to look over the empirical universe and to pick out certain general phenomena which are found in many different disciplines, and to seek to build up general theoretical models relevant to these phenomena. The second approach is to arrange the empirical fields in a hierarchy of complexity of organization of their basic 'individual' or unit of behavior, and to try to develop a level of abstraction appropriate to each.[1]

These two approaches are complementary, and the ones which we should use in this book. The phenomena which are common to some of the areas of logistics will be investigated with a view to developing models which have some commanality and transfer from one area to another. For example, the principle of fixed and

---

[1]Kenneth E. Boulding, "General Systems Theory--The Skeleton of Science," Modern Systems Research for the Behavioral Scientist ed. by Walter Buckley (Chicago: Aldine Publishing Co., 1968), p. 5.

variable costs can be applied throughout the entire field of logistics. Models will be developed using this principle. There will be many variations in application, but the principle will have some universality.

The second approach may require a variety of models, ranging from simplistic to very complex. For example, where the problem involves determination of average cost on a single commodity between two points where the average load is always the same, average cost is simply $\frac{\text{total cost}}{\text{total miles}}$ = average cost per mile. Other simple measures would work as well in this case. However, for highly complex situations like inventory cost in a food chain, there is a need for very sophisticated model development. The variables of time, variation in turnover, dollar differences per unit, customer traffic, and product substitution demand much higher level of analysis.

Model Search and Organization Theory

The search for models or general phenomena which can be used in different disciplines or subject areas centers around various aspects of the theory of organization. Generally, organization theory deals with the principles of combinatorial arrangements of the components of a particular system to achieve desired goals.

Organization theory has been approached by economists largely from the standpoint of the size of the firm. The factors they have considered have been market size, market uncertainty, and management limitations. Market size and uncertainty will be considered in some detail in later chapters. At this point we are concerned with the exercise of the planning and control functions by organization managements.

Planning and control of logistics systems may be centralized or decentralized. Centralization may be at one geographic point, or performed by a central group. Decentralization concerns planning

and control done at many geographic points and/or by several groups
at these points.

The literature of business organization has well documented
considerations of centralization versus decentralization of production facilities. As L. R. Amey states:

> The problem is essentially one of reconciling the need
> for centralization in the interest of unification of policy
> . . . with the need for decentralization of responsibility,
> particularly in the production departments, without which
> inefficiency is likely to increase because of remote control,
> 'bureaucracy,' imperfect coordination, and lack of particular
> knowledge.[1]

This reconciliation has resulted in varying kinds of
integration, principally horizontal and vertical. Horizontal
integration denotes units engaged in the production of the same
class of products. Vertical denotes the integration units manufacturing successive product stages; the output of one unit becomes
the input in sequence of productive stages.

Based on this categorization we have the following types
of integration, the letter H or V indicating horizontal or vertical:

1. uniform functions - H
2. divergent functions
    a. joint products - H
    b. further processing of a by product - V
    c. similar processes but different products - H
3. convergent functions
    a. complementary products - V
    b. auxiliary products - V
    c. similar markets - H
4. successive functions - H
5. unrelated functions like conglomerates (neither H nor V).[2]

---

[1]L. R. Amey, The Efficiency of Business Enterprises (New
York: A. M. Kelley, 1970), pp. 116-117.

[2]Ibid., pp. 117-118.

The extent of integration for better management planning and control depends to a considerable extent on the types of production processes to be joined. Beyond this, however, there is a need for a quantitative expression for guidance purposes. A method will be outlined later to develop planned and actual profit by segmental units. Traditionally, the combined units were cost centers to which standard costs were assigned. Comparative cost alone cannot furnish adequate information to determine the efficiency of proposed or actual integration.

Therefore, profit centers will be developed to help consider the market as an integral part of the theory of organization. This will involve defining the basic segmental units of the company for profit planning and control. The management information system should provide all data in terms of these basic segmental units. For each segment, the system would include a market forecast, proposed operation plans and budgets, and control of variances of operations from budgets. Such information on an on-line, real-time basis would enable better planning and control of a logistics system.

There has been progress made in organization theory in other areas, too. The most rigorous work has been done in topology (relational mathematics), cybernetics, and decision theory. From topology has come network theory, which will be useful to interrelate the component parts of alternative organizational systems designed by management. Information theory, derived from cybernetics, will help to provide yardsticks for measuring the organization. Game theory, derived from decision theory, will help to arrive at plans which will serve as guides for action under competitive operating conditions of the proposed systems.

Hierarchies of Model Complexities

There are two broad areas of systems theory. These are:

1. Modeling theory, which deals with the development of a model from the models of the components of a system; and

2. Behavior theory, which is concerned with the use of a systems model to study the behavior of a system in response to changes in the structure of the system.[1]

Modeling theory concerns the procedures involved in obtaining a mathematical description of certain features of classes of systems. One approach is to view the system externally, without concern for internal system operations; this is essentially a "black box" approach. Another approach is to mathematically model the components of a system, look at the patterns of interconnection, and arrive at a total model for the system.

In the "black box" approach, the system is not known structurally; it is modeled on an input-out basis. The format in this case would be a statement of the problem and a statement of $0 = F(I)$, where (0) is some measurable output for the system related to overall measurable system inputs (I). An illustration of this is in capital budgeting problems.

In the flow of funds statement constructed for a given period of time, it is usual to show the sources from which funds come and places to which funds are applied. It is seldom that these are paired or directly related to each other. Rather, the funds are summed together and applications shown separately as deductions. This is not to say that there is an analysis of both outputs and inputs. Analysis is conducted through such techniques as comparative returns on investments, but these

---

[1] For an excellent treatment of the qualitative aspects of systems theory see John Griggs, Evaluating Marketing Change: An Application of System Theory (E. Lansing: Graduate School of Business Administration, Michigan State University, 1970), M.S.U. Division of Research.

generally do not pair a specific output and input unless they are both large and purposely causally related.

In the component modeling approach, we are concerned basically with the analysis and synthesis of networks of functional components that are interacting in some specific and related manner. A simple electrical system is constructed in Figure 1.1 to illustrate this. The components in the system are a comparator (N), a forward amplifier gain (A), and a feedback amplifier gain (P). An excitation signal (i) is fed into the comparator. A feedback signal (u) regulates the response (o) as a function of the error signal (e); e is generated by substracting u from i. Since we can mathematically model each of the components (A, P, N) and their interconnections (i, e, o, u), we combine these components into a total system.

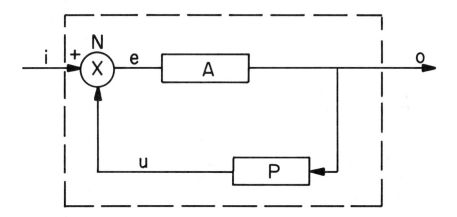

N = Comparator   i = Excitation Signal
A = Forward Amplifier Gain   e = Error Signal
P = Feedback Amplifier Gain   u = Feedback Signal
                                   o = Response Signal

Figure 1.1. Feedback Control System.

We can model the output or response as a function of the excitation or input as we did in the "black box" approach. The difference at this point is that we can include everything inside the black box and express these relationships mathematically.

In the component modeling approach, the format of analysis would be as follows:

1. Statement of the problem
2. Identification of the components in the system
3. Statement of the interaction pattern of the components
4. Definition of measurement units
5. Modeling of each of the components
6. Joining the components into a systems model.

The nature of the problem will determine the specific format of the modeling steps. Theoretically, there is no limit to the number of components that can be included in a system. It may be as simple or as complex as the problem, time, and available funds permit. This procedure follows the suggestion of Rapaport and Horvath:

> Analysis is an attempt to understand a complexity by examining its constituent parts. The parts being simpler, they are supposedly more amenable to understanding. The idea of analysis, then, is to understand the working of the parts.[1]

Since the component modeling approach is concerned with the analysis and synthesis of networks, let us proceed to an understanding of these terms. In network analysis we are concerned with determining the response, given the excitation and the network. If from Figure 1.1 if we know i and the network, then we would be interested in the determination of o. In network synthesis, the given excitation and desired response are used to develop the network; if from Figure 1.1 we know i and o, we would use these to develop the network.

---

[1]Anatol Rapaport and William J. Horvath, "Thoughts on Organization Theory," Modern Systems Research for the Behavioral Scientist, ed. by Walter Buckley (Chicago: Aldine Publishing Co., 1968), p. 71.

In the electrical field, where network theory had its earliest development and applications, the excitation and response functions normally would be time variant voltages and currents. When applying some of the principles of network theory to logistics, force (or propensity) and <u>flow</u> will be used to denote relevant variables in the network.

In electrical network applications, the excitation and response functions are handled either in the time domain or the frequency domain, and there are very well developed mathematical tools available to translate the information from one domain to the other. This is done primarily to facilitate the handling of the transformation. Similar translations or transformations are available for problems in logistics.

Network Graph Theory

Network theory has a highly powerful off-shoot called "network graph theory," or simply "graph theory."[1] Graph theory provides simple, accessible, and powerful tools for constructing models and solving problems concerning discrete arrangements of objects. In either analysis or synthesis of complex systems there are numerous problems that pertain to specific configurations of specific components. These systems include such wide ranging problems as industrial scheduling processes, PERT and critical-path analysis, communication systems, and information transmission. For such diverse and extensive application, graph theory offers combinatorial construction techniques for finding the appropriate solutions, which often are quite different and simpler than the arithmetic or algebraic computational approach through the equations of classical analysis.

---

[1] R. G. Busacker and T. L. Saaty, Finite Graphs and Networks: An Introduction with Applications (New York: McGraw-Hill, 1965), Chapter 1.

10

By definition, a graph is a set of points known as vertices connected by a set of lines known as edges. If the graph is a set of points interconnected by a set of non-intersecting continuous curves it is known as a "geometric graph."[1] If the set of edges of a graph represents components and the vertices represent the interfaces between these components, the graph is known as a "systems graph." Similarly graphs drawn in two-dimensional Euclidean space are called "planar graphs." Graphs can also be "directed" or "undirected" and "finite" or "infinite."

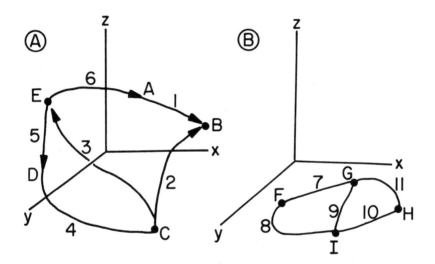

x-z plane contains points A, B
x-y plane contains points C, F, G, H, I
y-z plane contains points E, D

Figure 1.2. Illustrations of Graphs.

[1]Frank H. Mossman and James P. Hynes, Systems Theory: Approach to Mathematical Modeling (Braintree, Mass.: D. H. Mark Publishing Co., 1968), pp. 8-10.

In Figure 1.2A we have points in all three planes. Each edge is directed from one point to another, and all points are joined. This is a directed, finite, non-planar graph. In Figure 1.2B, all points are in one plane, the edges are not directed, and all points are joined; this is an undirected, finite, planar graph.

In logistics, systems graphs of different kinds are used extensively to characterize the systems. Analyses can be made of these graphs with network theory techniques.

Control and Regulation of a System

A four-step approach has been utilized in logistics systems methodology:

1. To establish a need for a more systematic consideration of the various parts of logistics systems
2. To establish systems theory as the means for this holistic treatment
3. To consider organization theory as a basis for spatial organization
4. To introduce systems theory, including graph theory and network representations

It has been stated that this approach is aimed at providing better means of controlling and planning the adaptability of systems. Management must be skillful enough in planning and controlling its operations to identify the components, measure them, model them, and combine them into a system that can operate within the economic environment, as defined by the firm.

This adaptation skill has been classified as planning and control by (1) error; (2) rule; and (3) purpose. Systems are error-controlled when the results of their behavior return to them as a signal to control their subsequent behavior. Control by rule uses similar successes of the past as the basis for current behavior. Control by purpose selects a behavior pattern because it is likely to have a foreseen and desired result.

Certainly all of these control processes will have to be used at some point in defining the firm's most favorable combination of markets, skills, and resources. The decision process means making choices between acceptable alternatives. This is an extremely difficult task. At times one may have to use the "black box" approach; at other extremes one may be fortunate enough to have the resources to apply the systems concepts to problem solutions.

CHAPTER 2

LOGISTICS OF DISTRIBUTION SYSTEMS

The Societal Environment in Which
Logistics Systems Operate

The level of economic development in any society can be
analyzed through the interactions which occur between human wants
and needs, human technical knowledge and skills, and available
natural resources. Conceptually this would appear as a triangular
interrelationship (Figure 2.1).

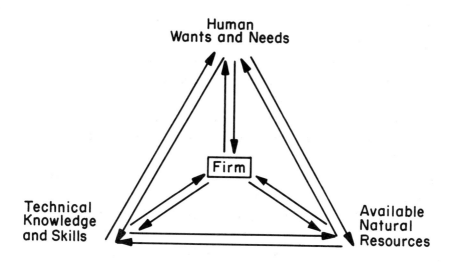

Figure 2.1. Interactions in an Economic System.

The triangular interaction in each of the three areas can
start at any one or more corners of the triangle and cause a change

in the other two. For example, a change in the level of human wants and desires of any sector of society will require new levels of utilization of existing skills, or require new ones to be brought into being. This new level of productive skill will require a new level of resource utilization.

The chart indicates that the change can work in either direction from a given corner. This is meant to signify that any corner of the triangle can cause change and will also react to change. For example, a newly discovered natural resource can increase the availability of materials and make possible the attainment of a new level of human wants and needs. Thus, any area is capable of both creating and adapting to change.

The extent to which the economic system is sufficiently flexible to allow this interaction to occur is a matter of concern to those involved with planning. There must be enough viability for improvements in technology and resources to satisfy the wants and needs of human beings who comprise society.

The individual firm also has its combination of human wants and needs, its combinations of technical knowledge and skills, and its available resources. The firm usually reacts to changes at the societal level since it operates within the confines of that society. Very few firms are large enough to cause changes in any one of the three corners of the triangle. There may be a few such instances, however, and so an indication has been shown that the firm can cause change.

Individually, firms try to discover their comparative advantage with respect to product offerings in the market place. Since these product life cycles are evolved over space, there are spatial changes between competitive firms. Individual firms must be flexible to adapt to changing societal conditions and have a relatively flexible, but sharp, ability to discover their comparative advantages relative to their competitors.

The Search for Comparative Advantage

It seems appropriate, at this point, to relate the field of distribution to the principle of comparative advantage, which is the basis of trade. This principle states that each individual, region, or nation will specialize in the production of those commodities or services for which it is best fitted, and will exchange the surpluses with the surpluses of other individuals or regions for which it is best fitted. The principle was stated in early classical economic literature by Ricardo,[1] and was later refined by John Stuart Mill.[2]

Later economists of both the classical and neoclassical schools refined the principle of comparative advantage and incorporated it into the marginal revenue and cost portions of general equilibrium analysis. The original theory, as developed by Ricardo and Mill, was in terms of labor inputs into production. Later economists converted these into monetary units, and pointed out the importance of proportionality among land, labor, and capital in seeking least cost combinations to maximize profit.

Distribution is one of the basic cost factors and, as such, will enter into determining the proportionality of the various factors for maximizing net profit. In the final delivered cost of the product to the consumer, if distribution cost is high, such costs will be important in determining the comparative advantage of a firm, region, or nation. If distribution costs are proportionately low, these costs will be less important than the other factors to be considered. However, even in those industries in which the transport cost is a low proportion of the commodity's delivered cost, these costs must still be considered in relation to other competition in the economic area.

---

[1]David Ricardo, The Principles of Political Economy and Taxation (London: John Murray, 1817), Ch. VII.

[2]John Stuart Mill, Principles of Political Economy (New York: Longmans, Green and Co., 1911), Bk. III, Ch. XVII.

Distribution assumes more importance in the principle of comparative advantage when the conditions of processing allow lower unit costs with increased volumes to be obtained by applying capital to the transformation process. This can readily be seen if one considers briefly the historical development of our economic system.

When man was a nomad, he was largely concerned with those wants whose satisfaction was necessary to the maintenance of his own existence. During this stage of economic development, man found it necessary to move to resources in order to satisfy his own wants. However, as he began to utilize the resources of the land for producing goods, he became more stationary. Gradually, individuals accumulated goods beyond their own particular needs and began to look for ways to exchange surpluses for those of other individuals for mutual advantage. In this stage, man first attempted to conquer space, since the extent to which he could trade these surpluses was in large part determined by his ability to overcome spatial obstacles.

Trade at first was on a purely local level. As man used surpluses and applied capital, in the form of tools, to the productive process, hence acquiring a declining unit cost curve, he began to spread out geographically in order to trade his products with others who were likewise beginning to specialize. Attempts were made, as trade spread, to bring raw materials from more distant points to the production site and to deliver the finished products to more distant geographic locations. Not until spatial differences were overcome did regional specialization begin to occur.

If the level of economic development is spatially limited to the village or city, the principle of comparative advantage will be worked out only within that particular location. However, if the problem of spatial relationships is overcome, the principle of comparative advantage can operate over a broader geographic area. Thus, movement is significant in determining the extent to which the principle of comparative advantage can operate in the triunal interaction of human requirements, human skills, and utilization of the natural resources of any population.

Macro- and Microdistribution Systems

In the analytical approach to macrodistribution systems, attention is focused on the distribution system as a whole, rather than on its individual components. For example, social scientists are concerned with the aggregative forces at work in the nation, considered as a universe. On the other hand, the analytical approach to microdistribution systems is concerned with the various forces at work in sub-segments of a given universe or macrosystem. For example, social scientists could study particular production and distribution problems of an individual firm.

The study of distribution systems should include investigation of both macro- and microdistribution systems, if the various parts of the movement system are to serve economically the requirements of the market place. The selection of either approach depends, to a great extent, upon the problems to be studied and the objectives to be attained. For example, the over-all cost of movement in a given intercity movement agency can be determined from the general approach, but the range of cost within the agency must come through the particular approach.

While it is clear that the general approach is concerned with the overall aspects of a universe and the particular approach deals with an individual system, the dividing line between the two approaches is difficult to discern. It is usually a comparatively arbitrary division at best. Where a relatively small number of firms are interrelated, the same forces that determine the level of interrelationship might apply to both the general and the particular approaches. As the number of firms and individuals increases, so does the complexity of the interrelationships.

The relationships of the forces at work in the larger universe should be studied so that the individual company, or other segment of the system, can tie in its own efforts with the trends of the larger universe. Although it is often extremely difficult to ascertain trends correctly, managements in charge of planning and control often must at least estimate them in order to make commitments for future actions. Examples of this are commitments made by the federal and state governments for the interstate highway system, the construction of airports to handle projected volumes of traffic, and the development of master plans by urban planners.

Logistics Systems Components

Definition

A logistics system is the logical conceptual arrangement of the functional areas of an operation which moves goods and persons from one location to another. The system includes all movement from the shipment of the raw materials to the final resting point of the end products. The application of scientific methodology to alternative combinations of the functional areas has as its purpose arriving at the most logical arrangements to achieve a desired goal.

Logistics has many functional areas, some of which have become interdisciplinary in recent years. A useful method of classifying functional areas in the system is by type of movement, basically three types.

1. Intercity movement between cities or regions. These moves may be short or very long in distance. The emphasis in this case will be on the line haul aspects of the move, i.e., the movement occurring between major terminal points.

2. Intracity movement between points within a city or metropolitan area. The moves in this case will be relatively shorter than intercity moves. The emphasis will be more on terminal costs and less on line haul costs.

3. Intrasite movement occurring within a given warehouse, plant, or retail store location. Moves are the shortest distance-wise at this level and emphasis will be on handling costs in the given location.

These categories are sufficiently understandable in a general sense, even though the divisions may be arbitrary at the margin. In each of these levels there is necessarily a combination of the physical components of a logistics system. These components are the power unit, movement unit, control unit, right of way, and terminals. These components are placed in varying combinations, dependent on the market being served. Each of these components is discussed relative to the three types of moves-- intercity, intracity, and intrasite.

Power Unit

The power unit gives the propulsion providing for the move. Diesel, electric, jet, and internal combustion engines are common types. They vary greatly, depending on the job they are to do. The following typical ratios of horsepower to load indicate the great variety of power in relation to load.

	Horsepower	Load (1000 lbs.)	HP/Load (horsepower/ pound)
Inland barge train[1]	10,000	30,000	1/3000
Railroad freight train[2]	7,500	10,000	1/1320
Motor truck[3]	500	100	1/200
Automobile	300	5	1/17
Space module[4]	4,000,000	7,000	1/1-3/4

[1]Assumes a train of 12 units and one pusher unit.
[2]Assuming merchandise freight with three units of 2500 horsepower each.
[3]Assuming one trailer 40 feet long.
[4]Based on 6,000,000 pounds of thrust.

Movement Unit

The movement unit contains and supports the payload, freight or passenger, being moved. These are sometimes moved as multiple units, or in other instances as single units, depending on the relationship of the technology to the market being served. Operating conditions on some inland waterways often permit multiple movement units per power unit, e.g., the trains operating on the lower Mississippi and Ohio rivers. Railroad freight trains are also operated with multiple movement units.

At the other extreme technology requires that in air transport the power and payload move in the same unit. Motor transport basically operates the power and payload in separable units but sometimes, where legal restrictions permit, multiple movement units are used. Other types of movement units are forklift trucks, conveyor systems, lighters aboard ship, and other intermodal containers.

Control Unit

Generally, there are two types of control units--a closed system and an open system. In the closed system there is a set course; in the completely open system, there is none. The use of a set course reduces the human element and increases mechanical or automatic controls. The use of a nonset course increases the human element and reduces the opportunities for automatic control.

Intercity carriage usually provides a mixture between these two extremes. Much intrasite movement is increasingly moved via closed systems in order to lower costs.

Right of Way

The space over or through which the power and movement units operate are the right of way. Generally, the intercity and intracity moves involve the use of land, water, and/or air

and the appropriate legislative body has control over granting
the right to use the right of way. Although the right of way may
be privately owned, as in the case of the railroad, the legal
right to grant such use rests with the governing legislative body.

Intrasite movements generally involve moves on privately
owned property; an example would be an intraplant, intrawarehouse,
or intraretail store move within the given site. Such intrasite
moves are not usually subject to legislative control unless the
property rights of others are contravened.

Terminal Units

A terminal is a point where movement size requirements are
equalized for different parts of the distribution system. Under
this definition, four types of services are provided by terminals:
dead storage, assembly, break-bulk, and reassembly.

Dead storage facilities are provided for commodities
because of seasonal production, seasonal consumption, or combinations of both. An example of dead storage is the cold storage
warehouse, where such items as eggs are stored at the time of
production and taken out of storage as needed for consumption.

Assembly terminals are provided for commodities where the
shipments do not meet the volume requirements of the carrier;
there the commodities are concentrated and handled from there on
as volume shipments. An example of an assembly point is the
grain elevator in agricultural production centers, where the
grain shipments are carried on trucks to elevators and moved as
carload quantities.

Break-bulk terminals are for receiving inbound volume
shipments from the distribution system and moving out less than
volume shipments into the system again. Beyond the processing
point, the requirements of the system are determined by the consumer's purchases of the end product. Since ultimate consumers
buy in relatively small quantities and at locations near their own

habitats, the distribution system must move successively smaller volumes per shipment from the plant to the wholesaler, wholesaler to retailer, and retailer to consumer. The job, then, from processing point to consumer includes successively breaking down the shipment into smaller quantities. In both the assembly and the break-bulk operations, the institution, by whatever name, is a location that equalizes the movement size requirements for different parts of the distribution system.

The fourth type of terminal facility, break-bulk and reassembly, is simply a combination of the second and third types in one physical facility. Break-bulk and reassembly facilities usually occur on the dispersion side of the movement system. They serve the many thousands of retailers and/or producers who do a volume of business so small, with consequent small and single shipments, that volume shipments direct from producer to retailer are not economically feasible. Physically, this may serve as an economic justification for the wholesale structure. Shipments of single commodities usually occur in volume to the warehouse or wholesale point. The wholesaler then reassembles these commodities so that there are many commodities in the outbound shipment, and delivery takes place to the retailer.

From the standpoint of movement alone, the presence of a terminal in the movement system is a diseconomy that raises immediate movement costs, but that may be desirable, since overall total costs are lowered. For example, on the concentration side, a less than volume shipment might be moved direct from the raw material producing point to the processing plant. However, the pooling of these less than volume shipments enables the movement to take place at a lower per unit cost than if each less than volume unit moved as a separate shipment.

The railroads and inland barge carriers are multiple-movement-units-per-power-unit operations. For the most part, on the concentration side the diseconomies of terminals in these operations are offset by the economies from the volume operation. As pointed out earlier, as the movement approaches and end consumer, the average size of the shipment tends to become smaller. In order for the distribution system to serve the customer under these conditions, the movement system must provide adequate terminal and movement facilities.

In more specific terms, this means that as the size of the shipment becomes smaller, there is more need for the single-movement-unit-per-power-unit operation, and for terminals to serve as equalizing points between the requirements of the shippers and the requirements of the movement system. In a sense, the diseconomy of the terminal operation is being compared with the economy of the volume movement operation. If the customer does not buy in large enough quantity to justify direct shipment from the plant he must expect the shipment to travel through a distribution channel before he may take possession physically of the goods from the producer or other vendor.[1]

In the movement system itself, the same four types of terminals are used for the movement equipment. Dead storage facilities must be provided for the movement equipment when it is not in use. Terminal facilities must also be provided for the assembly of movement units at one location, where the power unit is then attached and moved in trainload or other volume quantities. Break-bulk terminal facilities must be provided for breakup of the multiple movement unit or trainload into individual movement unit delivery to the customer at destination. Good examples of these are the classification yards of the railroads, where carloads are assembled from various shippers in a given city and then assembled into trainload quantity; the reverse process occurs at destination.

_____

[1]As a corollary of this situation, as the size of the shipment becomes smaller, the proportion of variable costs to total costs rises, and the turnover rate on capital also tends to rise.

Terminals might be utilized for breaking bulk and reassembl-
ing, as in the terminals of many common motor carriers. For example,
pickup trucks pick up the shipments from several shippers around a
given city and bring them into the motor carrier terminal. At this
terminal, shipments are unloaded and reassembled into line haul
units, which take the goods to another city, where the reverse
process takes place at the destination terminal. Thus, both for
the goods and the equipment, the terminal is a point at which the
shipment size demands of the shippers and the desires of the movement system are equalized.

Concentration and Dispersion Systems

Fundamentally, two jobs are performed by the commodity
movement system: first, the concentration of raw materials into
volume quantities for movement to production points; and second,
the dispersion of the finished goods from producer to consumer.
In each of these jobs, the size of shipment is an important consideration.

If volume shipments are accumulated as quickly as possible,
capital in the form of power, movement units, or rights of way may
be applied to the transport of the raw materials and, consequently,
goods may be moved at a lower cost per unit. Therefore, shipments
which do not meet the volume requirements of the carriers (less
than volume) are brought into concentration points and handled
as volume shipments beyond that point (Figure 2.2). Typical of
such shipments are grain shipments which, as mentioned earlier,
are carried on trucks to elevators and moved as carload quantities
from country elevators to the terminal elevators of milling
centers. Where the individual shipments are large enough, the
concentration process can take place at a single raw material
producing point and be moved as a volume shipment to the processing
point. For example, in shipping a trainload of coal from a single

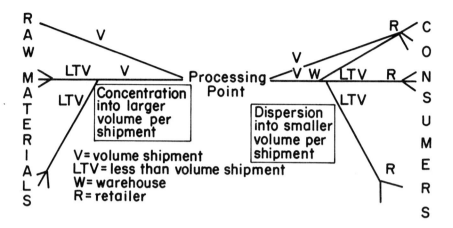

Figure 2.2.   Concentration and Dispersion Systems.

mine to a utility plant, the coal is concentrated at the mine and
moved in trainload quantities, eliminating the necessity for an
intermediate point.

Beyond the processing point, the requirements of the movement system are determined by the ultimate consumer. Since the
quantities demanded beyond this point are relatively smaller per
move, the movement system must transport successively smaller
volumes per shipment from the plant to the various middlemen.
The job, then, from processing point to consumer, includes successively breaking down the shipment into smaller quantities.

Since the ultimate consumer does not normally buy in
quantities which warrant volume shipments direct from the processing point, the retail structure has come into being as an intermediate point between the two. If the retailer is large enough,
he may buy direct from the processor in quantities which will
justify volume shipment. However, if the retailer's purchases
do not justify the volume shipment, he may buy through a wholesaler or other middleman. Volume shipments can then be made from

the processing point to the wholesaler, and less than volume shipments from the wholesaler to the retailer.

To summarize: the primary functions of the movement
system are; (1) on the concentration side, to concentrate shipments as quickly as possible; (2) on the dispersion side, to
break the shipments into successively smaller volumes, in order
to serve the ultimate consumer.

The extent to which capital may be applied to the movement process in the form of power, movement units, or rights of
way differs between the concentration and dispersion operations.
The application of capital to movement results in a declining
unit cost curve whose shape will depend upon the relationship of
fixed and variable costs.

Fixed and Variable Costs in the
Distribution System

Some authors divide operating cost into the following
categories: short-run variable (out-of-pocket) costs, intermediate costs, and long-run variable (fixed) costs. Short-run
variable, or out-of-pocket, costs are those traceable to a specific
movement of goods. Intermediate costs, then, would concern the
replacement of assets which were depreciated over a period of time.
If the period of time is long enough, all costs might be considered variable; therefore, the differences among the three are
relative. For our purposes, it is sufficient to make a simple
division between variable and fixed, with a full understanding
that the time period selected to distinguish between the two is
purely arbitrary.

If one assumes the capacity of a given distribution system
as fixed for a particular period of time, variable costs will be
those which vary with the volume of freight handled. Such costs,
when compared to total costs, are variable in total but remain
constant per unit of business moved. Theoretically, these costs

may be assigned to a specific volume or movement, i.e., those costs which would not have been incurred if the service had not been rendered.

Fixed costs are those that are fixed in total and, theoretically, are unaffected by increases or decreases in the volume of freight handled. Since these costs are unrelated to volume, they would continue even if all movements stopped. Fixed costs might be considered as the capacity cost of a particular distribution system: the cost of providing the physical plant for a given system to handle a given volume of freight within a given geographical area, at a given period of time, and within given time limits. Examples are the capital required for line haul equipment, for terminals, for materials handling equipment, for maintenance shops, and for rights of way.

J. M. Clark illustrates fixed and variable costs in the following analogy:

> The quantity and quality of equipment which it pays to install depends on the amount of use that will be made of it. It may not pay for a settler to lay a water pipe to save carrying three pails of water a day from a spring a few hundred yards from his camp. If the camp grows to a tiny settlement, it may pay to lay some sort of a trough or pipe to save the carrying of one hundred or more pails of water every day, and if the little settlement grows into a town, it will pay to install a reservoir with underground pipes and perhaps a pumping system. A pipe is a fixed expense and the work of carrying pails of water is a variable one, and the fixed expense is for equipment which makes variable expenses unnecessary. This is the type of all labor-saving machinery and all enlargement or development of labor-saving equipment. The saving is measured by the number of pails that have to be carried. If this amount bulks large, it would pay to install a considerable amount of equipment to avoid it, while if it is small, the equipment may be uneconomical.[1]

We can say that the average total costs of a process are determined by the relationship of the degree of use of the process

---

[1]J. Maurice Clark, Studies in the Economics of Overhead Cost (Chicago: University of Chicago Press, 1923). See also W. Arthur Lewis, Overhead Costs (New York: Rinehart and Co., 1949).

with varying proportions of fixed and variable costs. This relationship to the average total cost is illustrated as follows.

A salesman must rent a car. He has two alternatives.
The first rent-a-car service charges ten dollars a day and eight
cents per mile. The second charges eight dollars a day and
twelve cents per mile. Since both services include gas, insurance,
etc., the optimum choice will depend on the expected use of the
car. The first service represents higher fixed cost but lower
variable cost than the second. The salesman, on a cost basis,
should be indifferent between the two services if he plans to
drive fifty miles. If he plans to drive more than fifty miles,
he should choose the second plan. The two levels of fixed costs
(FC_1 and FC_2) are illustrated in Figure 2.3. The corresponding
total costs of each plan are represented by TC_1 and TC_2. The
areas between the FC and TC lines represent the variable costs
which vary directly with the number of miles traveled. These are
converted into unit costs, and the effect to the varying proportions of fixed to variable costs and the relationship to the
degree of utilization can be seen in Figure 2.2.

Therefore, when two cost structures are compared to each
other, with one having higher fixed costs but lower variable
costs, the one with higher fixed costs causes the average total
cost curve to decline at a more rapid rate than the lower fixed
cost alternative. If enough use, beyond the break-even point,
can be made of a process with such a cost structure, the initial
higher fixed costs cause lower average total costs. In the
salesman's case, the expenditure of ten dollars in fixed costs
provides him with lower average total costs for any use beyond
fifty miles.

If the producer can realize lower variable costs by increasing the proportion of fixed costs, and enough utilization of
the productive factors is possible, he will obtain lower average

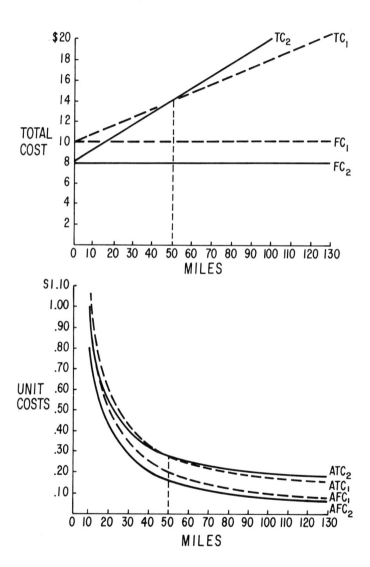

Figure 2.3. Fixed Costs as a Part of Total Costs.

total costs. Hopefully, lower costs mean a more competitive position. A second result of such a cost structure arises when a
producer sets his price on the basis of variable costs. Pricing
to cover variable costs allows lower prices to be quoted. Therefore, the relationship of fixed and variable costs with utilization can have a direct relationship to the competitive position
of a producer, in terms of the prices he must charge to cover
variable or total unit costs.

The Concentration Movement and Fixed Costs

        In an earlier part of this chapter, it was pointed out
that one objective of the distribution system is to concentrate
goods into large volumes per shipment as quickly as possible
for the purpose of applying capital, in the form of machinery,
to the movement process. Four factors which determine the extent
of capital application to the movement process include: the total
volume of the resource to be moved, the characteristics of the
goods, the extent to which the movement operations are repetitive,
and speed in transit.

        Volume is implied in two separate ways in the discussion.
The first meaning refers to the sheer quantity of the natural
resource available for shipment; the second, to the amount of
goods offered for single shipments. The resources referred to
in the concentration movement are generally coarse, unrefined, or
semi-refined materials such as lumber, coal, iron ore, bauxite,
taconite, and other bulk materials. In general, as the volume
available for shipment increases, it is possible to apply larger
amounts of capital in the form of machinery to the movement process,
with a resulting increase in the proportion of fixed costs to total
costs. As the volume available decreases, smaller amounts of
capital will be applied, usually resulting in a higher proportion
of variable costs to total costs.

Characteristics of the goods to be moved refers to those factors that determine the transfer characteristics of the commodity in the movement system. From an engineering point of view, it is generally easier to apply machines to the movement of raw materials than to the movement of finished goods. Raw materials are often homogeneous and uniform commodities, shipped in bulk or unpackaged units and, as a result, are susceptible to the application of the gravity flow principle. Finished goods tend to move in packaged form as discrete units. In such movement, the transfer into and out of the movement units requires more care to minimize loss and damage, with a resulting increase in handling costs. For example, it is often possible to apply gravity loading and unloading to rail cars for such materials as coal, wheat, and iron ore, whereas it would be very difficult to apply these to finished packaged commodities.[1]

Repetitive nature of the operations is, in a sense, a corollary of the characteristics of the goods. Capital is more readily applied in movements which can be routinized so that a given process can be performed repeatedly, without a substantial change in the arrangements for right-of-way, movement equipment, and terminals. Transfer operations are often necessary on both the concentration and dispersion sides of distributions to either assemble or break-bulk the individual shipments. These tasks are more readily accomplished with bulk or unpackaged units, typical of the concentration side, than with the packaged units, typical of the dispersion side. As noted, the repetitive nature of the line-haul operation phase of the movement is a corollary of the volume to be moved. If the volume to be moved is small, either as a total amount or as an individual shipment, there is little

---

[1]Other factors which might also be included under characteristics of the goods include: density, possibility of damage to equipment or other commodities in the movement unit, perishability.

possibility of a repetitive operation. As the volume per shipment increases, so does the possibility of a repetitive operation and applicability of capital.

Speed must also be considered in applying capital to the movement process. Since it is difficult to vary transportation space or carrying capacity from load to load, an optimum size of power unit, movement unit, and right of way is selected, and one must work within the physical transport limitations of the engineering alternatives. For example, the ratio of space to the rate of movement of that space will vary with the physical means available and is usually designed or constructed to fit the physical limitations. Great quantities of goods can be moved at a slow speed on a Great Lakes ore carrier, or smaller quantities might be moved faster via rail. Another example is a pipeline, where the cross sectional circumference of the pipe times the rate of movement of the liquid or gas through that space is the volume. By varying both space size and the movement of the cube at various rates within the economic factors of cost (pipe and pumping), one can arrive at the size of the pipe to be used in the installation. In general, the attainment of speed in movement comes at an increasingly high cost and sometimes requires more than proportionately higher investments of capital.

The element of time, aside from speed in transit, has not been included in the above list because it will be governed by such factors as availability of funds in the capital markets for particular kinds of investments, engineering capabilities of the movement machinery, and applicable tax laws that may determine depreciation rates. Time in this context has two aspects: first, the total period of time over which the machinery will be used; and second, the rate of use of that machinery within the period of time selected. If the life of the movement machinery is longer, it becomes more feasible to apply large amounts of capital; and if a shorter period of time is selected, a smaller amount of capital may be applied.[1] For example, if the machinery is to be written off over five years, as opposed to ten, then the amount which can be expended will be less for the five-year period than for the ten-year period.

The utilization of the equipment will also affect the amount of capital applied to movement. If utilization is high, it will tend to enhance the application of capital to movement, while low utilization tends to restrict its application.

A low unit value of resources makes it more desirable to accumulate such materials into relatively large volumes for single shipments. This allows the carrier to apply power to the movement process. Another contributing factor would be the small number of buyers and sellers of a commodity being shipped. This is clearly the case in the extractive industries, such as petroleum, copper, and aluminum, where either there is an integration of the mining and production processes into one company or there are few buyers and sellers at the mining and production levels. In the perennial industries, such as lumber, there is less tendency towards oligopoly, and in the agricultural industries there are thousands of producers but a relatively small number of processors. Thus, since the number of buyers and sellers are usually fewer on the concentration than on the dispersion side of distribution, the accumulation of commodities into larger volumes per shipment is more easily performed on the concentration side.

Fixed Costs and System Flexibility

The distribution system depends to a large extent upon the economic characteristics and markets of the industries it serves.

---

[1]This refers to the period of time over which the machinery will be depreciated. The depreciation period may be affected by technological obsolescence as well as by the capabilities of the machine.

When major changes occur in the economic complexion of the market, distribution systems with a heavy investment in existing facilities may find it difficult to adapt to these changes. A higher ratio of fixed costs to total costs tends to bring with it an economic rigidity which may present a reallocation of space and weight movement capabilities, and can result in non-utilization of that space.

Those distribution systems possessing lower levels of fixed investment have great flexibility of physical equipment and can adapt more readily to these changes, but only at a higher unit cost for the article or commodity moved. Generally, investment in equipment is based upon the expectation of a lower cost for each particular movement. Where this expectation is high, or at least with low risk, a greater outlay is feasible. When the demand for movement is uncertain, less outlay is made in the form of a smaller load capacity. Yet there is an advantage to smaller space facilities, in that small quantities permit greater speed or rate of movement of that space. Definitively, the nature of the investments made in fixed facilities will limit the spectrum of commodities to be moved by a distrubition system.

The Dispersion Movement and Fixed Costs

The dispersion system, which successively subdivides a shipment into smaller quantitics, is largely due to the relatively short distance customers drive in order to purchase commodities, the small average sale per customer at the retail level, and the emphasis on merchandise turnover at this level. The application of capital from processing point to consumer still depends upon the volume to be moved, the characteristics of the commodity to be shipped, the extent of repetitive operations, and speed in transit. In the movement process, however, the application of these factors to the dispersion side differs from application to the concentration side, since practice must be changed to meet the needs of the market.

Even on the dispersion side, the objective will still be to ship in as large a volume per shipment as possible so that capital can be applied to the movement process to obtain minimum cost. The extent to which this may be done will be determined by the needs and desires of the consumers of the product. Let us, therefore, consider the distance the customer will travel to make a retail purchase, the average sale per customer at the retail level, and merchandise turnover in the retail store.

Very little definitive work has been done on the distance that a customer will travel to a particular kind of retail store for a particular commodity. This is readily understandable when one considers the tremendous number of variables, including the many hundreds of different types of commodities, the many types of locations of retail outlets, and the many different human reactions to spending time in travel for a particular kind of commodity in a given type of store.

In order to show the relative variation between the time-space factor and the type of commodity, consider the differences among goods of the marketing classification: convenience, shopping, and specialty goods. Convenience goods are items which the customer desires to buy with a minimum of effort at the most accessible location. Shopping goods are items for which he is willing to exert a little extra effort to compare prices, quality, or some other characteristic. Specialty goods are similar to shopping goods, except that price comparison by the consumer is less important. The customer will not travel as far for a convenience item as for either a shopping or a specialty item. In recent years, city retail structures have been forced to relocate nearer to the customers, who have tended to move into suburban areas.

Average sale per customer at the retail level also influences the size of shipment from the producer to the consumer. Generally, the customer buys only a very small amount of goods at any one time. Normally, the customer has enough goods in his own home to meet his needs for current consumption. Of course, the extent of this inventory will vary with the nature of the goods and the income level of the individual concerned. For example, bread may be purchased with relative frequency, but an automobile or a refrigerator may be purchased infrequently. An automobile may be kept on hand for a relatively long time by a low-income family, but be traded in for a new model rather regularly by a high-income family.

Pressure within the retail and wholesale structures to lower operating expenses through increased merchandise turnover also affects the size of shipment. Merchandise turnover is defined as the ratio of sales to the average amount of inventory on hand for any particular period of time. This may be computed in either dollars or physical units. For example, if a retail store had sales of merchandise of $100,000 for a month and an average inventory of $25,000 on hand at all times, the merchandise turnover for that period would be four times ($100,000/$25,000).

The desirability of increasing merchandise turnover may be seen from the following. Assume annual sales of $100,000, with an average inventory of $25,000 at all times (an inventory turnover of four times). If the interest cost on this inventory is computed at 10 per cent per year, it would be $2,500. If this inventory turnover can be increased to 10 by decreasing the average inventory to $10,000, the interest cost declines to $1,000, a savings of $1,500.

There are many advantages and disadvantages to increasing merchandise turnover, but the sole purpose here is to indicate that as inventory turnover increases (assuming that sales remain constant), the average size of shipment tends to decrease. The effect is smaller, more frequent orders than would be the case with the higher inventory, and an increase in the performance of break-bulk and reassembly would ensue.[1]

The Dispersion System Compromise

From the producer's point of view, the ideal dispersion situation would be a straight line, with consumers placed at intervals along the line. This would be somewhat similar to a conveyor system, with the consumer placed at various points along the belt removing required items as they pass his particular station. All output placed on the conveyor would be removed, and subsequently consumed, by the time the end of the belt was reached. This method would allow a constant rate of production and an equal rate of consumption, assuming that the rate of consumption is constant and that the consumer cannot be at the point of production to obtain the desired goods. The water system serving householders most nearly approaches this model. Water is transported by pipes from the production unit directly to the consumer and is consumed as soon as it is obtained; the need for the consumer to store any of the product is eliminated. After the pipeline is initially filled, the producer pumps into the system only that amount of water that has been consumed.

---

[1]From retailers' and wholesalers' points of view, the advantages of a more rapid stock turnover are the following: a decrease in the amount of space required to do business; reduction in interest costs, insurance costs, and taxes; reduction in risks due to price change; reduction in depreciation and obsolescence of inventory. There are also limitations to a rapid stock turn-over, however; lost sales through shortages of merchandise, cost of paper work on increased numbers of orders, losses of quantity discounts and savings on freight rates of volume shipments, and a possible increase in the cost of the buying function due to increased orders.

Dispersion is, in reality, a compromise between the desires or exigencies of the producer and those of the consumer. The producer would like the consumer to take possession of the item directly at the time and site of production. The consumer, on the other hand, would like the item brought directly to him in consumable quantities at approximately the time he would like to consume them. Obviously, neither one has sufficient power to impose his desires completely on the other. Hence, the dispersion system has evolved from interaction, competition, and compromise.

Institutions have come into existence as a dispersion bridge between the producer and the end consumer. Distribution channels for industrial goods include: (1) manufacturer-user; (2) manufacturer-industrial distributor-user; (3) manufacturer-agent middleman-user. Distribution channels for consumer goods include: (1) manufacturer-consumer; (2) manufacturer-retailer-consumer; (3) manufacturer-wholesaler-retailer-consumer; (4) manufacturer-agent-middleman-wholesaler-retailer-consumer. These channels are commonly used for the job of demand creation and physical fulfillment of that demand.

Industrial goods are sold primarily direct from manufacturer to user, without the necessity for an institutional setup to perform the break-bulk and assembly in movement. The average amount per sale is much larger in industrial goods than in consumer goods. Because of larger average sales, the manufacturer can accumulate a large enough volume of goods for a single direct shipment to the customer without a break-bulk and reassembly point. From the demand creation point of view, manufacturers prefer this channel of distribution because of the highly rational and qualified buyers in the industrial market. Manufacturers feel that highly technically trained salesmen are required. Many of them feel that the industrial distributor, since he must by his very nature handle several lines, does not

have the technical competence in each line to represent them
adequately. In any case, the typical physical movement is direct
from the manufacturer to the customer, in sharp contrast to the
rather elaborate structure for dispersion of consumer goods.

In order that one may understand the dispersion system
for consumer goods from a physical movement point of view, it is
first necessary to investigate the nature of the retail structure.
Duncan, Phillips, and Hollander classify retailing into four distinct
methods:

> The retail functions are performed by organizations
> that reach customers in one or more of four ways: through
> stores, the mail, house-to-house salesmen, and automatic
> vending machines. Of these ways - commonly termed 'methods
> of retailing' - stores are most important, accounting for
> about 97 percent of all retail sales. Mail-order retailing
> and house-to-house selling are each responsible for nearly
> 1 percent.

Thus, nearly all retail sales are at locations where the
customer comes to make selections. There is, however, a considerable range of distances traveled and sizes of purchases which
depend upon the individual, the type of goods desired, and the type
of location to which he travels.

If the retailer's volume of business justifies volume
shipments direct from the producer, these may take place. However, many thousands of retailers and/or producers do a volume
of business so small, with consequent small single shipments, that
such volume shipments are not economically feasible. From the
physical movement point of view, this justifies the wholesale

---

[1]Delbert J. Duncan, Charles E. Phillips, and Stanley C.
Hollander, Modern Retailing Management: Basic Concepts and
Practices (Homewood, Ill.: R. D. Irwin, 1972), pp. 4-5.

structure. The nature of this physical function is shown in Figures 2.4 and 2.5.

Producers ship volume quantities to a warehouse, as indicated in Figure 2.3, and then shipments of less than volume quantities are made to the retailer. The reassembly operation is demonstrated in Figure 2.4. On the inbound side of the warehouse, either a rail siding or a truck dock handles inbound truckloads or carloads of particular kinds of commodities. These goods are then unloaded from the rail car or truck and placed in storage in the warehouse, as indicated by the arrows in the chart. A particular retailer's order might consist of five cases of pears, three cases of peaches, four cartons of orange juice, and three cartons of coffee. An order picker will than take these quantities from storage and reassemble them on the outbound dock as a single shipment for delivery to the retailer. Many times these so-called order picking lines are mechanized, in an attempt to modify or lower the reassembly cost in the warehouse.

Authors in the marketing area usually consider the wholesale structure to consist of the following: merchant wholesalers, manufacturers' sales branches, petroleum bulk tank stations, retailer owned wholesale operations, agents and brokers, and assemblers. The break-bulk and reassembly operation is normally performed by all of the first four. Agent middlemen do not normally perform physical break-bulk. Many large manufacturers and retailers perform their own break-bulk and reassembly operation, either in their own warehouses or in rented spaces. These branch warehouses might also be called part of the wholesale structure, since essentially the same physical operations would be performed in them as by an independent wholesaler.

41

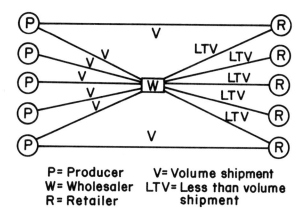

P= Producer   V= Volume shipment
W= Wholesaler   LTV= Less than volume
R= Retailer   shipment

Figure 2.4.   The Wholesaler's Break-Bulk Process.

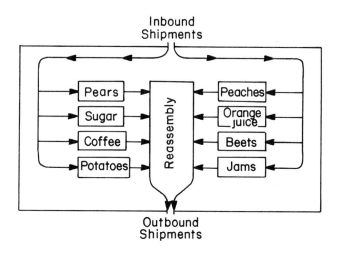

Figure 2.5.   The Wholesaler's Reassembly Process.

The Effect of Customer Requirements on
Fixed Costs in Dispersion

All carriers, both on the concentration and dispersion
sides, want to apply capital to movement in order to obtain
declining unit costs. However, as noted above, since the consumer usually travels a very limited distance to make a purchase
and purchases small quantities at any one time, large volume
shipments direct from the producer to the consumer are considerably less feasible on the dispersion side. Therefore, as we
found earlier, the retail and wholesale structures have developed
to fulfill the needs of the dispersion system for break-bulk and
reassembly points between volume and less than volume shipments.

Quicker times in transit are demanded in dispersion for
a variety of reasons. One of the more important is the added
value of the goods after processing. Any delays in getting the
goods from the producer to the consumer will increase the amount
of interest expense on inventory while the goods are in this pipeline. Therefore, it is desirable to consider inventory interest
cost, then to select the means of movement which will keep this
at a minimum.

Faster transit time between producer and consumer usually
will require smaller shipments; consequently, the applications of
capital to the movement process will not be as feasible. Thus,
there is a very clear need on the dispersion side of movement for
a qualified service for smaller quantities per shipment, a capable
performance of the transfer operation, and faster times in transit.
This means a smaller number of movement units per power unit.
There is, correspondingly, less opportunity for the cost curve
of movement to be a declining unit cost curve. In fact, dispersion
movement tends to approach a constant unit cost curve because of the
high proportion of variable costs in the operation.

CHAPTER 3

LOGISTICS OF LOCATION

Terminal properties are important integral parts of the distribution system, and are necessary to equalize demand and supply considerations in distribution systems. Since retail stores and warehouses are considered important in terms of space preference of the consumers, the logistics objective of terminal location is to strike a balance between profitable operations and consumer convenience.

The networks of retail and warehouse terminals have particular importance when linked to population expansion and decentralization. Population shifts initiate a whole series of secondary adjustments in the retail structure of the community Many studies have indicated that the retail structure arranges itself so as to best serve the needs of the community. Outstanding evidence of this has been the rapid growth of the suburban shopping center.

In taking the micro approach to the study of distribution systems, it is not uncommon to encounter many cases of vertical integration, in which the entire distribution system is owned by one corporation. In such instances, terminal location would be a problem of real concern to the distribution organization. For the individual firm which is not vertically integrated, be it at the retail or plant levels, the location of such terminals would still be a problem. The manufacturer would have to consider what kinds of retail stores he would prefer to have handling his goods. To the independent retailer and/or warehouse operator, location may well be a matter of business life or death, when attracting customers from a given distance is concerned.

Retail Location

The retailer, in adjusting to the pressure towards large
scale retailing and the move to the suburbs of great numbers of
his customers, is faced with the problem of what type of store to
build and where to locate it. These questions are probably more
easily resolved for retailers of shopping and specialty goods than
for those in convenience goods or services. The former presumably
would make fewer decisions, and would be more limited in alternatives, because of the nature of these types of retailing.
Retailers of convenience goods, however, are faced with the problem
of locating near their market. They usually serve small segments
of the market, and so must develop good techniques for defining
markets. These techniques assume major importance as the metropolitan area becomes saturated with convenience stores, leaving
smaller and smaller segments open to development.

Consumer Space Preference

Production and distribution processes transform and transport
the product to the point where the final consumer will purchase it.
The retail terminal is the site at which the distribution system
and the consumer meet. The basic problem is to devise methods
which will allow a reasonably accurate estimate of the distance
which the consumer will travel to make his purchase, and to select
a compatible site for the retail store terminal.

Since the consumer is spatially situated, and is faced with
the task of satisfying his economic wants with an imperfect market,[1]

---

[1]This imperfection is twofold; first, the consumer's spatial
mobility in terms of time-distance movement rate is not equal in
every direction, due to such factors as rivers, limited access
freeways, and industrial developments; and, second, the consumer
does not possess perfect knowledge of the market place. His knowledge may range from complete certainty about such factors as the
available quantity, price, quality, performance characteristics,
to complete uncertainty over the range of goods that one would
normally purchase.

he would probably arrange his travel pattern so as to receive the most utility for the time and effort expended. In order to understand the consumer's attitude towards optimization of utility, we must analyze the component elements of consumer movement and space. The basic factors to be considered include a demand base point, unit of travel, differentiation of travel purpose, time period of reoccurring travel patterns, and quality of transport service.

For the purposes of analysis in connection with the distribution system, the base point of demand is most commonly the household of the individual. Therefore, the demands for transportation refer principally to the family, either as a unit or, more commonly, as households.[1] If the home is used as a base point, the most logical unit of travel is the round trip.

The distance a person will travel must also be identified in terms of the time actually spent in travel, and in terms of recurring travel patterns. The time spent in travel consists of both actual and psychological time--the impact of a given period of actual time on an individual--the most violent reaction occurring in the event of a delay. A five-minute delay due to a traffic jam is much more frustrating, and seems considerably longer, to a driver than to a passenger; a similar delay in starting seems longer to someone waiting at a bus stop than it does to someone sitting in the bus. It is probable that the importance of actual time decreases as psychological time increases.

Travel patterns tend to recur in daily, weekly, monthly, and yearly cycles. Most people have had the misfortune of observing the effects of the daily cycle on a first-hand basis in the form of the "rush hour," or daily peak time demand. In the United States the daily peak time demand typically occurs from 7:00 a.m. to 9:00 a.m. and from 4:00 p.m. to 6:00 p.m. The relationship between time demand

---

[1]The analysis here does not attempt to go into the ecological reasons why consumers live in given locations.

46

and travel purpose is most clearly evident in daily demand at the beginning and end of the normal work day. Similar cycles can be established for travel patterns for different kinds of commodities in differing market combinations.

The relative quality of each alternative also helps determine how far a person will travel in order to make purchases. The quality of transportation includes the factors of speed, access, frequency, reliability, safety, comfort, convenience, and cost. Changes in these factors will show some changes in the respective demands. The majority of these factors can be lumped into the general classification of comfort. If a passenger feels safe, and is traveling by a reliable, convenient, and low cost vehicle, he feels more comfortable. In a sense, the factors are so closely interrelated with each other and with time, both actual and psychological, and purposes of travel, that to attempt to separate them often results in an artificial differentiation that has little or no meaning. However, in spite of the difficulty of establishing cause and effect relationships, retailers must consider these factors when making location decisions.

The source of demand is the difference between what is available at home and what is available away from home.[1] In any given time period, an absolute amount of time is allocated by a person to achieve maximum satisfaction. Some of this time is spent in travel. The traveler necessarily foregoes what is at home during his travel period. But in foregoing home satisfactions, the traveler gains the total travel product. This is defined as the result of travel; the anticipated travel product is defined as the reason for travel. These two products are frequently, but not necessarily, the same. The total travel product and the anticipated

---

[1]Emery Troxel, Economics of Transport (New York: Rinehart, 1955). See also Martin T. Farris and Forrest E. Harding, Passenger Transportation (Englewood Cliffs, N.J.: Prentice-Hall, Inc., 1976).

travel product both vary with the time absent from home. The
traveler establishes some hierarchy of goals he expects to achieve.
He will accomplish his most important goals first, then will
attempt to accomplish secondary goals. For maximum satisfaction,
the traveler selects a time order of losses of satisfactions at
home just as he selects a time order for travel satisfactions.
To obtain the net travel product, the loss of at home satisfactions
and the consideration of travel effort, both of which presumably
increase with actual travel time, are subtracted from the total
travel product. As time elapses, more home satisfactions are lost,
and more time is spent in travel, the net travel product is reduced
until zero is reached. At this point, the traveler must be paid
to continue traveling. A good example of this payment is the use
of premiums and special services in retail stores to attract the
customer a longer distance. The retailer is, in a sense, paying
the customer to travel.

The single most important factor in any consideration of
passenger travel is time. Time is not only money; it is more
important than money. The problem facing the decision maker on
retail store locations is to establish the amount of time that
customers will travel to a given site in order to purchase his
commodities.

Selection of the Retail Site

The objective of the retailer should be to locate where
he offers the customer a maximum of utilities in order that, as
a minimum, he attains a threshold level of sales. Beyond this
consideration, he must select a site which will strike a balance
between profitable store operation and consumer convenience. The
individual retailer has an added burden in that he is required to
make this decision in a competitive vacuum. At best, he can only
guess what competitive action will be taken to counteract his

decision, and a competitor, by appropriate location strategy, could disturb his balance.

The term "trading area" has diverse meanings in different disciplines. The economist often considers it as a "perfect" selling zone, with its boundaries determined by plant location and transport costs. The individuals within the trading area are treated as not being subject to promotional or psychological pressures, and react in the best traditions of the "economic man" in their purchasing. The geographer views the trading area as a complex phenomenon, in which the geographical imperfections of the area determine the direction and degree of travel of the inhabitants. A somewhat blurred perspective is presented in the marketing literature because of the common practice of accepting the customer as "spatially given." The individual space preferences of the consumer are implicitly regarded as being determined by the product. Increasing suburbanization of the consumer and resulting retail decentralization have focused new attention on the usefulness of the trading area concept.[1]

The American Marketing Association defines a trading area as "a district whose size is usually determined by the boundaries within which it is economical in terms of volume and cost for a marketing unit or group to sell and deliver a good or service."[2]

---

[1] For an excellent case study in the development of the trading area concept, see Bernard J. LaLonde, Differentials In Super Market Drawing Power (East Lansing, Mich.: Bureau of Business and Economic Research, Michigan State University, 1962. Major portions of this section of Ch. 3 are from LaLonde's study. See also David L. Huff, "Defining and Estimating a Trading Area," Retailing--Concepts, Institutions, and Management, ed. by Ron J. Marking (New York: MacMillan Company, 1971).

[2] A Glossary of Marketing Terms (Chicago: American Marketing Association, 1960), p. 22.

This definition is not operational, since it sets no objective
criteria for evaluating the limits of a trading area. Others have
offered as criteria drawing power, per capita sales, time the
customer will travel, and population.

All of these criteria have certain weaknesses when applied
to all retail units or groups. As stated by Applebaum and Cohen:

 As a broad definition, the authors suggest that the trading
 area is the area from which a store gets its business within a
 given span of time. This does not exclude the reality of overlap. It also emphasizes the trading area. People must come to
 a store from a specific area. If other stores offer equal
 attractions, then the trading area of a given store will be
 related to the store's distance and the convenience of access
 from the origin and destination of the potential.[1]

The individual retailing firm must choose a particular site
in connection with its network expansion. Two objective measure-
ments--drawing power and per capita sales--provide a useful framework for trading area analysis to meet the two objectives. Drawing
power indicates the geographical nature of market coverage and,
therefore, is relevant to the problem of optimal network expansion.
On the other hand, per capita sales provide a measurement of the
quality of any individual site, in terms of sales penetration. The
two taken together provide a framework for decisions on site location
and development planning.

Application of drawing power and per capita sales measurements is by no means a simple matter, and judgment must be employed
in using these objective measurements. Distinct location profiles
could be developed on the basis of past experience, if relevant

---

[1]William Applebaum and Saul B. Cohen, "The Dynamics of
Store Trading Areas and Market Equilibrium," The Annals of the
American Association of Geographers, Vol. 51, No. 1, March, 1961,
pp. 73-101. See also David B. McKay, "A Microanalytic Approach
to Store Location Analysis," Journal of Marketing Research, Vol. 9,
May, 1972; and Applebaum, "Store Location Research--A Survey By A
Retailing Chain," Journal of Retailing, Vol. 8, February, 1971.

variables could be isolated and integrated into the analysis of the proposed site. An example is the influence of population density or income on the drawing power and per capita sales of a store in a given size community. It is entirely possible that if enough observations are made, a reliable statistical relationship can be formulated.

Drawing power is the average distance traveled by a fixed percentage of the actual or potential customers of the store. Per capita sales are simply the dollars of sales per person within a designed area. In order to calculate per capita sales in an area, three types of data must be available. First, the segment of the market must be clearly delineated for analysis, so that both population totals and sales may come from the same reference point. Second, accurate population data must be available. Third, sales figures must be available for the market. The effects of store complexity and size on drawing power were investigated by LaLonde for a selected sample of food supermarkets. He discovered that store complexity significantly affects drawing power, and that as the level of product offering at the retail site increases, drawing power increases, but not proportionately.[1] Although store size and store complexity are related to some degree, there was no systematic or reliable connection between store size and drawing power.

Store complexity significantly influenced the amount of per capita sales, although the amount varied considerably at varying distances from store site for each type. There was no systematic or reliable connection between store size and per capita sales.

A concept of store complexity can be useful in several ways in developing sound location policy. A supermarket chain has

---

[1]There is considerable variance in the applicability of this statement to the different categories of store investigated. The types studied included: urban strip, urban cluster, small town, neighborhood shopping center, and regional shopping center.

many types of stores within any metropolitan area. If these types are isolated and analyzed and their drawing power characteristics determined, an optimum network of distribution points can be established and maintained by adding or closing individual distribution points. New stores should be located so that the geographic limits of the market match a given store complexity situation. Since consumers are always changing locations and travel habits, the retailer must keep up constant research to maintain an optimal network of distribution points.

Delineating Retail Trading Areas in Urbanized Centers

A site decision may be concerned with whether or not to place a store in an established shopping area, or with the feasibility of store location in a commercially undeveloped area. In either type of location decision, a certain amount of inference and judgment will be required. Still, the gathering of applicable data for a given site decision can aid considerably in improving retail store location decisions.

For either kind of site decision, two basic approaches may be used to collect data: the empirical approach and the gravitational approach.[1] The principal methods used in the empirical approach are customer interviews, automobile license plant analysis, prize contests, check cashing analysis, credit record analysis, newspaper circulation analysis, and area customer surveys.

Gravitational models define the trading area as a mass which is structured according to certain principles. These principles are believed to govern, in an over-all fashion, the behavior of the individuals in the mass, acting both as constraining and initiating influences.

---

[1]For a good discussion of the principal empirical approaches, see LaLonde, pp. 150-166.

Gravitational models concern the interaction of many variables, much as the interaction of masses is viewed in the physical
sciences. In the Stewart-Zipf hypotheses, three primary examples
of gravitational models are presented. Stewart defines demographic
force as a constant times the product of two masses divided by the
square of the distance separating these masses. Where the population of cities I and J, designated Pi and Pj, respectively, are
taken as the relevant masses, demographic force F is:

$$F = \frac{GPiPj}{d_{ij}}$$

where G is a constant corresponding to the gravitational constant.
Steward defines gravitational energy as:

$$E = \frac{GPiPj}{d_{ij}}$$

Gravitational potential is demographic potential produced at point
I by a mass at J, which may be designated iVj and defined as a
constant times the mass at J, say Pj, divided by the intervening
distance. That is:

$$iVj = \frac{GPj}{d_{ij}}$$

Although many problems arise in connection with the use of
gravitational models, Isard feels that spatial interaction can
best be analyzed through this approach.[1] Some of the more

---

[1]For a good discussion of gravity models in transportation
and location, see Edward J. Taafe and Howard L. Gauthier, Jr.,
Geography of Transportation (Englewood Cliffs, N.J.: Prentice-Hall,
Inc., 1973).

significant problems include the use of factors other than population as an index of mass; the selection of weights to be applied to the various masses; the selection of exponents for variables in both the potential and demographic concepts; and the connections that occur between constraining and initiating forces. Reilly proposes the following list of factors that influence the spatial size of a retail trading area:

1. Lines of transportation
2. Lines of communication
3. Class of consumer in the territory surrounding the market
4. Density of population in the territory surrounding the market
5. Proximity of the market to a larger city market
6. Business attractions of the city
7. Social and amusement attractions of the city
8. Nature of the competition offered by smaller cities and towns in the surrounding territory
9. Population of the city
10. Distance which prospective customers must travel in order to reach the market, and the psychology of distance prevailing in that part of the country
11. Topographical and climatic conditions peculiar to the city and its surrounding territory
12. Kind of leadership offered by the owners and managers of various business interests of the city.[1]

In 1929, Reilly formulated a gravitational model when he stated that "under normal conditions two cities draw retail trade from a smaller intermediate city or town in direct proportion to some power of the population of these two large cities and in inverse proportion to some power of the distance of each of the cities from the smaller intermediate city."[2]

---

[1]William J. Reilly, "Method for the Study of Retail Relationships," Research Monograph No. 4, University of Texas Bulletin No. 2944 (Austin: University of Texas Press, 1929), pp. 21-22.

[2]Reilly, p. 16.

Various adaptations of Reilly's original formulation have been presented in the ensuing years. Two illustrations are presented here to show the use of such models and store location. P. D. Converse adapted Reilly's principle to predict the amount of fashion goods business that should be located in any town.[1] The formula was stated as:

$$\frac{Ba}{Bb} = \frac{(Pa)}{(Hb)} \quad \frac{(4)^2}{(d)}$$

where Ba = Proportion of trade going to the outside town

Bb = Proportion of trade retained by the home town

Pa = Population of the outside town

Hb = Population of the home town

d = Distance to the outside town

4 = Inertia factor

An interesting formulation of the drawing power of shopping centers was made by Harry J. Casey, Jr.,[2] expressed as follows:

$$Bia = \frac{\dfrac{Fa}{(Dia)^2}}{\dfrac{Fa}{(Dia)^2} \ \dfrac{Fb}{(Dib)^2} \ \dfrac{Fc}{(Dic)^2} \ \dfrac{Fd}{(Did)^2} \ \dfrac{Fe}{(Die)^2}} \ X \ B_1$$

Where

B_1 = Buying power of neighborhood 1.

Bia = Purchases made by residents of neighborhood 1 in the shopping center A

---

[1] Paul D. Converse, "A New Application of the Law of Retail Gravitation," Opinion and Comment, Vol. XII (August, 1947), and Converse, "New Laws of Retail Gravitation," Journal of Marketing, Vol. XIV (October, 1949), pp. 382-383.

[2] Harry J. Casey, Jr., p. 82. See also L. A. White and J.B. Ellis, "A System Construct for Evaluating Retail Market Locations," Journal of Marketing Research, Vol. 8, February, 1971.

Fa, Fb, Fc, etc. = The square feet of retail space in
the shopping centers A, B, C, etc.

Dia, Dib, Dic, etc. = Driving time distances between
neighborhood 1 and other retail
centers.

A high degree of judgment is required when using either the
empirical or gravitational approach in selecting a retail location,
and in defining the retail trading area of that site. If information is available on the factors affecting consumer travel, these
approaches can be reliable. However, students of distribution must
examine thoroughly the reasons underlying a consumer's travel
behavior. Considerable empirical and theoretical research still
needs to be done on retail store location.

Warehouse Terminal Locations

Terminals were defined as points in the distribution system
at which the shipment size requirements of the market, and the
shipment size desires of the movement system, are adjusted to each
other. Four types of terminals were described: dead storage,
break-bulk, assembly, and break-bulk and reassembly operations.

In assembly, less-than-volume shipments are accumulated
into volume quantity in order that power may be applied to the
movement process, as either multiple-movement-units-per-power-unit
or more payload in relation to deadload. The assembly terminal
allows a shift from less-than-volume to volume movement. It tends
to be located toward the origin point of shipments, either near
the raw material or the producer-oriented locations. Assembly
terminals might be located between the processing point and the
market if there are multiple plants, or sources, from which volume
shipments may be made. This is typical when nondistributional
costs favor dead storage at a point midway between the processing
point and the market.

A fundamental point in this discussion is the assumption of minimum distribution costs consistent with the requirements of the market place. It is possible, of course, to compute the costs of giving different levels of service and inventory replacement with terminal locations at various points in the distribution system.

Since break-bulk terminals are places to shift from volume to less-than-volume movements, such terminals will be oriented towards the markets in which they sell, although they may be between the processor and his primary markets. At a break-bulk and reassembly terminal, volume movements of single commodities are shifted to volume movements of mixed commodities. For example, individual carloads of separate commodities may come in from many separate origins and be placed in the terminal for temporary storage. They are then reassembled in smaller quantities, still as individual commodities, but each outbound shipment will constitute a volume move. There are many such warehouses. Break-bulk and reassembly terminals tend to be located toward the market and away from the processing points. The mixing point, of course, will be where the distribution cost of the products will be minimized.

If the customer's size of physical order and the volume requirements of the movement system are approximately the same, a volume shipment can be made direct from the processor to the customer without the necessity of a terminal operation. If the customer's physical requirements are smaller than the physical requirements of the movement system, a break-bulk operation may occur, in order to allow a less than volume shipment direct to the customer. However, if the customer's size of shipment requirements are lower than the less-than-volume requirements of the movement system, a break-bulk and reassembly terminal will probably have to be placed somewhere in the distribution system. The retail store is a break-bulk and reassembly terminal to which the customer comes to make his purchases.

As shown by LaLonde, the larger the assortment of merchandise, either in an individual store or in a store complex,
the farther the customer will travel to make his purchase. In
order to fill the physical demands of the retail store where its
purchases are below the volume requirements and, in some cases,
the less-than-volume requirements of the movement system, break-
bulk and reassembly warehouse points are inserted in the distribution system. This permits the shift from volume to less-than-
volume and back to volume movement to the retail store.

There is a distinct difference in the extent to which
terminal operations are carried on in the industrial and consumer
goods market. The amount per sale and the amount per shipment
tends to be considerably higher in the industrial market. Therefore, on the dispersion side of distribution, the desires of the
market and of the movement system are closer together in the
industrial market than in the consumer goods market, and there
is more need for the terminal function in the distribution of
consumer goods.

Some Early Attempts at Location Theory

The origin of the theory of location may be attributed to
three writers:

1. Johann Heinrich von Thunen (1875)
2. Whilhelm Launhardt (1885)
3. Alfred Weber (1909)

Von Thunen was concerned primarily with agricultural locations. Although his theory was designed to explain the type of
crops that would grow at various distances from the market, it is
nevertheless applicable to manufacturing locations. Locational
cost differences were considered to be due to land rent and
transportation expanses. Thus, assume in Figure 3.1 that OA is the
cost of producing a dollar's worth of potatoes and A's (and A"T)

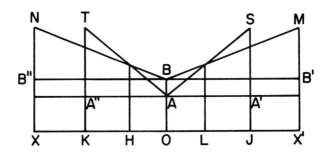

Source: Melvin L. Greenhut, <u>Plant Location in Theory and in Practice</u> (Chapel Hill, N.C.: University of North Carolina Press, 1956), p. 254.

Figure 3.1. A Graphic Representation of von Thunen's Theory.

the cost of transporting the potatoes over a distance of OJ (OK) miles. OB represents the cost of producing a dollar's worth of wheat, and the B'M (B"N) lines therefore represent the freight rate over a distance of OX' (OX) miles, the freight rate being higher on potatoes than on wheat.

Von Thunen's assumption of a uniform homogeneous plane signifies that labor and capital are equal in unit rate and productivity at all locations, and that the cost of production (exclusive of transport cost) is everywhere the same. The land rent and the cost of transporting the goods are thus the co-determinants of location. The producers of potatoes will be found in the OL (OH) region, while wheat will be grown between LX' (and HX).

Launhardt says the location of industry results from the difference in cost and demand at alternative locations. He presented the first significant treatment of industrial location theory, distinguishing between determining the site of production within or at the corners of a locational polygon, where the corners represented raw material sources and a one-point consumption space, and supplying a consuming area from a given point of production. Although he handled both problems comprehensively for his time, he made no attempt to put them together. In fact, Launhardt's studies of industrial location and market areas treated a narrower set of circumstances than were encompassed in von Thunen's isolated state.

Weber's theory of location is procedurally the opposite of von Thunen's. Von Thunen assumes a homogeneous land surface and one consuming center, though his general discussions are framed in terms of a given buying point.

Weber's theory is based upon three general factors of location: transportation cost, labor cost, and agglomerating forces. Figure 3.2 illustrates Weber's theory of location in terms of the transport and non-transport factors. It combines, in one illustration, the general regional influences (transportation and labor) with the general local forces (agglomerating advantages). It depicts the cost substitutions which take place in the search for the least-cost site.

Transport costs include the cost of shipping and the different costs of fuel and raw materials at given sites, plus the agglomerating factors (proximity to auxiliary industries, marketing advantages). Non-transport costs include the cost of labor and the land costs (rental, police and fire protection, economies of size, etc).

The curve of substitution SS is an isosale curve connecting a series of locations at which equal numbers of units may be sold. The isosale curve is less elastic from points D to A and more elastic from D to G. A movement from point B to A indicates a small saving in non-transport cost, but a larger increase in transport cost. Point D on the curve of substitution is the least-cost location; it is the point of unitary elasticity. Therefore, the plant is located at D; the point represents the unique

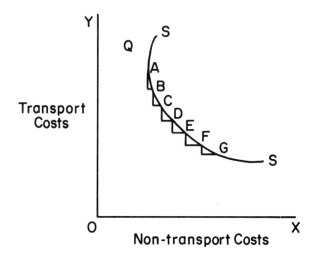

Source: Melvin L. Greenhut, <u>Plant Location in Theory and in Practice</u>
         (Chapel Hill, N.C.: University of North Carolina Press,
         1956), p. 13.

Figure 3.2.   Weber's Location Theory in Terms of Transport and
             Non-Transport Factors.

relationship between the transport cost factors and the non-transport
cost factors, which minimize the total unit charges.

     Weber's assumption of constant demand and omission of insti-
tutional factors left gaps which must be closed for a complete
understanding of plant locations in a capitalistic economy.

The Size and Shape of the Market Area

     Three individuals who have made substantial theoretical
contributions to spatial relationships in size and shape of the
market area are August Losch, Melvin Greenhut, and Walter Isard.
The major contributions of each are considered in this section.

     August Losch, in his studies, goes beyond partial analysis
and the mere recognition of the complex spatial interrelations of

economic factors. He presents succinctly a highly simplified
static model of a space economy operating under conditions of
monopolistic competition.

Losch depicts the hexagon as the most nearly perfect market
area shape; it is the shape which is required for locational equilibrium. Also, of all the regular polygons (hexagon, square,
triangle) which will exhaust a given area, the hexagon deviates
least from the circle form and, in consequence, minimizes the
transport expenditures in supplying a given demand; expressed
differently, it maximizes the demand of the population of a given
area.

For each commodity, then, the plane is dissected into a
honeycomb (a net of hexagons) of market areas. Losch groups these
honeycombs according to the size of their respective market units.
In a manner consistent with the established criterion of minimum
transport effort, he orders the resulting nets about a common,
central production point to obtain his system of nets. Losch's
equilibrium conditions are as follows: (1) the hexagon-shaped
market areas are determined by a system of equations for which
the initial condition is that each producer maximize his gains
(MR = MC); (2) all extraordinary profits must disappear; (3) the
area served by each individual is the smallest possible (to
prevent profits from existing); and (4) any consumer on a boundary
line is indifferent to the possible sources from which he can
obtain a given commodity at minimum cost.

After establishing the hexagon as the ideal market shape
and setting forth his equilibrium conditions, Losch views the
trading area of various products as a net of such hexagons. By
turning the nets around a common center, six sectors with most
production centers and six with fewest are obtained. The coincidence
of many of these centers concentrates the population, minimizes
the freight burdens, and enhances consumer demand by making
possible diverse purchases from many local mills. This, then,

is why Losch maintains that industry tends to agglomerate. These self-sufficient regions are considered ideal, economically.

While Losch's theory is highly informative, (1) he fails to include cost differentials, other than those attributable to agglomeration and transportation advantages, and (2) consequently he fails to combine an analysis of cost and demand factors in one model.

Melvin Greenhut attempts to combine the Weber and Losch approaches. Weber abstracted from the area concepts, failing to consider adequately the problem of maximization of total effective demand. Losch abstracted from the influence of forces causing intra-industry locational interdependence, failing to appraise adequately the private capitalistic economy. Greenhut not only believes that a fusion of the two approaches is possible, but offers understanding of underlying location factors, and from such evaluation endeavors to formulate a general theory.

Greenhut mentions that location factors are divisible into three broad groups: demand, cost, and purely personal considerations. Location theory has been moving towards an emphasis of the site that offers the largest spread between charge and receipts.

The demand factors include:
1. Shape of the demand curve
2. Location of competitors
3. Competitiveness of the industry in location and price
4. Significance of proximity, type and speed of service
5. Extent of the market area
6. Relationship between personal contacts and sales

The cost factors include:
1. Cost of land
2. Cost of labor and management
3. Cost of materials and equipment
4. Cost of transportation

The purely personal factors involve the extent to which the minimax principle outweighs the quest of maximum profits. This principle includes:

1. Importance of psychic income (size of plant)
2. Environmental preferences
3. Security motive

These factors are part of the system of plant location in a capitalistic economy, regardless of whether the particular focus be short-run or long-run. In every site selection, a balancing is involved among the three groups of factors. In his final note, Greenhut emphasizes again that locational equilibrium exists when spent energy units equal received energy units. Adding psychic dissatisfactions to, or subtracting satisfaction from, the expenditures of energy units would completely generalize the theory of location.[1]

Walter Isard's studies are much broader than Greenhut's. He attempts to improve the spatial and regional frameworks of the social science disciplines through the development of a more adequate theory of location and space-economy.

Isard demonstrates the utility of the concept of transport inputs in the determination of a firm's geographical position, and starts with the locational equilibrium of the firm when the problem of transport-orientation obtains. He presents graphically the problem of transport-orientation quoted from Launhardt and Palander. In effect, he postulates (1) the absence of the various agglomeration economies and of geographic variations, and (2) uniform transport facilities.

Incorporation of labor into the Launhardt-Palander construction is obtainable, and it can be converted into a more generalized location problem which considers the pull of sites possessing advantages in factors other than transport and relative spatial position. Once again, Isard demonstrated that all such

---

[1]The authors particularly recommend to the avid student Chapters 5 and 6 in Melvin Greenhut, Microeconomics and the Space Economy (Fair Lawn, N.J.: Scott, Foresman and Co., 1963). Also see M. L. Greenhut and H. Ohta, Theory of Spatial Pricing and Market Areas (Durham, N.C.: Duke University Press, 1975).

analysis can be embraced by a general substitution framework involving substitution among transport inputs and among outlays and
revenues.

Isard treats economies of scale, localization economies,
and urbanization economies as three subsets of agglomeration
factors. Further, he adopts Losch's various other assumptions
and conditions pertaining to his market area analysis. But unlike
Losch, Isard locates major transport routes through the heart of
city-rich and city-poor sectors, rather than at their boundaries.
This catches more fully the significant scale (urbanization)
economies in the use of modern transport media, and obtains a
pattern of distorted hexagons which, in general, decrease in size
as one approaches the central city. Isard also attempts a second,
contrasting path of integration, one that follows mathematical
lines, to couple with the notion of a spatial transformation function the fusing of location theory and production theory.

Weight Loss or Gain in Processing

Generally, two kinds of industries locate at the point of
production of the raw material: first, those industries where a
high percentage of the raw material is lost in processing the
material into a finished product; second, those industries where
perishability of the raw material makes it necessary to locate
the processing plant near its resource region.

In the forestry and mining industries, for example, there
is a high proportion of weight loss in at least the initial stages
of manufacture. Only one per cent of copper ore, as extracted
from the ground, is commercially useful. Smelting plants are
located near the mining area, and the other 99 per cent of the
ore extracted and dumped near the smelting plant before the
refined copper is shipped on to other destinations. In the
lumber industry, the logs are trimmed, cut, and sized into rough

lumber near the production points. The lumber is then shipped
from the mill to ultimate destinations, where it is transformed
into various wood products in the market areas. In the beet
industry, only a portion of the beet as it is dug from the ground
is used for sugar purposes. Many fresh products, of course, are
moved intact to the market without any processing.

Agricultural commodities such as cherries, asparagus, and
tomatoes are other perishable goods processed near the production
point. In such instances, the produce must be left in the field
to ripen, then canned immediately, in order to maintain maximum
palatability. If these products were shipped to the market either
before or after reaching ripeness, they would deteriorate enough
so that the canning plants must locate near where the agricultural
products are grown.

Normally, products which gain weight in processing are
market-oriented. From a movement cost point of view, the material
can be more economically added at the market than at an intermediate point or the point of raw material production. For example,
in the soft drink industry, the basic syrups are shipped from raw
material-producing points to the market place, where carbonated
water is added. Such carbonation plants are usually located in
the market in which the product is to be sold.

Weight loss or gain definitely affects distribution system
requirements. Plants for weight-losing products are usually
located near the raw material source, and the raw material will
move a relatively short distance. The raw materials of weight-
gaining products will be shipped longer distances, with the
finished good shipped sub-regionally. In other words, the distribution system's transportation requirements for weight-losing and
weight-gaining products are exact opposites.

Effect of Scale Economics

Much economic theory concerns the effect of economies of scale on production costs of a firm. If a firm can realize economies of scale, the long run average cost curve will decrease over a wide range as output increases. This decrease means that successively larger scales of factor utilization are more efficient than smaller ones. Two of the greatest contributors to increasing efficiency and, hence, decreasing costs are (1) division and specialization of labor, and (2) larger and more efficient machines and/or advanced technological methods.

Not all increases in scale result in decreasing unit costs. Some firms have relatively constant costs, while others may have increasing costs. Constant cost firms do not realize substantial economies or diseconomies as they increase their output and, hence, can expand or contract their output with relatively little change in long run average total costs. Increasing cost firms, or "diseconomies of scale," mean that the long run average cost curve may first decline with an initial increase in output, but would reach its lowest point rapidly and continue with increasing costs over a wide range of output. Such diseconomies of scale can result from increasing prices in the firm's factor markets as it increases its demand, the hiring of labor which is progressively less efficient, or management's inability to control larger scale operations.

In normal economic usage, the term "production costs" and the average total cost curve would include the distribution system costs of a firm. In the analysis which follows, the distribution costs of raw materials and finished goods have been removed from "production costs" and are shown separately. Thus the effects of movement costs, as an input into the cost structure of a firm, can be considered separately. The three cases of decreasing, increasing and constant costs are shown in Figures 3.3, 3.4, and 3.5. The lower solid LAPC line represents the long run average production

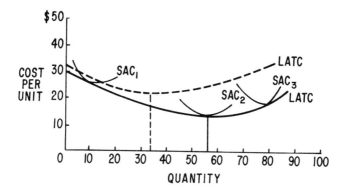

Figure 3.3.   Decreasing Unit Costs.

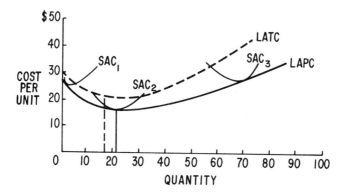

Figure 3.4.   Increasing Unit Costs.

68

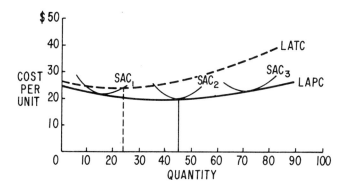

Figure 3.5. Constant Unit Costs.

costs (minus movement costs), while the dotted LATC line above
represents long run average total costs (production costs plus
movement costs). The smaller curves in each illustration represent three of the short run average production cost curves from
which the long run curve was derived. Assuming a competitive product market and no movement costs, the lowest point on the LAPC
curve would be the optimum output for the firm, from a production
cost point of view. Given the competitive product market, this
is also the point of equilibrium for the firm. The space between
the LAPC and LATC curves indicates the average movement costs at
any given level of output.

In analyzing distribution costs in relation to the level
of output, three effects may occur. First, increased output at
a given location may require that raw materials be acquired at
more distant sources. Second, expanding output may require the
firm either to cultivate more intensively sales in its given market
area, or attempt extensive sales cultivation in markets more distant from the plant. Third, both of the above may occur as output
expands.

In each of the illustrations, the distribution costs were assumed to be a constant cost per unit per mile, but the raw materials and finished goods both required longer shipments as output increased.[1] This increase in shipping distances causes the average movement cost to increase with output. Herein lies the general case of the effect of transportation costs in relation to increasing levels of output. Movement costs in a given location normally result in diseconomies of scale (increasing average movement costs) due to the sheer activity of overcoming increases in space resulting from increases in the level of output.

The interrelationship of production costs and distribution costs to the location of a firm can be analyzed with the help of Figures 3.3, 3.4, and 3.5. As noted earlier, the optimum output and point of equilibrium in each case is the lowest point of the respective LAPC curves. Likewise, when distribution costs are added to the production costs and a competitive product market is assumed, the optimum output and point of equilibrium is the lowest point on the LATC curve. In each case, this point with movement costs included is at a lower output than the previous point. Therefore, in the general case (increasing average movement costs) the effect on all three types of production costs firms is to cause the optimum output and equilibrium point to be at a lower level than if there were no distribution costs.

Thus, industries with declining average production costs tend to locate in or near their primary markets in order to

---

[1] It should be recognized that there are many other cases than the one above which could cause the average movement cost curve to take one of many shapes. The average movement cost per mile is not only affected by the distance involved, but also by the size of shipments. Like other components of cost, an increase in the scale of distribution operations (the size of shipments) can result in increasing, decreasing, or constant average costs. This is true since the same possibilities for using division and specialization of labor and larger and more efficient methods become available.

minimize finished goods movement costs (since raw materials move at generally lower rates than finished products). Under such conditions, a firm with decreasing production costs tends to deliver its products to markets at a point of distance, where the distribution cost increase approximately equals the production cost decrease.

Those firms with increasing production costs and a difference in raw material and finished goods rates will tend to orient themselves toward the primary markets in which they sell. Thus, firms with increasing average production cost curves decentralize, whereas those firms with decreasing average production costs centralize and ship their finished products over a wider geographic area.

Those firms having relatively constant average production costs will have a degree of plant centralization between that of decreasing and increasing cost firms.

Solution of the Unbalanced Movement Problem

Normally, rates on raw materials and finished goods charged by the various distribution systems differ. These differences make it desirable for processors to locate where their total movement cost from origin of materials to point of consumption will be minimized. If there were no difference between the inbound rate on the raw material and the outbound rate on the finished goods, the problem of industrial location would not be nearly as complex as it is.

If the carriers had a balanced flow of movement directionally on each portion of the movement system, and if population and raw material were equally distributed throughout the market area, it might be possible for the distribution system to follow a system of average pricing. The result, considering only weight and distance, would be an equal rate on the raw material and the finished goods. However, populations and raw materials are not located uniformly throughout the market place, and there are no uniform directional movements throughout the transportation system. Populations are clustered in geographic areas; raw materials are available only in certain locations. The consequent imbalance in the transportation system causes a difference in rates charged on commodities moved.[1]

Movement systems, therefore, have excess capacity from two points of view. The fundamental cause of imbalance raises from unequal distribution of population and raw materials. The other cause, not necessarily resulting from the first, is that the transportation system may have excess capacity between points in time throughout the whole system.

A map illustrating the effect of the first cause shows that the major population centers are located in the Northeast quadrant of the country. Raw materials from the West are moved to these centers for processing. Much of the equipment is empty on the return journey to the West because the market for finished goods in the West does not provide full volume for the equipment on the return trip.

The alternatives available to the movement system are: (1) to make the raw materials move bear the entire cost of the round trip[2] or (2) to price the return trip low enough to attract additional traffic. The carrier must, of course, recover full

---

[1]There are often cost reasons which result in different rates at different points in the movement system. A few such transportation cost-causing differences are weight, weight-density, distance, and the number of pieces in the shipment. However, temporarily abstracting from these cost-causing differences, the explanation of differences in raw material and finished-goods rates becomes considerably simpler.

[2]The round trip is an excellent example of joint cost, since the return trip is necessary for the equipment to be returned to origin for additional movements of raw materials. An increase in one results in an increase in the other.

cost, plus a reasonable profit for the total. He therefore tends
to charge more than the actual cost for moving raw materials and
to price the return portion of the journey at a lower level of
order to attract some movement of finished goods.

Therefore, directional excess capacity provides the mechanism for value-of-service pricing which, in turn, can lead to rate
charges of more or less than the full costs of movement. Specific
examples of directional excess capacity are: (1) the empty return
of movement units from the eastern part of the United States; (2)
the high ratio of empty miles to loaded miles for specialized types
of equipment such as tank cars, refrigerator cars, stock cars, and
petroleum tank trucks; and (3) the unbalanced movements into
automobile assembly centers, where the inbound move of parts may
be by motor carrier of general commodities and the return move
by specialized automobile haulaway truck equipment. In each of
these instances, the phenomenon of directional excess capacity lets
the carrier, if he so desires, utilize value-of-service pricing to
promote traffic in the direction of light loadings.

Seasonal or cyclical fluctuations in demand are another
aspect of excess capacity. The movement system must be prepared
to meet such variations in the sale of shipper's products by
having the necessary equipment on hand to move them. For example,
in the automobile industry both car and truck assembly varies
widely from year to year and the movement system must provide
enough equipment to meet the fluctuating demand. Such an excess
capacity, created by seasonal and cyclical fluctuations of shipper
demand, tends to create value-of-service pricing to induce traffic
to move.

Carrier competition and seller competition in common markets
also create a difference between raw materials rates and finished-
goods rates. To illustrate, assume as in Figure 3.6, that Carrier
1 has been operating between points A and B and now faces competition

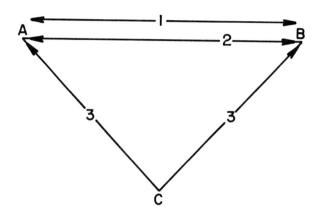

Figure 3.6.   Illustration of Carrier Competition.

with Carrier 2 between these two points.   Further, assume complete
freedom of competition within the field under consideration.   There
is (1) no agreement between producers to restrict competition or
production at any level; (2) no price agreement; (3) relative
freedom of the companies' managements to utilize the factors of
movement; and (4) an elastic demand curve for the firms' services.
Under such circumstances, the two carriers in the field must
attempt to compete on a price and/or service basis to secure
business from each other.   Under conditions of pure competition,
these two carriers would be willing to quote prices lower than the
full cost of furnishing the service in order to take business from
each other.

For further illustration, assume that a third carrier
operates between points A and B via point C.   In this instance,
Carrier 3 would be a circuitous-route carrier, and would have to
at least meet the price of Carriers 1 and 2 between points A and
B.   Carrier 3 may actually be in a fortuitous position since it
monopolizes traffic between these respective points in order to
compete with Carriers 1 and 2 between points A and B.

Such situations may exist at various times under pure competition regardless of the carrier's ability to obtain constant or
variable costs. This is well illustrated by the rate wars of the
railroad during the nineteenth century, and of the airlines and
motor carriers before regulation by federal and state law. In an
attempt to obtain business, carriers quite frequently lower their
rates, not only below the level of their full costs of operation,
but sometimes below the level of their variable costs. If such
a competitive situation continues for a long period, one or more
of four events is likely to occur: (1) the carriers may voluntarily
agree to restrict competition on either a service or a rate basis;
(2) there may be some business failures, resulting in less competition; (3) amalgamation, merger, or consolidation may occur
among the carriers; or (4) restriction upon entrance into the
transportation field may occur through outside control. Actually,
all four have occurred in the field.

The significance of the relationship between excess capacity
(directional and/or seasonal or cyclical) and carrier competition
is that the former provides the mechanism for value-of-service
pricing and the latter makes the carriers want to engage in this
pricing practice. Beginning about 1900, railroads developed rate
associations to minimize price competition among themselves. This
practice has been followed by other forms of transportation, particularly those engaging in common carriage.

In addition to the components creating value-of-service
pricing, vendor competition also helps explain the differences
between raw materials and finished-goods rates. This will be
treated in two phases: first, the competition of raw material
vendors who are spatially separated from a given market; and second,
competition of processing plants to supply given markets from
alternative plant locations.

Distant raw material vendors must compete with close sources
for sales to a given market. Assume, as in Figure 3.7, that suppliers at points A and B with raw material sources of equal grade
are competing for sales of this raw material to a plant located in
city C. Assume also that two different carriers are serving from
B to C and from A to C. In this instance, it is obvious that if
raw materials suppliers located in A are to compete with city B,
they must absorb at least 40 cents per hundredweight in freight
charges, the difference between the 60 cent A-to-C rate and 20
cent B-to-C rate. Only suppliers at A who can absorb this freight
charge may attempt to compete in market C. However, a common
result from such a competitive situation is that vendors apply
pressure to transportation companies to lower the rate in order
to compete in a competitor's more distant markets.

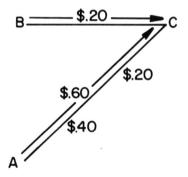

Figure 3.7. Illustration of Shipper Competition.

The net result on the carrier's rate structure will be the
same in terms of shipper pressure for depressed rates from geographically distant points to a common market, whether raw materials
or finished products are concerned. As was pointed out by J. H.

von Thunen, and later by August Losch, with a single seller in a market place and a constant transportation rate per ton-mile, the market area for the product from a given plant will tend to be circular. Losch points out that as more producers enter the market place, each producer's market area becomes hexagonal. Introducing the concept of a decreasing unit cost curve, the market patterns of spatially differentiated producers serving common markets will overlap at varying points in time. As presented later by Walter Isard, these hexagonal markets continuously overlap as producers competing in a common market constantly evaluate their unit costs of production, the costs of transport to the market, and the extent to which they can absorb freight into these common markets at any point.

As a result of these pressures from shippers of both raw material and finished products, the carriers have the dilemma of whether or not to lower the rate below full costs of movement to allow competition in a common market. These pressures, in the aggregate, force individual and competitive carriers to adjust their rate structure for maximum movement of goods (in keeping with revenue requirements to meet total costs of operation). This, in turn, leads to value-of-service pricing in order to maximize their total revenue.

A final consideration in the difference between raw material and finished-goods rates is the previously discussed difference in handling costs. This can easily be visualized in the case of coal. Coal cars are loaded directly from the coal tipple, and are un-loaded (in the case of hopper cars) by gravity flow from the bottom of the car at the shipper's docks. Or in transferring coal from cars to lake vessel, the cars are simply turned upside down and dumped into the laker, which then hauls the coal to other lake ports for further transfer. Another example is wheat, which may be un-loaded into a storage facility by gravity flow. The wheat is then

moved into the storage elevator by conveyor belt and reloaded by
gravity flow from a chute into the rail car.

At the other extreme, in the motor carrier terminal operation, a pickup unit gathers small, discreet packages from the
various shippers in the metropolitan area and brings the load into
the terminal for reassembly into an outbound line-haul motor carrier
movement unit. The individual packages must be hand moved from the
shipper's dock onto the pickup truck, then unloaded, by hand, from the
pickup truck onto the carrier's dock, then moved either by hand or
mechanically to the other side of the dock to the appropriate line-
haul unit. This process is reversed at the destination terminal.
Obviously, there is a vast difference in the cost per hundredweight
of handling raw materials and finished goods. These differences
in handling costs add to the possibility of the distribution systems
pricing movement to vendors on a value-of-service basis.

CHAPTER 4

MEASUREMENT OF SYSTEM CHANGE

Introduction

The advent of operations research and systems analysis techniques has given the manager new tools with which to inquire into
the workings of his organization. These techniques have made him
a scientist in his own right. He is now able to face problems with
objectivity and provide quantitative responses to complex issues.
The techniques have increased his capacity to study and learn new
fields, to provide new understanding of his position, and to study
the ability of his organization to survive in the crucible of the
marketplace.

As competitors avail themselves of these new techniques,
the manager has come to depend on specialists in each of the areas
that impinge on his operations. But he is still faced with the
problem of being able to provide an objective response to the range
of problem resolutions offered him by the specialist. All this has
brought the manager to realize that the organization which he
manages is but a segment of larger business systems.

Even though there are social considerations that the
manager faces, the emphasis must be on the profit aspect of
operations by which investors gauge his abilities. That vital
difference between sales and costs is the ultimate measure of
the marketplace. Only by observing a systems outlook can the
distribution manager keep pace with those other segments of the
organization which make demands on the financial resources of the
firm, and with which he must compete in order to function properly

and provide the owners of the firm with adequate insurance to maintain investor interest.

In this sort of an environment, where performance is the name of the game, the manager is continually planning changes in the current organization in order to keep pace and hopefully to advance on his competitors. He must foster an insatiable desire for facts as they pertain to his operation and then be able to organize these information bits into usable data on which to base decisions. The dependency on factual information increases as the predictive power of these techniques increases, and that can only occur as he applies a scientific methodology to his applications of these techniques.

The scientific method, in its ideal form, calls for this special desire for factual information. The ability to distill this information into utilitarian data is a special task for the manager; he must be able to specify the exact information required in the decision process and then apply this data in the methodologies available to him. This requires the manager to understand the concept of the model of the process that he is investigating or operating, the measures of effectiveness, the necessity for decision, and the role of the experimentation process.

Use of Models in the Systems Approach

The most frequently encountered concept in the systems approach is that of the model--a simplified representation of the process, action, or operation being considered, simplified to the extent that it includes only those aspects of the system that need be measured to exemplify the system. In most applications in the field of logistics, the model is a mathematical formulation of the operation, a set of equations relating the significant variables in the operation that relate to the operation. In fact, the mathematical model is required because of the inability of the manager to utilize actual operations as a laboratory, partially because of cost and partly due to the necessity for maintaining normal operations in the business community. Thus the manager must simulate the probable responses of the system as various environmental conditions are inserted into some sort of a model. The concept of the model then leads to the derivation of theories of the operation of the system. These theories lead to the postulation of hypotheses to be used in the interpretation of the model and the physical system it represents.

Performance Measurement of the System

In order to interpret the phenomena encountered in the model, the manager must be able to express the level of goal achievement of the model in the various operational modes he simulates. The question of goal achievement is simply how well does the system accomplish its purpose? The notion of an adequate response links four distinct spatial-temporal steps:

1. The identification of those environmental circumstances or events which act as stimuli and evoke the response.
2. The response.
3. The environmental circumstances which the response meets during its execution.
4. The occurrence of a certain event or state of affairs, viz., the so-called goal of the response as an effect of the interaction between (2) and (3).[1]

Schematically, this is shown in Figure 4.1, where we call the environmental stimulus S, the response R, the environmental circumstances encountered E, and the desired goal G. At time period t_0 a stimulus S_{t_0} evokes a response R_{t_1} which may or may not interact with environmental circumstances E_t in the same time period t_0 to t_1. This response contributes to the achievement of goal G in time period t_2.

---

[1] G. Summerhof, "Purpose, Adaptation, and Directive Correction," Walter Buckley, p. 282.

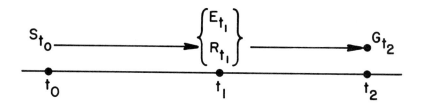

Figure 4.1. Schematic For System Adaptation.

The place of this schematic within the adaptive framework presented in Chapter 1 is that the interactions at either the macro or micro system levels will take this general form. The macro level of society will have interactions between human wants and needs, human technical knowledge and skills, and available natural resources. For example, the stimulus in t_0 might be an increase in the level of human wants and needs. The response of R in t_1 of human technology and natural resources interacting with the environmental influences of E_{t_1} would make possible the attainment of this demand as G_{t_2}. Responses at a more micro level, adjustments of the firm, would also take this same form.

Types of System Behavior

If we assume that the system is purposeful, then we also assume that the system will carry out certain actions toward specific goals. These system actions belong in three distinct categories:

1. Invariant behavior in changing environments (zero order)

2. Variant behavior due to changing environments (first order)

3. Variant behavior with alternative environments (second order)

Systems with Invariant Behavior (Zero Order)

The system which possesses invariant behavior in changing
environments is fairly easy to characterize, since the environmental changes around the system do not affect it. This type of
system is independent and behaves in a set routine. Most production processes are of this type, in that the behavior of a machine
is determined by the flow of inputs only and not the presence of
other machines in the plant. The processing of the information
needed for component operation may very well be handled in coordination with other components. However, in the case of the invariant
function, this information flow does not affect the operation of
that component possessing invariant behavior.

The schematic for adaptability in this type of behavior
becomes simply:

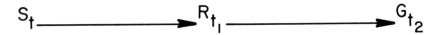

$$S_t \longrightarrow R_{t_1} \longrightarrow G_{t_2}$$

The effect of the environment is negligible and therefore not a
part of the adaptive process. Measurement tests in this type of
situation are not difficult to construct. By definition, the
behavior does not change. Clocks continue to run whether it is
hot or cold. Electric light switches work in widely varying
environments. Pipelines operate continuously with given pressures.
Delivery schedules can be specified. The test of this kind of
behavior is simply, "does it work or not?"

This zero order component offers no measure of goal attainment or objective achievement. Another analogy would be that
of an analyst attempting to discern trends in the operations of
the firm by having only a single year's balance sheet at hand.

This invariant behavior is also exemplified by the fixed
cost segment of the firm's distribution system costs. When the

firm's level of operation changes in response to changing environments, the fixed costs of terminal operations, management, and
financial portions of the total systems costs do not vary. The
equation

$$X = K + VY$$

where X = Total Cost
      V = Volume
      Y = Variable Cost
      K = Fixed Costs
describes the invariant function (the fixed cost element) component operation.

One critical aspect of this type of function is that there
is no inherent feedback, or memory. This type of component is not
capable of learning from a set of previous inputs and results. It
is essentially a steady state system providing a snapshot of the
component at a single point in time.

Variant System Behavior in Changing Environments (First Order)

The next level in the hierarchy of component behavior
(first order) is that of the simple element that provides a direct
feedback to the analyst and decision maker for the purposes of
controlling the component itself. The system is keyed to respond
to certain external stimuli or environmental changes. The first-
order system can be likened to a two position switch with an open
or closed node. This component possesses a conditional operative
behavior, so that when external environmental changes occur the
first-order system can alter its state to respond to programmed
levels of change. The thermostatic controls in heating and cooling
systems are typical of this type of system.

84

The adaptability of the second type is somewhat more difficult to measure than the invariant behavior. The schematic shown
in Figure 4.2 would be the basic adaptivity model. Fortunately,
the reaction between E_{t_1} and R_{t_1} will involve only one type of
behavior in any given environment.[1] Within the given environment,
information systems can be designed to record and signal the need
for adaptive action. The automatic temperature control can signal
the system on or off for given objective temperatures and if new
objectives are sought, new functions are used to attain the new
objective.

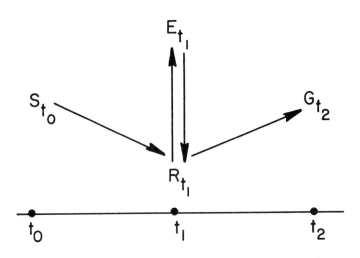

Figure 4.2. System Adaptation of Variant Behavior with Changing
Environments.

---

[1]S_{t_0} is presumed not to directly affect E_{t_1} which also does
not directly affect G_{t_2}. In macro systems some circumstances might
be of sufficient proportions to have direct relationships from
$S \longrightarrow E$ and $E \longrightarrow G$.

In the analysis of distribution systems, the first-order
component provides feedback information on system status by
signaling the expediture of amounts greater than standard cost
estimates in the various segments. The example below shows the
typical method of operation in this instance:

State I   When TA is less than zero, stop operations
State II   When TA is equal or greater than zero, continue
            operations
where   A equals (Standard cost minus Actual cost)
and   T equals the number of transactions in the
            period.

In actual operations, the order to cease operations is
downgraded to a cautionary signal to the system manager. He would
initiate the analysis of the conditions leading to the greater than
estimated costs, and institute suitable component changes or revise
the standard cost actuating level, depending on the circumstances
surrounding the variation in planned operational costs. The new
level of standard costs or the designation of a different filter
level to warn the decision maker represents the response necessary
for the system to respond to changes in the environment, and the
change in the component required if the desired goal is to be met.
The component is then reprogrammed to be triggered at these new
levels.

Variant System Behavior in a Constant Environment (Second Order)

Next in system complexity is the system that learns as it
operates and adapts internally to changes in external stimuli.
This second-order behavior expands on the first-order system's
inability to predict or make a conditional choice of actions to
be taken in response to external stimuli and internal variances in
the component. It incorporates the ability to remember what has
transpired in the past, and applies these memories to what is

apparently occurring within the component at the time. For example, the first-order component must be reprogrammed externally to respond to operational changes (i.e., the changes in actual costs), while the second-order system can recognize what is occurring in the component, uses the memory of the past to change the standard cost or the filter level, and continues to operate. The decision maker may desire a record of the changes made. A recording device may be appended to components to display these changes.

Measurement of adaptivity in the third type of behavior, shown schematically in Figure 4.3, is considerably more difficult. Let us assume that S consists of a set of stimuli, E a set of environmental circumstances, R a set of responses, and G a set of possible goals. Since in purposive behavior we state that there are alternative paths which may be followed to connect S, E, R, and G, a statement is needed to bring order to this set of alternatives. Sets of elements so arrayed can be referred to as "correlated" if a one-to-one relationship exists between the members of the sets. This has been very well summarized by Sommerhof:

> . . . The statements that R_{t1} is adapted to E_{t1} in respect of G_{t2} means that the organism or mechanism causally determining R_{t1} is objectively so conditioned that if certain initial circumstances had caused the occurrence of any alternative member of the set E_{t1}, E_{t1}, E_{t1}, . . . it would in each case have caused the occurrence of the correlated set R_{t1}, R_{t1}, R_{t1}, . . . of appropriate responses.[1]

It is not necessary that these elements, like S^1, R^1, and E^1, be correlated with G^1. From a measurement point of view, it would be helpful and much simpler in measuring system adaptation if this were true. In those instances where there is no correlation between the specific elements of S, R, E, and G, then non-correlation techniques must be used. A wide range of such measures is available. Indeed, most complex system response is in this category of problem.

---

[1] G. Summerhof, "Purpose, Adaptation, and Directive Correction," Walter Buckley, pp. 286-287.

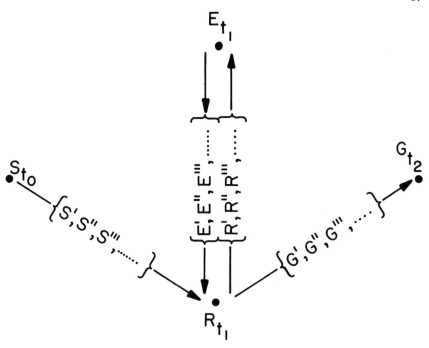

Figure 4.3. Schematic for System Adaptation of Variant Behavior
With or Without a Constant Environment.

In the daily operation of a distribution system, daily
operations reports can be utilized to present the system adaptations made in the course of the day. Flagging the changes made in
the component's operation and the new levels of decision as a
portion of the operations report can be made a part of the executive review. Completion of the review and the determination
of probable effects of the responses to stimuli encountered
during the period are the only requirements for the decision
maker working with the second order component.

Basic to this level of behavior is planning for changes,
and the installment of an array of conditional statements into

the memory and control element of the component. An example would be the establishment of an operating rule stating that whenever a required delivery date cannot be met using the normal shipping means, the component schedules the movement by premium transportation. Another action, used when the customer is purchasing the transportation, would be the dispatch of a message stating the new expected delivery date and inquiring whether the customer wishes the use of a faster delivery means.

In all three types of adaptive behavior, the definition of adaptation assumes the presence of initial circumstances in S which cause the occurrence of events in R and E to lead to G. These initial circumstances in S are the independent variables; there must be one or more such variables in every case of adaptation. In fact, it is in the actions of these independent variables that we seek to find an economic series which will give us some basis for forecasting trends in the independent variables.

This development of the probable effects of continued system operation under the present conditions, and a comparison of the possible operation using an improved criterion, give us the thinking portion of the component which allows learning and memory of past events to assembly an array of possible alternatives for the decision maker. All this requires the use of automated computation to be useful in something other than historical analysis.

Measurement of Profitability in the System

In the private sector of business enterprise, the individual firm relies upon the profitability of its efforts to determine the extent to which it is adapting to changing circumstances. In order to stay competitive, companies must have information on stimulus, response, environmental circumstances, and goal objectives to quickly determine the profitable and non-profitable segments of their business. This means an increased emphasis on planning and control of the system, regardless of whether the reason for change comes from externally imposed stimuli or from changes in the environmental circumstances constituting a response to the efforts of the firm to sell its products and services.

The planning and control of the system, with particular reference to the S, E, R, and G portions of the adaptive framework, necessitate three kinds of accounting: external accounting, functional cost accounting, and segmental profit analysis. Each one of these is defined in order to show how they relate to the measurement of system profitability.

External accounting needs of the business concern the preparation of summary statements, such as the balance sheet and the statement of profit and loss, which aggregate the operation of the business into the natural accounts. If the system is one of invariant behavior, then the traditional process of aggregating accounts into the form necessary for external statements will be quite adequate for measuring profitability. Since invariant behavior is not concerned with changes in environmental stimulus or in the environmental circumstances, the totals constructed for the firm would be quite adequate and we would not be concerned with information for changing component elements of the system. The totals for the firm itself would be sufficient.

Functional cost accounting is the determination of cost by function in order to assure the efficient operation of each of the functional parts of the business. A function is defined as a principal activity center of the enterprise: warehousing, selling, packaging, inventory control and management, terminals, or such other principal logistics activities. Functional centers are necessary for planning and control of systems adaptability. If the logistic system is responding to invariant behavior, then the need for functional cost accounting will be minimal and company totals might suffice. If, however, the logistic system is responding to variant behavior in both the stimulus and the environmental circumstances, then more timely information must be furnished to the functional center managers. This information must be broken down into as many response centers as are necessary to adapt the functional centers to changing stimulus and environmental circumstances.

Segmental profit analysis is the evaluation of the performance of the market segments of the enterprise. A segment is defined as an analytical unit to which costs and revenues can be specifically attached, so that it can become a focal point for planning and control. Typically, such segments include categories of customers, products, territories, and order or shipment size. The concept of segmental profit analysis is relatively new in many businesses, although in the more progressive firms this type of analysis has been going on for many years.

A segment is basically a collection of functional efforts being performed for a particular part in the market. For example, if the segment under consideration involves categories of customers, then the expenses will relate to the functional cost involved in producing and delivering to the particular customer a range of functional services.

The needed accounting information for segmental profit analysis consists of a sales forecast; plans for the promotional, physical distribution, and other functional mixes; construction of the budget; and monitoring of performance. The provision of this information is particularly important if the type of system is one of variant behavior, either in a changing or constant environment. Considerable attention will be devoted to developing this information on a timely basis for segmental profit analysis.

Use of the Contribution Approach as a Basis
for Measuring System Profitability

There are two approaches to segmental analysis: the traditional net income approach and the more modern contribution approach. The basic difference between the two is the extent to which costs are allocated.

Net Income Approach to Determination
of Segmental Profit

The net income approach allocates all costs on some basis, however arbitrary, to arrive at a segmental net income figure. This usually goes through at least a two-step procedure, in which the account balances and the natural accounts are allocated to the functional cost centers. These functional costs are then allocated to customers on some arbitrary basis. To illustrate this procedure, let us assume that we have two natural accounts-- wages of $2,500 and rent in the amount of $500. If the three functional cost centers are sales expense, packaging expense, and advertising expense, the wages may be allocated to each of the three functional cost centers on the basis of the number as indicated, of people involved; rent is allocated similarly. Let us further assume that there are three customers--A, B, and C--who produce sales revenues as indicated. Customer A produces 35% of total sales revenue; customer B, 30%; and customer C, 35%. The allocation of sales salaries of $1,000 would then be allocated to customer A in the amount of $350; customer B, $300; and customer C, $350.

Suppose that customer A did all his business through one order, but customer B required 99 orders and customer C, 900 orders. If the average cost per order were $1, let us see what would happen to customer costs if we allocated on the basis of the number of orders. The cost for customer A would be $1; the cost for customer B, $99; and the cost for customer C would be $900.

92

Natural Accounts	Sales	Packaging	Advertising
Wages $2,500 ⟶	$1,000	$900	$600
Rent $500 ⟶		$250	$250

Figure 4.4. Allocation of Functional Costs on Arbitrary Basis.

Customer	Sales Revenue	Percent of Sales
A	$87,500	35.0
B	$75,000	30.0
C	$87,500	35.0
	$250,000	100.0%

Figure 4.5. Allocation of Sales Salaries by Total Sales Revenue.

The point of this is that cost allocations are made on an arbitrary basis, both from the natural accounts to the functional cost centers and from the functional cost centers to the segment. The selection of the allocation basis will indicate the extent to which the segment is profitable. In no instance will the basis of allocation be "fair" to all segments of the market.

This raises very real problems in determining segment protitability. If we rely on segmental profit to determine segment response to environmental stimulus and environmental change, then we are on extremely shaky ground. We are employing a faulty system to determine segmental costs and, hence, segmental profit.

Contribution Approach to Determination
of Segmental Profit

The contribution margin approach charges to a segment only
those costs directly attributable to its production of revenue.
In the following illustration of Excalibur Mining Equipment an
income and expense account statement is shown for the Specific
Products Division. The division is charged with only the cost of
goods sold and expenses directly attributable to it. The division's
revenue of $10 million less the $6 million of cost of goods sold
and $1,650,000 of division expense resulted in a contribution to
corporate costs and profits of $2,350,000. Only when the same
thing had been done for all other divisions were corporate costs
deducted. Specifically, the $4 million, in corporate costs was
not deducted from the contribution of any particular division.
Rather, it was deducted from the contribution of all divisions in
order to determine corporate net income.

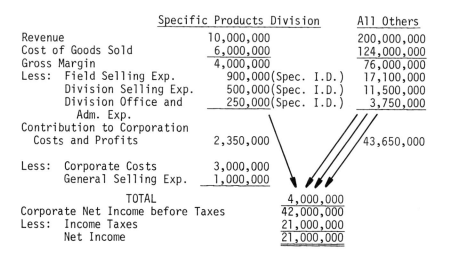

	Specific Products Division			All Others
Revenue	10,000,000			200,000,000
Cost of Goods Sold	6,000,000			124,000,000
Gross Margin	4,000,000			76,000,000
Less: Field Selling Exp.	900,000	(Spec.	I.D.)	17,100,000
Division Selling Exp.	500,000	(Spec.	I.D.)	11,500,000
Division Office and Adm. Exp.	250,000	(Spec.	I.D.)	3,750,000
Contribution to Corporation Costs and Profits	2,350,000			43,650,000
Less: Corporate Costs	3,000,000			
General Selling Exp.	1,000,000			
TOTAL				4,000,000
Corporate Net Income before Taxes				42,000,000
Less: Income Taxes				21,000,000
Net Income				21,000,000

Figure 4.6. Summary of the Contribution Approach.

In the net income approach, where all costs are allocated,
the net income of the Specific Products Division was $1 million, as
shown in Figure 4.7. In this fully allocated cost illustration,
the Specific Products Division had no control over the allocation

	Excalibur Mining Equipment Company		Specific Products Division
Revenue	210,000,000	Specific I.D.	10,000,000
Cost of Goods Sold	130,000,000	Std. (est.) Cost	6,000,000
Gross Margin	80,000,000		4,000,000
Less: Field Selling Expense	18,000,000	Allocate	900,000
General Selling Expense	15,000,000	Allocate	800,000
Office and Admin. Expense	5,000,000	Allocate	300,000
Net Income before Taxes	42,000,000		2,000,000
Less: Income Tax	21,000,000	Allocate	1,000,000
NET INCOME	21,000,000		1,000,000

NOTE: Sum of Division Incomes = Corporate Income

Figure 4.7. Summary of the Reconciliation of Net Income Approach.

of field selling expense, general selling expense, and office and
administrative expense to its particular division. Rather, the
costs were simply allocated on an arbitrary basis. The result is
a determination of net income, which means little to the manager
of the Specific Products Division. It would seem much better to
charge the division, at least in the segmental income statement,
only for those items which are controllable by the particular
division. In this sense, the contribution approach means a great
deal more to the division manager, since he has an indication to
him of the expenses over which he can exercise planning and control.

The needs for systems adaptability--where there is variant
behavior in either a constant or changing environment--are met much

more adequately by the contribution approach to the determination of segmental profit than by the net income approach. The determination of response by segments to environmental stimulus and to environmental change must be translated into the component elements of the system. In terms of the logistics and the component elements of the system, the functional and segmental managers should have the information available to them, on a timely basis, on those costs over which they have some responsibilities for planning and control.

An additional comparison of the net income and the contributional approach is made in the accompanying illustration.[1] Column 1 in the illustration shows the external accounting format of total company sales less total expenses equal net income. For invariant systems this type of system measurement would be quite adequate if only overall company reaction to change is desirable.

Column 2 illustrates segmental analysis, using the net income approach. Sales are divided into selected segments, and the various functional costs are fully allocated to the segments. Net income for the segments is equal to company net income. The need for understanding some adaptability of system components is indicated in column 2, where it is made to break down costs by segment.

The use of the contribution approach is indicated in column 3, where only costs directly attributable to the production of segment revenue are charged to the segment. These costs exist only because the segment exists. Segment margins represent contribution to the company net income. It should be noted in

[1]This chart is used with the permission of Frank H. Mossman, W.J.E. Crissy, and Paul Fischer, co-authors of various works in the financial dimensions of marketing management. Cf. Crissy, Fischer, and Mossman, "Segmental Analysis: Key to Marketing Profitability," Business Topics, Spring 1973, pp. 42-49; and Mossman, Fischer, and Crissy, "New Approaches to Analyzing Profitability," Journal of Marketing, Vol. 38, No. 2, April, 1974, pp. 43-48.

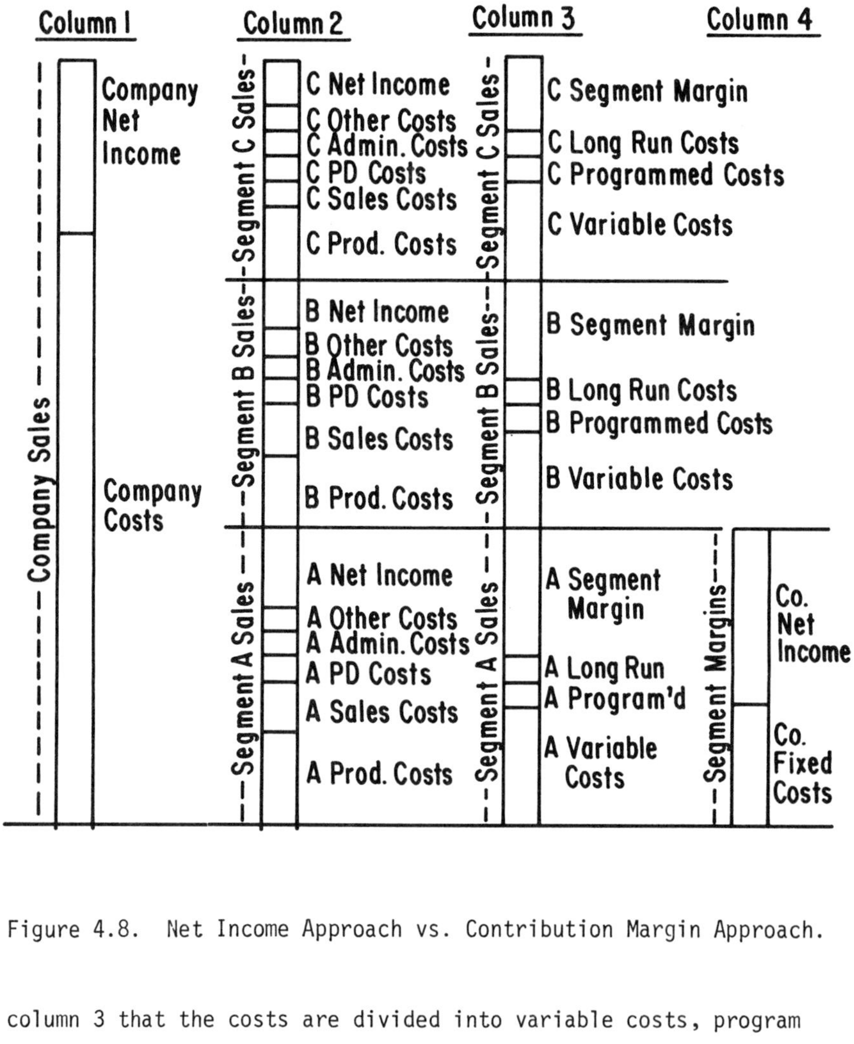

96

Column I	Column 2	Column 3	Column 4
Company Net Income	Segment C Sales: C Net Income, C Other Costs, C Admin. Costs, C PD Costs, C Sales Costs, C Prod. Costs	Segment C Sales: C Segment Margin, C Long Run Costs, C Programmed Costs, C Variable Costs	
Company Sales	Segment B Sales: B Net Income, B Other Costs, B Admin. Costs, B PD Costs, B Sales Costs, B Prod. Costs	Segment B Sales: B Segment Margin, B Long Run Costs, B Programmed Costs, B Variable Costs	
Company Costs	Segment A Sales: A Net Income, A Other Costs, A Admin. Costs, A PD Costs, A Sales Costs, A Prod. Costs	Segment A Sales: A Segment Margin, A Long Run, A Program'd, A Variable Costs	Segment Margins: Co. Net Income, Co. Fixed Costs

Figure 4.8. Net Income Approach vs. Contribution Margin Approach.

column 3 that the costs are divided into variable costs, program costs, and long range costs. The variable costs are those which vary directly with the volume of revenue produced. Program costs are those which are programmed for the period and will remain semi-fixed for the time period under consideration. Long range costs are those which remain fixed over more than one time period

and are the least controllable of all of the segment costs.
In all instances, only costs attributable to the segment are
chargeable to the segment, whether they are variable, programmed
or long range.

The total of the contributions to company net income
is shown in column 4. The total of these segment margins less
the company's non-allocable costs equals company net income.

Weaknesses of the Net Income Approach

There are three weaknesses to the net income approach.
The first is that application of net income approach to system
profitability is not a continuous process. It creates a need to
desegregate data from natural accounts. In the process, costs
are often improperly identified and arbitrary allocation occurs
for both relevant and irrelevant costs. In particular, general
and administrative costs are frequently assigned to segments not
responsible for them. Consequently, the results of the decisions
and actions of the segment may not be reflected accurately in
measures of its performance.

Secondly, traditional allocation methods make no attempt
to allocate costs on the basis of controllability. This obscures
the relationship between controllable inputs and resulting outputs, especially when costs and revenues are not clearly related
to particular segments. Further, it distorts the cause and
effect relationship between decisions made and actions taken,
and the cost of revenue results of such decisions and actions.
This weakness is particularly significant when it comes to
measuring systems adaptability where the systems have variant
behavior either with or without constant environments.

Third, when fully allocated costing is used, the performance
evaluation of one segment is influenced by the performance of other

98

segments. Poor performance of one segment inadvertently may be
affected in the performance measures of other segments, as shown
in the following illustration.

	Total	Product Lines		
		A	B	C
Net Sales	300	100	100	100
COGS	158	50	50	58
Gross Profits	142	50	50	42
Allocated Non-Manufacturing Costs*	120	40	40	40
Net Income	22	10	10	2

*Allocated in direct proportion to sales volume.

Figure 4.9. Illustration of Overhead for Time Period I.

Assume that there are three customers--A, B, and C--who make
equal contributions to the net sales of the company. After the
costs of goods sold are deducted from each of the customers revenues
for product lines, the non-manufacturing costs are then allocated
to the three products on the basis of proportion of revenue. In
this instance, each product line will receive one third of the
$120,000 of allocated non-manufacturing costs. As is apparent
in the illustration, the net income of all product lines show a
net profit.

In Time Period Two, the sales volume in terms of number of
units remains unchanged. However, product lines A and B require
price cuts to compete effectively. Product lines A and B now
contribute a lower proportion of net sales than previously, and
as a result bear a lower proportion of allocated non-manufacturing
costs. The result is that product lines A and B on the net income
approach basis show a net profit, whereas product line C shows a
net loss.

Results of Time Period Two:

(sales volume in units remains unchanged; however, product
lines A and B required price cuts to compete effectively)

| | Total | Product Lines | | |
		A	B	C
Net Sales	280	90	90	100
COGS	158	50	50	58
Gross Profits	122	40	40	42
Allocated Non-Manufacturing Costs *	120	38.6	38.6	42.8
Net Income	2	1.4	1.4	- .8

*Allocated in direct proportion to sales volume.

Figure 4.10.   Illustration of Allocation of Overhead for Time
               Period II.

Advantages of the Contribution Approach
to Segmental Analysis

There are several advantages to the use of the contribution
approach in determining segmental profit. It provides recognition
that different segments generate different input-output relationships. The segment operating statement emphasizes the behavior of
segmental costs, the extent to which the costs are attached to the
segment, and the degree of controllability that the segment has
over these costs. This is a particularly strong advantage over
the net income approach, in that it provides an incentive at the
segmental level to plan and control the component elements of the
logistic system when the component elements are variant with
environmental circumstances. The use of the contribution approach
makes possible the establishment of the extent to which system
adaptability is occurring.

A second advantage is that the building of aggregates from
specific costs and revenues is facilitated by the use of a modular

100

data base. Source documents are coded so that costs and revenues
can be specifically assigned to the segments responsible for them.
This single data base can be used to generate accounting information
for external use as well as internal needs.

Third, costs are attached in a meaningful hierarchy. Since
most elements of system planning and control mean planning and
control at the segmental level, it is important to know the nature
of controllable costs in each component part of the logistics
system. The segment variable costs are the most controllable, the
program costs are a little less so, and the long run costs are the
least controllable. However, all segments can be added to get
applicable costs. Attachment goes from the specific segments to
meaningful aggregates of segments, thereby avoiding the disadvantages of the fully allocated cost net income approach.

Other specific advantages of the contribution approach
include: appraising alternatives with respect to price changes,
discounts, and advertising campaigns; calculating desired profit
levels to be obtained by determining the volume of sales necessary
to reach them; determining the most efficient use of resources by
stressing products with the highest contribution margin; and
aiding management in deciding which segments to push and which
ones to de-emphasize.

An Operational System for Cost
and Revenue Flows

An operational system for cost and revenue flows should
provide for the flow of data so that it will meet the timely needs
of management at all levels in the analysis of segments and functions, assuring more effective planning and control. The results
should be improved decision making in the whole process of putting
goods and services before the proper customer-prospect mix. Alternative segmental combinations are a fundamental requirement in making
such planning and control possible.

In the recommended information system for cost and revenue flows, shown in Figure 4.11, provision is made for one input into a data base from source documents which should be sufficient to accommodate all subsequent analysis on an on-line, real time basis. These subsequent analyses relate to the needs for external reporting, functional cost analyses, and segmental profit analyses.

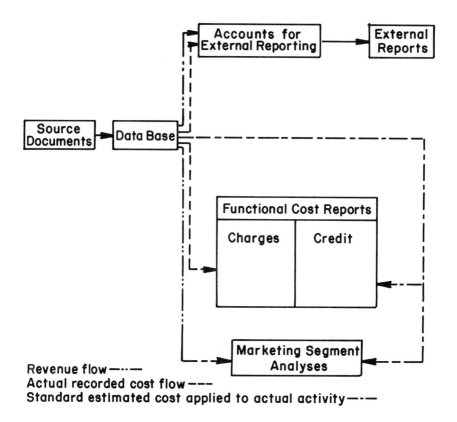

Revenue flow —·—
Actual recorded cost flow ———
Standard estimated cost applied to actual activity —·—

Figure 4.11. Information System with a Modular Data Base.[1]

---

[1]This figure originally appeared in Mossman, Fischer, Crissy, p. 45.

Functional Costs

Costs should be capable of being totaled, both by function and by segments for which the costs are specifically incurred. Regrouping of cost modules should also be provided in three ways. One is the consolidation of costs into functions that are under common responsibility, allowing a comparison of estimated and actual cost by function. As indicated in the graph, the function costs, including production costs, are charged out of the modular data base to the appropriate functional cost center based on the standard estimated costs of actual activity.

The use of standard costs is, of course, an accepted practice in production cost accounting. Actual recorded cost flows are charged into the functional cost centers to determine cost variance. Adjustments are made periodically on the standard estimated cost to keep it accurate on a timely basis. A new view is that the functional cost should be charged to the functional cost centers of business at all levels, as well as in production.

It is suggested that the functional cost centers constitute a "cafeteria" of standard costs. When a product is charged as it moves from functional cost center to functional cost center, a standard cost will be attached to the product as it moves. To illustrate this, let us assume that we have the following situation:

Functional Cost Center	Standard Unit Cost
Inventory cost	$1.20
Transportation	.05
Warehousing and handling	.05
Personal Selling (commission)	.15
Credit and collections	.02
Distribution finance	.02
General distribution	.10

The product is purchased by the company and costs $1.20 per unit. As it is received it is charged into the appropriate functional

cost center of inventory at $1.20 per unit; transportation and
warehousing unit costs are added as it moves out of the transportation flow and into the warehouse. As personal selling, credit and
collection, distribution finance, and general distribution expenses
are incurred or as the product is sold, these standard unit costs
are attached to the unit. These costs in sum total are then
transferred out of the functional cost centers and into the appropriate marketing segment. In this instance we may specify this
as product A sold to customer 1 in territory 1. The sum total of
the standard costs from the functional cost centers would be $1.59.
As the sale is recorded and the revenue recorded to this particular
segment, the standard revenue per unit of $2.00 minus the standard
cost accumulated as it passed through the functional center would
be $1.59 and the segment contribution would be   41¢.

Usually, program costs and long run costs of the segment
will come in lump sums at the appropriate period, and do not vary
directly with the segment's level of output. In a district office,
the decision to add a secretary for a period of time usually will
be a result of considering whether or not to pay overtime to
existing staff members or to add a new secretary, which would result
in a new lump sum cost for that segment for the time period under
consideration. This results in the familiar step cost in the total
cost curve, the outcome of the step cost function of the programmed
and long run costs.

Segmental Costs and Revenues--Cost modules also need to be
regrouped to charge costs to the marketing segments for the services
of the various functional cost centers, utilizing standard estimated costs for the functional cost activity and according to actual
use. Thus, a total set of applicable functional costs can be
determined for any marketing segment and deducted from the revenue
of that segment to determine the contribution of the segment toward
the net profit of the company.

Enough flexibility should be built into the marketing segments and functional cost centers to determine alternative courses
of action at a given time. This flexibility, plus the timeliness
of being able to draw relevant costs and revenue information from
the data base, gives the planning and control activities of
management much greater opportunities for profitable decision
making than heretofore has been available. Three illustrations
will demonstrate some alternative segmental combinations.

External Costs and Revenue Reports

The aggregation of cost and revenue modules into the natural
expense account categories is necessary for external reporting
purposes. This continues the traditional role of accounting, in
which the natural accounts are maintained for purposes of pre-
paring the balance sheet, profit and loss statements, and such
other reports as are required for purposes external to the business.

Forecasting System Change

A simulation model will contain a feedback, or learning,
function, which takes new management options and iterates them
into the model. This function is referred to as the controller.
The controller system and the necessary behavior section of the
controller provide an insight into the learning of the operations
by the simulator itself.

The initial behavioral pattern for the controller must
come from a basic set of preinstalled behavioral patterns, which
are selected from the past actions of the firm and the consequences of those actions. This historical summation of past
behavior is identical to the learned behavior patterns of the
human mind stored for future use in our brains. It provides the
necessary first recognition of the need for change and systems
modification. This segment of the controller provides the

management options and decision set from which the controller selects appropriate actions within the firm's operating structure. The processing segment of the controller simulates the effects of the selected adaptation mode and then provides the set of options available to the firm.

An additional behavioral guide in the controller is a continually updated forecast of what the future may hold. This exogenously oriented portion of the controller allows it to pace itself with the estimates of the future, as seen by the analyst. It also provides the requisite behavioral framework for the system controller to adjust itself within the competitive situation facing the firm. As the controller manipulates the information available to it and the decisions are readied for review by the manager, the system iterates into the succeeding time period and prepares to accept new information, in the form of forecasts and decision alterations, made by the manager and analyst.

The feedback process provides the model with the renewal of its positional information, and with the ability to move forward in the time period. By revising its behavioral patterns and learning the consequences of its actions, the controller stands ready to smooth out any overreactions to stimuli presented to it. An example of the behavioral review process based on planning forecasts is shown in Figure 4.12.

The feedback process is a continuous action, constantly updating itself in learning the situation facing the firm. An analogous situation would be the intravenous feeding of a hospitalized patient while the patient's own bodily functions are still operating, in an attempt to bolster the patient for an upcoming operation. The importance of the planning inputs based on forecasts cannot be overstated. Just as routing and scheduling provide bases for vehicle operations in the distribution system, the forcast provides the controller with a device for measuring

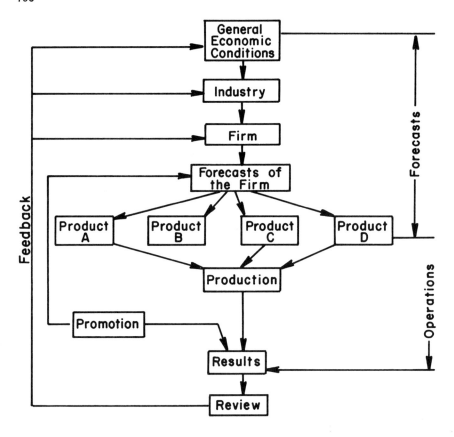

Figure 4.12.   An Example of the Behavioral Review Process in
Planning Forecasts.

the progress and rate of the approach to the optimized system
actions that the controller develops.

In summary, the values of forecasting to the operation of
a second-order controller are:

A.   The orderly development of the planning and forecasting
process provides more definitive objectives on which the model can
operate, and can generate expectations and outcomes on which the
management of the firm can assess its decisions.

B. More precise and better controlled scheduling of
distribution system activities are products of the planning and
modeling activity.

C. Long run improvement of system controller options are
gained as the model learns the consequences of its actions.

Typical Period Measurement Techniques

The system controller provides an effective link between
the analyst and the manager by providing comprehensive examin-
ations of the alternatives considered in the model. In the near-
term, day to day operations of the firm, use of actual short-term
data can cause severe and significant differences between forecast and actual data; the system controller who acts on such
information might arrive at some overreactions and alternatives.
One well known technique for overcoming the variations in short-
term data is exponential smoothing. This method weights actual
demand data for late periods of operation and earlier periods at
varying levels, and corrects for abrupt shifts in volume from
those forecast. The use of this procedure is a great asset in
keeping the immediate operational and production facilities from
making large changes in operations due to minor short life swings
in expectations.

Exponential smoothing uses the concept of moving averages
and adds more weight to various periods in demand history,
dependent on the history of the firm's operations. By using
exponential smoothing, the manager can emphasize either early
or late periods of demand to influence the operations of the
controller operations. In a firm that is growth oriented, the
latest period of demand experience can be weighted more than
later periods, while in firms that are more conservative the
earlier periods can be weighted to give more dependence on experience. The specific weighting value used is called the smoothing

constant (or alpha factor); each segment of the forecast is weighted. Where the smoothing constant for the latest period is .30, the earlier period weighting is 1.00-0.30, or .70. If the latest period demand was 60 units and the earlier period demand was 80 units, the use of the smoothing constant values above would result in a forecast of 74 units (.30 X 60 + .70 X 80 = 18 + 56 = 74) for the next period.

The smaller the alpha factor used for the latest period demand, the slower the convergency toward correcting the forecast. The larger the alpha factor, the more rapid the convergence. Generally, the larger the alpha factor, the greater the likelihood of overcompensating variations in demand. In order to prevent the possibility of over correction, the controller incorporates a self-correcting mechanism called a tracking factor. The tracking factor acts as a homeostatic mechanism; it provides the controller with a self-correcting mechanism to warn of impending danger just as the temperature sensing function in the human body warns the circulatory system of changes in outside temperatures.

The smoothing constant may be chosen in the same manner as one chooses the number of periods in a moving average; the following table indicates equivalencies:

	Equivalent Number of Periods in a Moving Average
.500	3
.400	4
.339	5
.300	5.67
.286	6
.200	9
.154	12
.105	18
.100	19
.080	24
.050	39
.038	52
.010	199

As one can see, the lower the smoothing constant, or alpha factor, the lower the effect of periodic changes in the forecast. Thus, a firm employing a private trucking fleet, faced with a short term shortage of capability in its own fleet, would not purchase immediately additional equipment based on the single or short term variations from forecasted requirements, but would purchase the services of other carriers to augment its fleet. Given the cost of new equipment, the controller can state the trade-off between the purchase of service or new equipment. The convergence timing to a large extent determines the nature of the firm's management, i.e., whether it is aggressive or conservative. The controller would balance forward the costs of providing additional inventory in the company system against the variations in demand.

The entire concept of the exponential smoothing technique is based upon the concept of regression analysis. This statistical device is used to disclose the relationships between variables. The primary purpose of regression analysis is to predict the value of one dependent variable from knowledge of the fixed value of the other variables, independent or predictive. In regression analysis, the controller derives a "regression equation" which measures the change in the dependent variable in relation to one or more independent variables. In the univariate regression analysis, relationships are established between a dependent variable and any of a number of variables established in the controller. The regression analysis is used by the system controller to establish the future limits of the firm's operations. When the trend line established in the regression analysis is emplaced in the management options and decisions segment of the controller, the modeling process of predicting the future, as the firm moves through the present set of activities, establishes the accepted relationships among the various segments of the firm's operational activities, and searches

out the variations within these segments for analysis based on the
documentation presented to it from the firm's records.

Joining the concepts of the exponential smoothing technique
and the trend line, the controller can measure the modifications
and adjustments needed to equilibrate the operations of the firm.
The controllable (endogenous) variables within the forecasting
section of the model are the natural candidates for first adjustment. Included in these variables are the customers of the firm,
the product mix, and the various logistics activities within which
the firm can control its operations. The most difficult set of
variables to control internally is that which requires sequential
decisions. It must necessarily rely on partial information, and
it is in this category of decisions that the second-order controller
functions. The dynamics of the system controller and the actual
operations of the firm are simulated to establish the actual
decision rules for sequential decisions, which provide the forward
look into the future, especially into the long-term.

A longer term problem in forecasting is determining the
seasonal variations in firm operations. Here the tracking factor
emplaced in the controller senses that there is a consistent, more
than one-period, variation produced sequentially; by the experience of the trend lines, of past time periods, it is able to produce
and verify that, in fact, a change has taken place. The manager
must now be aware that the controller is sensing the seasonal trend
in the operations of the firm, and is establishing the needed adjustment factors, even though these changes may seem to be counter to
expectations. The correlation of the various factors affecting the
level of activity of the firm is of prime importance in the estimating equations used in the controller, and on which the manager
and analyst have constructed the first set of learning factors
which have been placed into the controller. Establishment of the
coefficients of correlation among these various sets of information

depend, to a large extent, on stochastically generated exogenous
changes over which the firm has little direct control.

Forecasting Related to Segmental Analysis

When the forecast is extended to the various elements of
the firm's marketing mix, the problems are compounded and magnified.
They become more constrained by the actual elements of the firm's
competitive and operational status. If the level of forecast
sophistication could be brought to the level of the individual
segment, then one could ascertain in advance the attachability
of these accounts, for budget purposes. This segmental forecast
would involve assessment of segment potential by identifying, for
both present and potential customers (1) a definition of the buying
unit; and (2) the number of buying units, their willingness to buy,
and their ability to buy.

Budgeting Related to System Change

When the operation and control system is capable of providing
new operating rules for the manager, and there are departures from
planned levels of expenditures or changes in revenue expectations
from the distribution sector of the firm's operations, some consideration must be given to the impacts on the firm's operations.
Provisions for these impacts are made usually through budgets,
which are either fixed or variable in their formats.

Fixed Budget

The simplest components of a budget represent a static
description of the firm at the time of exposure. During the normal
operations of a firm, these exposures correspond to the operating
periods used in the control of the distribution system. These
might be weekly, monthly, quarterly, or even annual statements
of the performance of the component.

In distribution system controllership, this type of system audit corresponds to the fixed budgeting type of planning. Such budgets have two characteristics:

1. They are prepared for one level of activity, corresponding to a target volume of production within the operating period, and

2. They provide a static comparison as a measure of component performance.

An earlier example of the single balance sheet for both beginning and ending times of the period applies here, providing a single time perception of the condition of the firm.

The static budget is a useful tool for the development of single subsystems within the entire firm; consideration of the possibilities of variances from expected levels of operation, and the use of learning controls of components, requires some other method to observe the firm's operations during the operations period. In the establishment of the different types of behavioral systems explained earlier, the components responded implicitly within the bounds of acceptable reactions. They did not exceed the limits within which the control system was capable of operating without destroying the controller itself.

The same problem faces the developer of the learning component in a data analysis system of the firm's distribution function. When departing from the static budget and the connotations it represents, a different set of operating rules is required. The static budget, as used in our first-order type of component, must necessarily order the stopping of a particular segment of the distribution system component when the planned level of operations is exceeded.

The control of the system is centralized to a higher level within the firm's operating structure than at the distribution

management level. This is tantamount to setting an arbitrary level
of operations and expenditures within the component which cannot
be exceeded without authorization from some higher level within
the firm's hierarchy.

The analogy of the thermostat control applies. If the
voltage inputs for operating the thermostat are exceeded, a
circuit breaker protects the operation of the component by cutting
off the supply of electrical power. The static, or fixed, dollar
budgeting control program does not allow the system to learn as it
progresses through an operating period.

The fixed budget provides an estimate of functional costs
by component or account associated with an anticipated level of
distribution system activity. The budget becomes a basis for
analysis and comparison of desired performance in advance of the
operating period with actual performance after the period is
completed. The budget represents a joint management attempt to
set the desired level of performance. System operational updates
are performed as interim reports are compiled, but the fixed budget
does not allow for corrections at the operational level.

Variable Budgets

In contrast to the zero-order system, the second-order
behavioral system allows the component to learn within the accounting period as it strives to achieve the desired goals and
objectives. Planning the objectives for the period in the control
system that learns is a complicated task. It is concerned with
variations in volume, traffic, inventory, customer location, and
operating costs, as well as all the other variables that can
possibly occur within the period.

While the second-order system is concerned with coping
with changes in operating conditions and environment, it must also
track these changes and report them to the manager for consideration

in planning for the next time period. The resulting condition
reports provide for the development of sets of standardized
responses to changes in the environment. The past reactions to
changes in the environment become the predictive actions for the
future, and provide the measures for estimating future performance.

Should the system be incapable of internal change during
operating periods, strategy development and alternative creation
must be accomplished externally and programmed into the system.
Again we have devolved into a first order-control system with no
feedback amplifications to direct the thrust of environmental
alteration.

The development of strategy is of paramount importance and,
in fact, the reason for the development of a component controller.
Strategies must be developed before decisions are made. Sets of
decision rules must be inserted into the automated controller;
the information processing system and user simulator operate on
these rules.

The second order system is capable of providing a decision
rule change for consideration by the manager as a portion of the
management options, and conditions output of the controller. In
this way, the controller becomes an innovator of strategies. We
do not imply that the second-order system is a "thinker," but the
developer of alternatives on the basis of decision rules programmed
into the machine. An example would be the occurrence of greater
than programmed inventory costs in one segment of the firm's
operation; a second-order controller would offer as options the
transfer of inventory to other locations, new inventory levels,
or possibly state new production batch sizes, even discount options
for sales and marketing personnel. By incorporating each of these
options into the projected operations, relative costs for each
alternative are developed for decision by the manager, and offered
as options in the output from the controller.

Development of strategies on the basis of information stored in the controller requires a rigorous examination of data available for inclusion in the data bank, in an attempt to limit the uncertainty of future decisions. As the time period of each decision step or operations period expands, the possibilities for environmental change increase; so do the factors that affect the decision maker's control. When these states of nature become so broad, the only solution is to present a statistical distribution of alternatives. In most cases, a matrix solution can be constructed as tableaus for the decision-maker. Environments and decision alternatives from the rows and columns, with entries of decision costs at each intersection. From the tableau, the component controller can select the best alternative and program for the acceptance of that change. Only an accounting system based on variable budgeting can achieve such internal response to environmental change.

The location of fiscal documentation in the controller provides the necessary legal reporting requirements for the financial manager. The most difficult problem in this system is the necessary commutative ability for the system to move from operating documentation to legal and fiscal documentation.

Obviously, the control of the component actions in the second order level of behavior requires the development of extensive instruction sets for the conditions to be encountered during operation. Each condition requires the establishment of a threshold value which, when reached, will trigger the new control reaction. Thus, the response-stimulus pattern of system change is readily exemplified in the behavior of the second-order component. This is the cornerstone of the development of the data base system.

Basic Elements of a Data System
for Measuring System Change

Definition of a Data Base

A data base is a central data storage system which contains revenue, cost, and performance information in readily accessible form. The concept of a data base can be visualized in a simplified form for a small jewelry store chain, as follows:

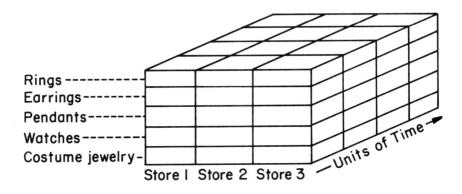

Figure 4.13. Concept of a Modular Data Base.

Each store, product line, and time unit forms a basic module of data. The columns represent store numbers, the product lines are shown on each of the rows, and the units of time are shown in the depth part of the module.

The columns can be added to obtain store data. The rows can be summed for overall product line data. Any combination may then be extended over time to get daily, weekly, monthly, quarterly or any unit of time provided for on the data base.

In the illustration, the modular data base is shown in three dimensions. More dimensions may be added, but it is not possible to present these graphically. The system could be extended to n dimensions, dependent solely upon the physical capacity of the computer or information system of the business.

The data can be retrieved from the modular data base in any one of the forms by which it is inserted into the base. This is because alternative combinations may be desired in measuring system adaptability. Provision is also made for varying units of time. The reason here is equally valid that for planning and control purposes there will be alternative time periods that will be desired by functional and segmental managers. The value of data from the data base for planning and control purposes is particularly important in most types of systems where there are variant components which will be different even with constant or changing environments.

A simple illustration of coding will give some idea of the approach used to establish the data base. The left-hand side of the illustration indicates the more or less normal procedure utilized to establish codes. The following steps were used in the illustration:

1. Identification of the functions to be used. Production, marketing, finance, and logistics are numbered 1, 2, 3, and 4.

2. It was decided to record the territories and the products as the segments for analytical purposes. Territories were numbered 1 and 2. Products A and B were numbered 1 and 2.

3. In order to determine whether the item was revenue or expense, revenue was coded 1 and expense coded 2.

4. Provision was made to add expenses into further functional categories. Examples are selling, warehousing, and advertising, which were coded 1, 2 and 3, respectively.

> 5. The rest of the field in the coded card was to be used for the amount of the transaction.

Let us assume that we wish to enter a sale in territory 1 of product A in the amount of $100. The first figure to be punched would be 2 to reflect Marketing. The second figure would be 1, to recognize Territory 1. The third figure would be 1, to record the sale of Product A. The fourth figure would be 1, to indicate that it was a Revenue. The rest of the field would be $100.00, the amount of the sale.

As a second illustration, let us assume that there is an expense of $500. incurred for the advertising of Product B in Territory 2. This would be coded as follows: 2 (Marketing); 2 (Territory); 2 (Product); 3 (Expense); 3 (Advertising); $500.00 traded. In the real world, the situation would prove to be more complex. The above does show how costs and revenues could be attached to a function and a segment on a behavioral basis.

Operation of the Data System

The bases for the data storage system are operating documents such as warehouse receipts, bills of lading, and other transportation control documents used primarily within the distribution operating function. After analysis of the documentation for applicability and inclusion within the information bank, these essential elements of information are indexed into the automated storage equipment, either in the form of punched cards, magnetic tape, or disc stored. The user, either staff distribution manager, traffic manager, or the decision-maker, translates these elements into options and conditions. He submits them for processing, where they flow through the processing or through the firm's operating system as feedback responses within the system, to be returned to the controller for analysis as operating documents.

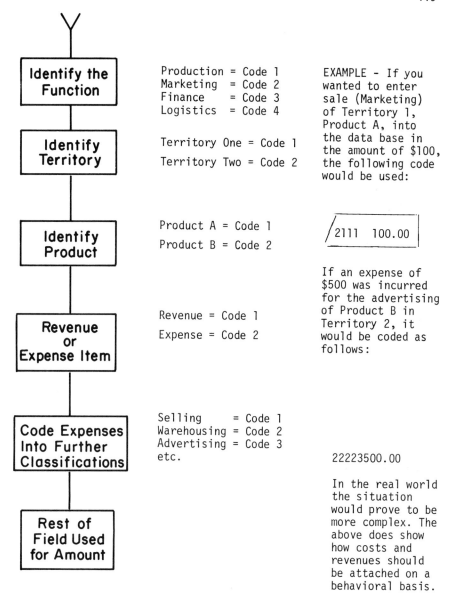

Figure 4.14. Coding Revenue and Expense Items to Segments.

The storage function of required decision information is separated into a fiscal documentation section where the documents are stored for future uses such as audits and required business reports. The second element of data storage consists of the index or machine storage of the elements of each of the documents selected for inclusion in the controller component as essential to the formulation of decisions in the distribution system.

The user segment of this system is actually the simulation model of the system. As in most operations in dynamic situations, this model shares some manual inputs from the analysis function for decision criteria to be used in the compilation of management options. While most designers of simulation models are reluctant to discuss this aspect, it is true that unless the system can be designed to feed back within itself between the user and processing subfunctions, the component is not actually operating as a second-order component.

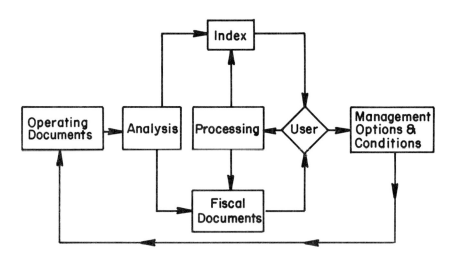

Figure 4.15.   Diagram of Operations of the Data System.

Information Requirements for the Data Base

The elements of the data base are directly related to the requirements of the operations of the system and the extent of control exercised in the use of the system. Returning to the second-order system described above, the data to be included in the information storage subsystem is derived from the operating documents the firm uses in its everyday operations. The envelope in which the data storage and operating controls reside is comprised of files, analytical routines, processing functions, and the printed data which forms the raw input to the controller component. Use of company operating documentation for the data inputs or raw information for the controller provides for the commutation of the facts and alternatives, which constitute the output of the controller component. The controller provides the feedback or learning function for the system. This connotes that the user develops new operating rules as the system iterates through the development of management options.

The company operating documentation stands at the primary level of data base organization. From this set of information bits, the operating management must obtain all its internal data. The most complex and comprehensive data set would be the documentation itself, but the volume of this type of input coupled with the obvious problems of designing a recognition system in an automated system mitigates against this. Some abstraction of the documentation must take place for the system to be practical and relatively simpler than actual manipulation of the raw documentation. The most commonly used level of abstraction is an abstract of the document, which attempts to convey the meaning of the document without including all the information.

At this juncture, the problems of assigning segments of the abstract priority appears to confound the designer of the operating system. From the earlier discussion of segmental cost

analysis, the operating system must consider these requirements in
order to provide data for both systems, and to provide common data
elements which can be used to determine the marketing analyses of
operations and feed into the user sub-system. Another level of
abstraction would be to utilize the library key word type of
documentation recognition as an entry into fiscal documentation
storage. This type of user system fails to build an adequate
meaning for the documentation and loses those items which do not
fit the classification pattern.

Still, the problem remains for the development of sufficient
information on which to base decisions at several levels of managerial interest. The index section of the controller provides the
vehicle for the necessary translation of data elements used in the
simulation of the system. It may utilize all the data used for
decision at the functional manager level to provide generalized
and abstracted information outputs at the firm management level.

The user element of the system must provide the necessary
vocabulary for item representation when the fiscal documentation
is abstracted. This vocabulary can be the natural wording (the
language of the document) or an artificial one related to the
machine language used in the hardware/software on which the controller is being utilized. The National Bureau of Standards has
developed a generic information recovery system based on classes
of information[1] which can be used to derive a suitable vocabulary
for the controller.

The relationship of data inputs for the controller and the
necessary permutation of data for operational use is provided by
the syntactical translator. Syntax provides the necessary relationships among vocabulary words. Those elements of the shipping

[1] General Aspects of Storage of Scientific Information,
National Bureau of Standards Report NBS 6675, February 15, 1960.

documents which are common to sales vouchers would be located from different commutational locations by the syntax. Having developed a vocabulary, based on a machine language, and the syntactical relationship, the abstract must be coded for use in the controller. Here the use of natural language or the use of a mnemonic coding represents the range of options available to the designer of the system.

The designer or analyst must always be aware of the necessity for provision of decision information for the system. The use of machine coded language sometimes alters the basic pattern of information recognition, thereby destroying the ability to achieve a usable decision criteria.

Another aspect of item storage and organization is the format of information based on the vocabulary and syntax selected. A primary decision to be made is whether to provide data in fixed or random length fields. The complex problems encountered in using random length fields almost mitigates against its use. A fixed field representation, where each element of data has a significance and meaning associated with it, may require more total storage space in the index but in the end provides a much more utilitarian data base.

Within the field used for data display, portions may be set aside for use for different purposes. Some purposes are identification of the item used for output controlling, or specific identification for processing and immediate operation. For example, the sales document could be used to bill a customer and the shipping document record shipment of the item. Each of these documents contains some common items used for operating system control. When the customer's account is interrogated for use in deriving distribution costs, some information is not used. The syntactical relationship uses some of the information for processing and some merely to identify the output. Our earlier

requirement for a modular data base must take into account these
factors of manipulative requirements. The index segment of the
operating system provides the entry and output consolidation
needed to make the system universal in the firm's requirements.

The organization of these data fields into classes of
documentation is fairly simple. It is the interrelationship of the
possible uses of the various data elements when combined for
analytical and control purposes that provides the most complex
problem. The usage of data in multiple applications occurs in
non-standard auditing situations. For example, sales data may
be analyzed for factors causing cost differences in service for
various customers, and also used for fiscal and budgetary uses.

File organization in these situations requires complex
syntactical entries and cataloguing. The actual addressing of
data elements in the file amounts to rigorous search routines
applied to the accumulation of the significant data elements
needed to construct a suitable substitute for actual operations.
An example of the establishment of hierarchical arrangement of
data fields is the standard library coding systems and the
Standard Industrial Code (SIC) developed by the United States
Bureau of the Census. This coding ranks industrial products
from the most general category (in a two-position symbol), to
a seven (7) position code for a specific product. The following
example portrays the progression and construction of a coding
designation for digital computers and for industrial fans and
blowers. The elements of the simulation are a complex of sub-
structures providing entry to the data elements. These entries
can be categorized by product, customer, region, warehouse, or
any analytical category. The field organization must provide
the necessary entry capability for the analysis to be accomplished.

The index develops the necessary hierarchical structure
for entry at the various system operational levels. The decision

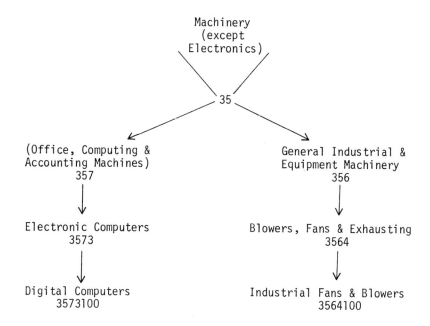

criteria used in each managerial level provide the key for these entries. The limitations of the storage media used provides the bounds of the data stored and the complexity of the analyses being done. The organization of the file must be dedicated to reducing search time and simplifying access to data elements. The classification of data elements by multiple syntactical relation statements through some type of dictionary term equivalents on a standardized basis is a necessity. Analysis of distribution systems is encumbered with numerous relationships which must be developed in order to simplify the data acquisition needed to complete the requisite computations. Access to the index of elements through the index on the randomized file access routines used in automated applications accomplishes minimizing of search routine times.

The processing of data in analyses corresponds to the steps of the logic involved in the construction of the analysis. This

automated version of the methodology used to derive the selected
decision points in logistic system analysis comes from the user
developed, pre-established processing of the files from fiscal
documents through the index and through the stated management
options and conditions segment of the operation system.

Information Element Processing

The file classification and organization determine the
parameters of the processing available to the analyst. To the
extent that these files are established, the limits of the capability to manipulate data are set. The pre-existence of file
organization forces the processing into established paths; any
alternative paths must also be pre-established.

The system which operates as a second-order system must
also be capable of learning. As decision criteria are encountered,
the management options and conditions segment of the operating
system allows the establishment of new file organizations, for
the purpose of providing the needed criteria for new operating
rules. As the system iterates, the new criteria are presented
in output formats for the manager to accept or reject, based on
the information presented from the analysis. Use of the operating
system to perform other processes, such as marketing review and
analysis, budget status, or other company operating information
are included in the index and can be formated in the same manner
as the operating system reporting.

The life of the operating system depends on the input of
current information into the data file, index, and management
options, and conditions segments of the operating system. The
use of character reading machines or key punching to enter data
into the system depends, to a great extent, on the ability of the
human element inherent in the system. Verification of data inputs
is an exacting and demanding activity, but is critical to the use

of the system as a decision tool. After data are verified, this information must be posted into the system. Predetermined or random input cycles may be used as long as the audit trail required in fiscal operations is maintained.

When functioning as a second order system, some non-standard file inputs will occur. These must be handled in such a manner that the audit trail developed for repetitive file updating is maintained. This type of operation could occur when the system derives a file on customer activity to be used for possible shipping volume determination or for possible shipment combination.

Those most active customers in the file can be categorized on the basis of their dollar volume and ranked within the file, as a portion of the learning aspects of the operating system. As the customer file develops over time, the inactive customers are separated from the remainder of the file and not considered in distribution cost and operations analyses. When an order does issue from one of these customers, the system can react by moving the customer into the active status again. This would be handled on an exception basis. The customers are ranked on the basis established criteria, possibly on several criteria: sales dollar volume, number of shipments, total weight of shipments, number of required delivery dates not met. By itself, the automatic aspects of such file organization on the basis of activity and importance in company operations is worth the development of the system.[1]

As the system operates through the routines and develops new criteria, the establishment of new decision criteria must continually be brought forward for consideration by the manager responsible for the function being analyzed. The dissemination of reports on the status of the distribution system are a necessary

---

[1]John Becker and Robert M. Hayes, Information Storage and Retrieval; Tools, Elements, Theories (New York: Wiley and Sons, 1963).

and vital part of the operating system. The system must continually
report the comparison of what the distribution modeling operation
is doing and what the company is doing in the concurrent fiscal
control system. Information on the possible changes in activity
due to changes proposed by the model must be coordinated with all
the other functional managers within the firm. The critical necessity for maintaining open lines of communication within the various
segments of the firm cannot be overstated, because it is the understanding of the second order effects on other segments of the
company operation and the acceptance of these changes by other
managers that will predicate the success of any operating system.
The production manager, comptroller, traffic manager, and warehouse
manager are all concerned with the decision criteria being used.
The traditional measures of activity may be replaced by complex
formulae which state the level of success and attainment in the
system. One thing is certain, the day of system is here. An
operating system capable of self-organizing and producing current
decision criteria is a necessary adjunct to an organization. In
a one-man organization, the human is unsurpassed, but in large
organizations the complex interrelationships can only be examined
by automated systems.

Data Base Flexibility

A well structured data base should take into account the
following factors:

1. The information needs of various levels of management
   in the company.

2. The meaning and use of the information elements as
   shown by the number of requests for various kinds of
   information.

3. Provision for estimating the effects of alternative
   courses of action prior to the implementation.

   4. Flexibility in updating and meeting changing informa-
       tion requirements.

Information Needs of Various Levels of Management

       The planning and control of changes within a system to
adapt to changing environmental conditions occurs at many levels
within the business enterprise. Therefore, within the organization
structure of a business system there is a need for alternative
segmental combinations for different types of decisions, different
levels of decision making and different time frames. Two examples
are given of companies who use different segmental combinations
for different decision making levels in their respective companies.

       In the large industrial company, the segments used were
the corporate entity, divisions on a product basis, and districts
on a territorial basis. At one time, the company was administered
through corporate headquarters. When the company became sufficiently large, it was decided to establish divisions for better
planning and control. These divisions were established on a
product basis, since in this particular company it was felt that
there were major product lines that could be grouped together
into principle divisions. However, the salesman in the field
specialized by product type. In a given geographic area, all
salesmen work out of the same office location; hence, the use
of the district or territory as a basis for organizing the
company's distributive efforts.

       A small retail chain uses the individual stores on a
territorial basis, and product lines within each store. Some
people often think that a complex computer setup is necessary to
enter into the establishment of a data base. Nothing could be
further from the truth. In this particular instance, a single
entry accounting system is used; coding of the cash register tape,
plus some elemental expensing, was all that was necessary to

determine the net segment margin for each of the stores. However, in addition to knowing the net segment margin of each of the stores, it was also thought desirable to determine the segment contribution margin by product line. This is shown for one of the stores in the illustration. Through more timely information, the owner of this particular enterprise increased his profit position substantially by having better information on products in each of these stores and so be able to merchandise more effectively.

In order to get a feeling for the state of the art with respect to types of decisions, different levels of decision making, and different time frames, the American Accounting Association conducted a study of the firms in 1971, using the contribution approach to segmental analysis. The AAA formed a committee on marketing costs and revenue analysis and conducted a study of 75 firms in Fortune 500.[1]

In the questionnaire, five specific decision areas were listed, encompassing marketing and physical distribution. Of necessity, the decision areas were broad. Each of the firms was requested to report the number of requests for data by type of decision. It was interesting to note that sales forecasting data were requested most often. Second in importance were budgeting and variants from budgets. The planning area, including both the marketing mix and the physical distribution mix, ranked considerably lower. Although more definitive work would be required in order to rank the importance of these decisions, the role of the planning function in marketing and physical distribution is considerably lower than the sales forecasting and budgeting functions.

The most important segment used in segmental analysis in the market area is the product line, with the customer second.

---

[1] Paul Fischer et al., "Report of the Committee on Cost and Profitability Analysis in Marketing," The Accounting Review, supplement to Vol. XLVII, 1972, pp. 575-615.

Type of Decision	Total Requests	Rank
Sales Forecasting	611	1
Planning the Promotional Mix	378	4
Planning the Physical Distribution Mix	388	5
Budgeting	491	3
Variance Analysis	506	2

Figure 4.16. Total Requests for Data by Type of Decision.

Other segmental alternatives rank considerably lower in terms of
the numbers of firms using each of these alternatives. The
preference for product line is apparent in all decision areas
surveyed. There were some exceptions to the use of customers
right across the board in all decision areas as a second choice
for the alternative for segmental analysis; channels of distribution were equal to customers in terms of planning the physical
distribution mix; territories were second in terms of budgeting;
and customers and territories were equally popular in terms of
grants and houses.

It is important that data be provided at the appropriate
decision level for planning and control of systems adaptability.
In terms of the numbers of decisions made, the departmental level
is by far the most important of the five. The second choice was
the division level. These statements only relate to the number
of decisions and not the qualitative importance of them to the
company. The question was simply how many decisions are made in
each of the decision levels.

Type of Decision	Product	Order Size	Customers	Territories	Channels
Sales Forecasting	1	4	2	3	5
Planning the Promotional Mix	1	4	2	3	5
Planning the Physical Distribution Mix	1	3	2	4	2
Budgeting	1	5	3	2	4
Variance Analysis	1	4	2	2	5

Figure 4.17.   Rank Choice of Segment Type for Use in Marketing Decisions.

	Sales-man	Sales Territory	Depart-ment	Divi-sion	Corpo-rate
Sales Forecasting	4	3	1	2	5
Planning the Promotional Mix	5	4	1	2	3
Planning Physical Distribution Mix	5	4	1	2	3
Budgeting	5	3	1	2	4
Variance Analysis	4	3	1	2	4

Figure 4.18.   Type of Decision by Decision Level.

Type of Decision	Daily	Weekly	Monthly	Quarterly	Yearly
Sales Forecasting	5	4	1	3	1
Planning the Promotional Mix	5	4	3	2	1
Planning Physical Distribution Mix	5	4	3	2	1
Budgeting	5	4	3	2	1
Variance Analysis	5	4	2	3	1
Specific Order or Product Pricing	2	5	3	3	1

Figure 4.19. Timing of Decisions.

Certainly, the timing of decisions is also extremely
important to systems adaptability. The annual basis is the first
choice in all decision areas listed. Second choice was quarterly
in the planning areas and in budgeting, monthly for variance
analysis, and daily for specific order or product pricing. It is
interesting that the sales forecasts are made apparently both
monthly and annually in order to keep in touch with the trends
of the market. Setting up modules of time so that the implementation of decisions can be made on a timely basis is an important
part of flexibility in the data base.

The Meaning and Use of Information Elements

In the previous section, examples were given of alternative
segmental combinations. Evidence is also given with respect to
certain specific types of decisions, different levels of decision
making, and different time frames. An important part of any
schematic for providing maximum systems adaptability to changing
environmental circumstances and stimuli is an understanding by the

134

decision makers of the meaning and use of information elements.
It is extremely important that internal managements of the functional cost centers and the segmental activity centers evaluate
the information they need for planning and control. The points
of emphasis are the important decisions of their respective functional cost centers and segmental centers which keep the system
adaptable to changing conditions.

An illustration of the kind of work that needs to be
done is the analysis of the decision types, decision levels, and
time frames at the small retail jewelry chain, as shown in
Figure 4.20. The staff of the chain consisted of the owner, one
manager, and three assistant managers; the job was relatively
easy. For example, on the decision of whether to add or delete
a store in the chain, the owner had a high responsibility, the
manager a low responsibility, and the assistant managers no
responsibility; the time frame of such decisions was "as needed."
At the other extreme of decision levels, the question of scheduling substitutions of employees was high with the assistant managers
and the owner had no responsibility; the time frame was daily. In
between these were, of course, many decisions where the responsibility rested with the manager and the time frames were of varying
lengths of time. Generally, the kind of analysis that needs to
be done in order to furnish information of the kind needed for
decision makers to keep the system adaptive to changing circumstances can be provided in a modular data base.

Estimation of Alternative Courses of
Action Prior to Implementation

The very essence of a modular data base is its ability to
provide information to decision makers who plan and control these
systems' adaptability to changing circumstances. The modular
data base is probably of greatest help to the systems which have
variant behavior with either constant or changing environments.

In addition to the owner, there is one manager responsible for all three stores. Each store also has an assistant manager. The relative participation of each in the decision making process is shown below.

Decisions	Decision Levels			Time Frames
	Owner	Manager	Ass'ts	(Frequency of Decision)
Adding or Deleting a Store	Hi	Lo	None	As Needed*
Adding or Deleting a Product Line	Med	Hi	Lo	As Needed*
Changing Product Mix	Med	Hi	Lo	Semi-Annually
Merchandise Buying	Hi	Med	None	Monthly
What Items to Mark Down	Lo	Hi	Lo	Semi-Annually
How Much to Mark Down Items	Lo	Hi	Lo	Semi-Annually
Scheduling of Employees	None	Hi	Med	Weekly
Schedule Substitutions	None	Lo	Hi	Daily, as Needed

*With the proposed controls for variance supported by the modular data base providing timely segmental information, product line and store reviews could easily be programmed for regular intervals.

Figure 4.20. Analysis of Decision Types, Decision Levels, and Time Frames.

It may be of help in the system which has invariant behavior, but it probably makes its greatest contributions towards systems flexibility, where there are alternative variant behavior systems.

The modular data base really pays off with the second and third types of systems adaptability. The second type, in which the system changes its behavior if the environment changes, begins to utilize the flexibility of the modular data base. It is extremely important to know what alternatives there are in arranging the components as the system responds to environmental stimulation. Fortunately, in this type of system there is normally only one alternative reaction between the environmental circumstances on response. The important thing is to know the relationships between S, R, and G, and to be able to utilize systems analytical techniques to measure and select the best alternative to accomplish the given goal objectives within the constraints of the problem. Certainly, simulation techniques are needed here and, fortunately, we have a wide range of these available for simulating alternative courses of action.

The third type of system consists of objects exhibiting different types of behavior, even in a constant environment. In these circumstances, S could consist of a set of stimuli, E a set of environmental circumstances, R a set of responses, and G a set of possible goals. Since the alternatives connecting S, R, E, and G are large in number, it becomes necessary to use correlation techniques to seek relationships between the alternatives. Thus, the job of simulation is much more sophisticated in the third type of system than in the other two. The value of the modular data base in this case is the feasibility in using correlation techniques which heretofore would simply have been impossible to accomplish even elemental simulations.

Flexibility in Updating and Meeting
Changing Information Requirements

Since environmental circumstances and stimuli do change, it is important that provision be made in the modular data base for updating and meeting changing circumstances. Some of these circumstances can be changed in the economic conditions of the market in which the firm sells, in its raw material components, in the customer-prospect mix, and in the service level mix of the company as it redefines its market to meet changing circumstances. A properly conceived modular data base will contain in its structure the flexibility for adding or deleting functions and segments to keep the system adaptable to changing market conditions.

CHAPTER 5

GRAPH METHODOLOGIES AND APPLICATIONS

General Considerations

Modern society is dominated by a complex of networks for the transmission of energy, the transportation of people, the distribution of goods, and the dissemination of information. This complex consists of such diverse systems as the telephone network, gas and oil pipelines, highway systems, and networks of computers which serve as data banks and remote processing units. The cost to develop these networks demands that they be used rationally, and new ones be planned and developed intelligently.[1]

The basis of their structure consists of branches along which flows are transmitted; and nodes, the points where flows originate, are relayed, or are terminated. These structural elements are combined into mathematical entities called "graphs," the connected branches and vertices.[2,3]

Network applications such as Program Evaluation Review Technique (PERT) and the Critical Path Method (CPM)[4] state the

---

[1]H. Frank and I. Frisch, Communication, Transmission and Transportation Networks (Reading, Mass.: Addison-Wesley, 1971), Chapter 1.

[2]H. Koenig, Y. Tokad, and H. Kesavan, Analysis of Discrete Physical Systems (New York: McGraw-Hill, 1967).

[3]Frank and Frisch, Chapter 2.

[4]R. Miller, Schedule, Cost, and Profit Control with PERT (New York: McGraw-Hill, 1963), Chaps. 2-4.

flows only; the element of "force," or demand, is not present.
Additionally, dynamic programming and linear programming
offer solutions to some network problems, especially those
with time and state sequencing.[1]

Management does not have the choice, "To plan or not to
plan." It must plan to survive, perform, and strive towards the
organization's objectives. The planner analyzes the problem, and
fixes the steps that must be achieved to reach the goal defined
in the solution. The plan must be conceived before decisions can
be made. Once the plan has been put into action, management needs
measurements and progress reports to assess its success toward the
goal. This information is required not only for the evaluation
of performance against the plan, but also to provide a basis for
any corrective action.

The first and most successful techniques, procedures, and
systems have been developed in manufacturing industries, especially
continuous production. Planning and control have been difficult
to apply to custom and project work; many have resisted the concept
that definite planning and control is feasible. Only through
recent successful applications have objections lessened.

PERT for Planning

PERT is the work of a project team of the Special Projects
Office of the Navy's Bureau of Ordnance. In 1958, the Navy was
looking for improved planning and control methods for its Fleet
Ballistic Missle System program, known today as Polaris. This
effort was intended to continue the reporting and evaluation
procedures of the contractor; in effect, it was a set of measurements for the Navy's own use, on this and other Navy projects.

---

[1] G. Hadley, Dynamic Programming (Reading, Mass.: Addison-
Wesley, 1964), Chaps. 1-3.

At the same time, DuPont was studying a similar technique, Critical Path Method (CPM), which has been used successfully in reducing costs and time required to bring new products from the research laboratory into actual production. CPM, it is noted, comprises the basis of the PERT system as it is applied today. This PERT-CPM technique has been applied in the chemical, construction, education, and manufacturing industries.

The basic techniques in PERT, Network Diagramming, and Critical Path Determination are outgrowths of earlier techniques. Before World War I, the U.S. Army Ordnance Bureau was faced with the problem of coordinating production work in military arsenals and private industry. The Chief of Ordnance asked Henry L. Gantt to establish a simple chart system to show the comparison between promises and performance. These charts portrayed scheduling and performance of all single items, subassemblies, and completed units supplied by or through the arsenals. They were updated daily, and photographed weekly; prints were sent to the Ordnance Bureau for scrutiny and production coordination.

Concurrently, other researchers were developing flow process charts. They portray the sequential relationship of activities or operations, but not the time relationship; they are a visual representation of how the work is to be done. Consequently, often they are overlooked as means for analyzing a problem and understanding its ramifications.

It is difficult for the human mind to comprehend complex problems without reliance on some aid, and these simple, graphic representations show the important features of the problem concisely, on one piece of paper. Still, a technique was sought that would portray both the sequential and time relationships of activities.

The "line of balance" technique incorporates methods of the Gantt and flow process charts. This procedure portrays key operations

and events on a time scale, according to their sequential and
lead-time relationship to the final event. Connecting lines
between events merge until the final objective is reached. The
line of balance technique has been used in both government and
industry; adaptations have proven valuable in various programs
and projects. There are shortcomings in its application, however.
The display of information tends to become too complex to portray
efficiently the performance milestones that the manager needs to
evaluate the progress of the project.

These tools sharpened the manager's awareness to the
complexity of his own problems, and the shortcomings of earlier
techniques. Often, necessary tasks were overlooked; upon dis-
covery, corrective actions generated increased costs, time, and
risk relative to the objective. It became more difficult to estimate the time required to complete a project. Errors were the
result of crash efforts, and since projections were difficult,
entire programs were accelerated rather than the few that would
have brought the project back on schedule.

PERT and CPM evolved as the most effective tools for project
management planning. The complexity of the planning task requires
explicit portrayal of important times and dates, the activities
that lead to the milestone dates, and the time required to complete
each phase of the task leading to the objective.

PERT accomplishes this through a network diagram, based on
the combination flow process and Gantt charts, which depicts all
the items that the manager must be able to control in order to
optimize the march to the objective.

We shall consider the PERT planning schedule only in the
time context, as originally conceived by the Navy, to show the
applicability to the requirements of the transportation planner.
The method has the following basic requirements:

1. All of the individual tasks to complete a given program must be visualized in a clear manner and recorded in a network comprised of events and activities. An event represents a specific program accomplishment at a particular instant in time. An activity represents the time and resources necessary to progress from one event to another. Emphasis is placed on defining events and activities with sufficient precision so that there is no difficulty in monitoring actual accomplishments as the program proceeds.

2. Events and activities must be sequenced on the network under a highly logical set of ground rules which allow the determination of important critical and subcritical paths. These ground rules state that (a) a successor event cannot be considered completed until all of its predecessor events have been completed; and (b) "looping" is not allowed, i.e., a successor event cannot have an activity dependency which leads back to a predecessor event.

3. Time estimates are made for each activity of the network on a three-way basis: optimistic, most likely, and pessimistic elapsed-time figures are estimated by those persons most familiar with the activity involved. The three time estimates are required as a gauge of the "measure of uncertainty" of the activity, and represent full recognition of the probabilistic nature of many of the tasks in development-oriented and non-standard programs. It is important to note that for the purposes of computation and reporting, the three time estimates are reduced to a single expected time (t_e) and a statistical variance (standard deviation). Interpretations of the concept of optimistic, most likely, and pessimistic elapsed times are based on probability, and can be defined as follows:

Optimistic--an estimate of the minimum time that an activity will take; a result which can be obtained only if unusual good luck is experienced and everything "goes right the first time."

Most likely--an estimate of the <u>normal</u> time an activity will take; a result that would occur most often if the activity could be repeated a number of times under similar circumstances.

Pessimistic--an estimate of the <u>maximum</u> time an activity will take; a result which can occur only if unusually bad luck is experienced. It should reflect the possibility of initial failure and fresh start, but not be influenced by such factors as "catastrophic events"--fires, power failures, strikes,--unless these hazards are inherent risks in the activity.

These time estimates are reduced by averaging formulas and then producing the probability of meeting an established schedule date. The results of the calculations are the most important segments in the determination of the planning network's critical path. It follows that the network diagram is the arterial representation of the connections of these estimates into the critical path determination. A critical path is that particular sequence of activities in a network diagram that defines the earliest time for the accomplishment of the objective. Slack paths are sequences of activities having excess time, as opposed to the critical path. Slack may exist in varying amounts; it indicates where flexibility exists in scheduling within the path. When the critical path has been identified and the activities and events related to calendar dates, the critical schedule has been determined.

The manager must be informed constantly about this sequence of events; these reports generally occur on a biweekly or monthly basis. Because time prediction and performance data are available in a highly ordered fashion, managers can concentrate on the important critical path activities. The manager must determine valid means of shortening lead times by applying new resources or additional funds from those activities that can afford it because of their slack condition. It should be noted that the PERT system requires constant updating and reanalysis; the manager must recognize that the outlook for the complexion of activities in a complex program is in a constant state of flux, and he must be concerned with problems of re-evaluation and re-programming. The military users of the system have developed highly systematized methods of reporting using computers. When new data and status reports from activities are received, new critical paths and critical path schedules are computed.

The creation of a valid network is a fairly demanding task, and an excellent indicator of an organization's ability to visualize the number, kind, and sequence of activities needed to execute a complex program. PERT presents a common language, vital to the many individuals and organizations that comprise the typical task force engaged in planning and implementation of large programs.

Prior to investing capital in a new endeavor, the firm's planning actions will be the subject of a typical PERT and CPM exercise, as it might be used in the business world. The example is kept simple purposely to present the basic procedures to the reader. Management, having found the company's product in a declining market, has two alternatives: dispose of its excess plant, or expand the firm's operations by introducing a new product line, thereby utilizing the firm's facilities.

Tentatively, the latter course is chosen; corporate management designates a planning team to evaluate the time dimension of introducing a new product. It will use the PERT and CPM method to determine the time frame and the actions of the firm in preparation prior to actual commitment. The managers of the actual operating divisions of the company which will be involved in the actual execution of the project should not be chosen on the basis of the company's organization, but on the actual function to be performed. The reason is two-fold: planning charts should be meaningful to the persons carrying out the work, and the time estimates presented should be free of any schedule biasing.

By planning backwards from the objective to preclude the inadvertent omission of an event, the planning group, analysts, and operators, list the activities and events from the future to the present time. The events, as developed for the example, and activity times, are listed prior to the establishment of the network diagram. Each event is assigned a code number to show the sequence of occurrence. The events in the plan are:

001-Decision to expand firm.

002-Initiate market survey.

003-Compete market survey.

004-Initiate product development study.

005-Complete product development study.

011-Initiate pilot model construction.

012-Complete pilot model construction.

013-Begin pilot model testing.

014-Complete pilot model testing.

021-Begin distribution system planning.

022-Complete distribution system planning.

031-Decision for implementation.

111-Begin production line construction.

112-Complete production line construction.

113-Begin production.

114-Begin deliveries to distribution centers.

121-Begin sales and advertising programs.

122A-Begin sales training.

122B-Begin advertising study.

123A-Complete sales training.

123B-Complete advertising study.

124-Begin sales promotion.

131-Begin site selection studies.

132-Complete site selection study.

133-Purchase sites for distribution centers.

134-Begin distribution center construction.

135-Complete distribution centers.

141-Select MHE.

142-Purchase MHE.

143-Deliver MHE.

200-Introduction of product.

In actual practice, the analyst should be prepared to call another planning meeting after the collation of the original data into the network diagram. This would ensure that all required events and activities will be included, that the sequencing of events is certain, and that all possible functional areas have been explored to the proper depth. The network derived from the planning meetings is shown in Figure 5.1; it is presented in this form to the corporate management body. The Critical Path will be derived in conjunction with the network diagram. The probability of meeting the scheduled objective date will be computed. Implementation costs will not be considered as being in the scope of this study, but would naturally follow any planning prior to implementation.

To determine the Critical Path, the longest path of the network, the values of t_e are determined by the following formula:

$$t_e = \frac{a+4m+b}{6}$$

where t_e = expected time

a = optimistic time

m = most likely time

b = pessimistic time.

Expected Time Formula

The value of t_e represents the 50% probability point of the Beta distribution, i.e., it divides the area under the curve into two equal portions. The three time estimates are presented on the

147

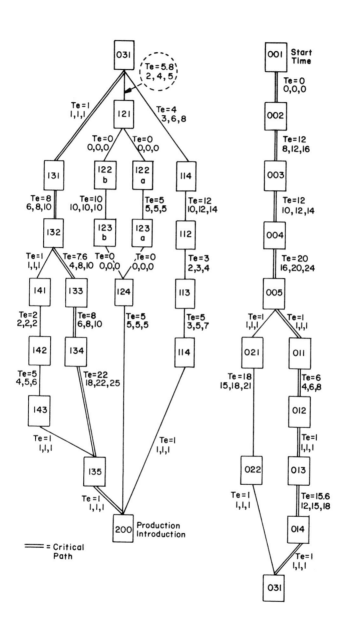

Figure 5.1. A Network Diagram.

activity lines as parenthetical expressions (optimistic, most likely, pessimistic). An expression such as (2,6,8) indicates the estimated elapsed times for the activity under each condition of time. When the term (0,0,0) is listed, it is called a "dummy" activity, and represents a tie-in point in the network. A measure of the statistical variance of this expected time is expressed in the formula:

$$(\text{Std. Dev.})^2 = (\frac{b-a}{6})^2$$

$$b = \text{pessimistic}$$
$$a = \text{optimistic}$$

Variance Formula

The higher the value of $(\text{Std. Dev.})^2$, the greater the uncertainty of meeting the date set by t_e. The greater the spread between the optimistic and pessimistic times, the larger the variance $(\text{std. Dev.})^2$ value; this indicates the uncertainty of the estimates concerned.

After the events have been assembled into the network diagram, expected times along the possible paths leading to the objective event are computed. In our example there are 10 paths between event 001 and event 200. The paths and the expected times for each activity in the path have been computed and are listed in Figure 5.2. The critical path for the planning schedule is labeled as #4 in the table, and can be identified as the path consuming the most time to accomplish the objective. All other paths have varying amounts of slack time; and the activities peculiar to these paths can slip from their forecast times without any effect on the objective, as set by the elapsed time estimate (T_e) for the critical path. The activity concerned with the accomplishment of event 123B can be postponed up to 3.6 time periods before it affects critical path times and the objective date. By setting up the

Path	#1		#2		#3		#4		#5	
From Event 001 to		t_e		t_e		t_e		t_e		t_e
	002	0	002	0	002	0	002	0	002	0
	003	12	003	12	003	12	003	12	003	12
	004	12	004	12	004	12	004	12	004	12
	005	20	005	20	005	20	005	20	005	20
	011	1	011	1	011	1	011	1	011	1
	012	6	012	6	012	6	012	6	012	6
	013	1	013	1	013	1	013	1	013	1
	014	15.6	014	15.6	014	15.6	014	15.6	014	15.6
	031	1	031	1	031	1	031	1	031	1
	111	5.8	121	4	121	4	131	1	131	1
	112	12	122A	0	122B	0	132	8	132	8
	113	3	123A	5	123B	10	133	7.6	141	1
	114	5	124	0	124	0	134	8	142	2
	200	1	200	5	200	5	135	22	143	5
							200	1	135	1
									200	1
Total Eatimated Time		95.7		82.9		87.9		116.5		87.9

	#6		#7		#8		#9		#10	
		t_e		t_e		t_e		t_e		t_e
	002	0	002	0	002	0	002	0	002	0
	003	12.3	003	12.3	003	12.3	003	12.3	003	12.3
	004	12	004	12	004	12	004	12	004	12
	005	20	005	20	005	20	005	20	005	20
	021	1	021	1	021	1	021	1	021	1
	022	18	022	18	022	18	022	18	022	18
	031	1	031	1	031	1	031	1	031	1
	111	5.8	121	4	121	4	131	1	131	1
	112	12	122A	0	122B	0	132	8	132	8
	113	3	123A	5	123B	10	133	7.6	141	1
	114	5	124	0	124	0	134	8	142	2
	200	1	200	5	200	5	135	22	143	5
							200	1	135	1
									200	1
Timed Estimated Time t_e		91.1		78.3		83.3		111.9		83.3

Figure 5.2 Expected Times for Project Completion.

150

slack values in a schedule of increasing values, the manager can
determine the activities which need to be allotted additional
resources, should the objective time be set forward by corporate
management.

Path #4---- 0	#5----28.6
9---- 4.6	8----33.2
1----20.8	10----33.2
6----25.4	2----33.6
3----28.6	7----38.2

The value of the schedule to the manager becomes apparent when the
original planning objective date is not acceptable and a decision
is made to compress the time frame. Assume the periods to be weeks,
the decision date is July 1st, and the objective date for introduction of the new product is September 25.   Further, we shall
assume that the corporate management wishes to know the probability
of meeting an introduction date of August 1st.   The analyst will
apply the variances formula to the time estimates and combine them
in the formula:

$$\frac{T_s - T_e}{Std.Dev.} = P$$

where T_s = Scheduled time
      T_e = Estimated time
Std.Dev.= Square root of sum of individual variances
      P = Probability of Meeting T_s; derived from Table of
          Areas under Normal Curve.

Probability of Meeting Scheduled Time

Computing the variances from the network diagram, we
tabulate the following table:

Activity from 001 to 002--0   031 to 121--- .44

```
Activity from 001 to 002--0          031 to 121--- .44
                 003--1.78                122A--0
                 004-- .44                122B--0
                 005--1.69                123A--0
                 011--0                   123B--0
                 012-- .44          123A to 124---0
                 013--0             123B to 124---0
                 014--1.0           124  to 200---0
                 031--0             031  to 131---0
          005 to 021--0                   132--- .44
                 022--1.0                 133---1.0
                 031--0                   134--- .44
          031 to 111-- .71                135---1.69
                 112-- .44                200---0
                 113-- .11          132  to 141---0
                 114-- .44                142---0
                 200--0                   143--- .11
                                          135---0
                                          200---0
```

Variances Table

The computations to arrive at the probability of meeting the designated date of August 1st are:

$$T_s = 108.5$$
$$T_e = 116.5$$
$$\text{Std. Dev.}^2 = 12.8 = (3.48)^2$$
$$\frac{108.5-116.5}{3.48} = \frac{-8}{3.48} = -2.3$$

The probability associated with a value of -2.3 is .001, or about one chance in a hundred that the date of August 1st could be met using the scheduled resources. The manager now goes to the critical path schedule to determine the most valid method of applying new resources along the critical path to shorten the time frame. He can determine which activities can afford to relinquish some resources by virtue of their slack conditions. By applying additional resources to the activity associated with the accomplishment of event 135 (Completion of Distribution Centers), the manager can accelerate the event time by 4 weeks without affecting any activities in the path with the lowest slack time (#9). The funds needed to reduce the construction time of the distribution centers might come from an activity peculiar to path #7, the path with the highest slack time. In this way, resources are applied to the activities which produce the greatest benefit to the program, i.e., those on the critical path. A reduction in the program of 4 weeks increases the probability of meeting the introduction date to .12. Any decrease in elapsed time from this point now must take place on both Path #4 and Path #9, for any reduction in time over 4.6 weeks makes Path #9 the Critical Path. Should the corporate management require a probability of .90 of meeting the introduction date, the program must be decreased by a period of 8.5 weeks; this necessitates the application of resources to Paths #4 and #9, both of which have path times greater than the required 108 weeks. The network diagram shows that application of resources to reduce distribution center construction programs by a period of 8 1/2 weeks will reduce the entire program to the required time frame. This example of the usefulness of the PERT and Critical Path Method illustrates how the procedure enables the manager to allocate effort only to those activities which will produce benefits to the program, rather than an indiscriminate, across-the-board application of resources.

The network schedule plan presented will be modified when the introduction date is set, and the determination is made as to the point of application of resources. Such updating should take place as the project moves forward. Most PERT applications have the biweekly or monthly report requirement built into the system, giving the manager or analyst the opportunity to directly communicate with operating-level personnel, and allowing direct inquiry into the status of all events scheduled to be started or completed during the prior period. During the course of this activity the

qualities and abilities of the manager, in terms of both understanding the substance of the work being performed and making
constructive suggestions on how to improve performance, become
particularly significant. The experienced PERT user will wish
to participate in the design review meetings of the program, in
order to have a deeper understanding of technical problems and
progress. During the updating process, he will inquire into new
time estimates for future activities, particularly in critical path
areas, or when new trouble spots are indicated.

Updating generally does not involve all activities of the
network, but it is likely to produce new critical path and slack
data. Thus, the formal process of analysis, replanning, and
review is started over again, and continues to recycle every two
weeks or every month until the end of the program. The amount of
effort involved in the updating process will be a function of the
quality of the original plan.

There is one particularly significant aspect of PERT time
scheduling, which represents a unique contribution of the technique: network condensation and integration. In large defense
and space programs, it is typical to have many different networks,
since many companies throughout the country are working on the
same program. One objective of the top manager of such a program,
whether it be a prime contractor or a government agency, is to
achieve a valid summarization of all these different networks.
The problem involves identification of all the interface events
common to two or more networks, and the ability to determine T_e
and critical path analysis for the totality of all networks. The
total of all networks may amount to more than 30,000 activities
on large programs. In these cases, network condensation, integration, and validation are best done through a computer program.

The PERT program has lent itself especially well to automatic data
processing; most Defense Department research programs are computerized

to minimize time spent in setting up and organizing the direction
of the research effort. By means of network condensation and
integration, and sometimes recondensation, an entire national
program can be viewed in one final, comprehensible summarized
network. Though the activity lines of such a network generally
do not have an identifiable meaning, the calculated expected times
derived from the underlying detailed network system are valid.
This process represents a contribution unique to the PERT technique; indeed, it would be hard to visualize how it could be
accomplished with any other schedule reporting system. It is
an example of the power of the PERT technique as an important
new tool for management of large, complex programs. The gains
to be achieved with PERT, in terms of both tangible and in-
tangible benefits, are summarized as follows:

1. A basic improvement in planning, in terms of more
realistic time estimates, allows for better decision making prior
to entering upon new programs. It is commonplace for programs to
be approved on the basis of optimistic or unrealistic estimates,
only to be terminated at a later date when the true facts emerge.
This situation produces severe waste of any company's resources.

2. The ability to control programs against original
objectives is greatly improved through early detection of un-
completed events and isolation of important problem areas by
means of critical path analysis. In other words, the possibility
exists of executing complex programs within plus or minus 20 per
cent of original estimates, rather than large increases in cost
and time through across-the-board increases in application of
resources.

3. PERT pinpoints the potential for actual cost savings,
increases in efficiency, and improvement in profits. These include such savings as the selective use of overtime on critical
path activities, rather than "crashing" a whole department; or

shortening total project time through network analysis and replanning. In the latter case, many tangible "down-stream" savings
can be achieved which are not directly related to the project
effort. In a combined engineering and production program, like
our example, the engineering release is made on schedule, or
earlier, thus allowing production buyers more time to negotiate
better prices. When PERT has been used in the areas of plant
construction, maintenance, and overhaul, significant profit gains
have been reported because of earlier schedule completion. These
gains involve minimizing production stoppage, or earlier entry of
a new product into the market.

For the kinds of programs where PERT is applicable, the
question management may well ask itself is not "Can we afford
PERT?" but "Can we afford not to have it?"

Dynamic Programming

Dynamic programming is a mathematical optimization technique which is useful for solution of some quantitative problems
involving a sequence of interrelated decisions. It provides
systematic procedures for determining the combination of decisions
which maximizes overall effectiveness.[1]

Dynamic programming deals with decisions that are dependent
on time or sequence. A time-dependent programming problem occurs
when the decision made in one time period will have an effect on
decisions in other time periods. In a sequence-dependent programming problem, the decisions made at previous stages become conditions for succeeding stages in the sequence. Recursive optimization
is a more descriptive term for the technique.[2] It is typically a

[1]Fredrick S. Hillier and Gerald J. Lieberman, Introduction
to Operations Research (San Francisco: Holden-Day, Inc., 1967),
p. 239.

[2]George L. Nemhauser, Introduction to Dynamic Programming
(New York: John Wiley and Sons, Inc., 1966), p. 8.

multi-staged process transformed into a series of single-stage
decision processes.

Dynamic programming starts with a small portion of the problem
and finds the optimal solution for this smaller problem. It
then gradually enlarges the problem, finding the current
optimal solution from the previous one, until the original
problem is solved in its entirety.[1]

The theoretical basis for solving the overall problem by
optimization of the sub parts is provided through the use of
Bellman's principle of optimality:

An optimal policy has the property that whatever the initial
state and initial decision are, the remaining decisions must
constitute an optimal policy with regard to the state
resulting from the first decision.[2]

The breaking down of the problem into a series of smaller
problems is called "decomposition." The smaller problems are
called "stages."

Typically, the first stage in a dynamic program formulation
refers to the last decision which must be made in a series
of sequential decisions. The results of this stage are then
included in the next stage of the dynamic program formulation. This recursive procedure is applied at each stage
until the last stage is reached, at which point we are able
to determine the optimal policy and value for the initial
decision of our problem.[3]

Setting Up a Dynamic Programming Problem

The accompanying flow chart is presented by Keuster and Mize
as an approach to setting up a dynamic programming problem.[4] The

---

[1] Hillier and Lieberman, p. 241.

[2] Richard E. Bellman and Stuart E. Dreyfus, Applied Dynamic
Programming (Princeton: Princeton University Press, 1962), p. 15.

[3] James L. Kuester and Joe H. Mize, Optimization Techniques
with Fortran (New York: McGraw-Hill Book Company, 1973), p. 157.

[4] Ibid., p. 159.

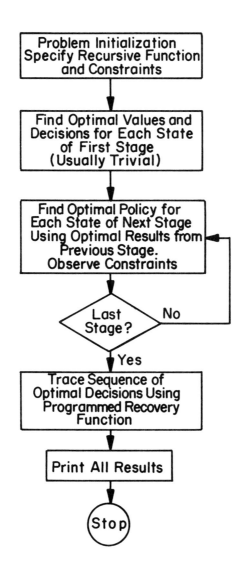

Figure 5.3.   Flow Chart for Dynamic Programming.

problem is initialized together with the recursive function and constraints. The program sets out to find the optimal values of the first stage and proceeds successively to the last stage. The optimal decisions are then retraced and used to program the optimal path.

An Example of the Use of
Dynamic Programming

An example of the use of dynamic programming to solve a complex problem was the design of an optimum system solution for the California State Water Project,[1] a massive water gathering, in-storage complex. Water gathered in the Delta Region about 50 miles from San Francisco is transported through Central California south through the Los Angeles region. When totally operational, the California Aqueduct will be the world's largest pure water delivery system.

The reservoirs for the system have no natural inflow; they serve as buffers during the winter when user demands are low. Water is released during the summer months when demand is high.

To move such large amounts of water requires pumping plants larger than have ever been built. The operation of the total aqueduct system requires enormous amounts of electrical energy. Clever operation of the aqueduct could reduce the purchase of certain types of electrical energy, particularly the cost of buying "on peak power capacity." The optimization problem is to determine operating schedules that produce the minimum yearly use of "on peak power capacity" for the entire system.

---

[1] John Matucha, "Don't Reject Dynamic Programming for Complex Systems," Computer Science, April, 1972, pp. 18-23. This application is presented with the permission of the author.

159

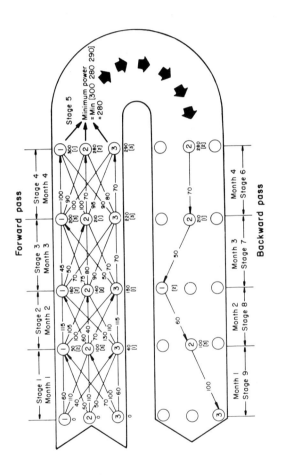

Figure 5.4.   Forward and Backward Pass Using Dynamic Programming.

A simplified example will show how the incremental, dynamic programming algorithm would determine a minimum "on peak power" operation for the system. The scheduling program must find a mode of operation for the California Aqueduct over a four-month period that will minimize "on peak power" requirements. Three sets of three total system values will be considered each month, where the ending storage values for one month will equal the starting values for the next month. During each month there are nine possible system "on peak" capacities.

The dynamic programming algorithm has two major phases. The first is a month by month forward pass through the network. This will produce the minimal values that can be achieved with the given set of values, but it will not reveal the proper path through the network. The second phase is a month by month backward path through the network that will find the optimal operations schedule-- the set of five total system storages that will give the minimum on peak for four months.

As the forward pass begins, note that three sets of possible end-of-month values are shown. These values satisfy all operating constraints, such as pumping capacity and minimum reservoir levels. Although some of the values shown are equal (two 50s from node 2, for example), they are total system values. The individual figures for all the reservoirs, therefore, might be different even though the total system values are the same. The numbers are related to on peak power costs, which are a function of changes in the reservoir system over the month.

The end values for stage 1 become the start values for stage 2. Note that each node at the beginning of stage 2 is receiving three values, one from each of the nodes at the start of stage 1. For example, at the end of stage 1 in month 1, supplies could have been drawn from three sources in the amount of 60 from source 1, 50 from source 2 and 70 from source 3. The program would have selected

source 2 as the source of power since it is the lowest cost of the
three alternatives with respect to location number 1 in stage 1.
Accordingly, the algorithm selects the minimum values at each node.
The lowest value, 100, from source 3 becomes the starting point for
point 2, and the value of 40 from point 1 becomes the starting
point for point 3 in stage 2. Under each of these values at the
start of stage 2 is the number of the node from which this minimum
value was received.

For the second month, the three minimal values from stage 1
are used as initial conditions. These are passed on to the node at
the end of stage 2. Selection of the minimum depends on the sum of
the minimum and the initial value and one of the passed values.
The calculation is demonstrated below node 3, where the minimum value
of 100 plus 50 equal 150 which was received from node 1.

Finally, at the end of stage 4, three values result: 300,
280, and 290. The minimum, 280 at node 2 represents the minimal
on peak capacity operation for the four-month period.

Now comes the backward pass through the network to determine
the path that was followed to reach 280. The objective is to track
back stage by stage to find the minimum path through the network.
This procedure shows that consecutive nodes 3,2,1,2,2 led to the
minimal operation.

The actual program used in solving the problem was essentially
the same as the example, except for a few modifications.

General Uses of Dynamic Programming

A standard mathematical formulation does not exist in which
a generalized dynamic programming solution may be used. Rather, a
set of equations must be developed to fit the problem at hand. It
may be visualized as a general strategy for problem solution rather
than a specific set of rules.

162

A major division of dynamic programming problems is usually made with respect to the nature of the decision variable. If the decision variable can take on any real value, it is said to be continuous. If the decision variable is restricted to integer values, it is said to be discrete.[1]

An additional division of the problems categories which may be handled by dynamic programming are those problems having finite horizons and infinite horizons. Finite horizons usually involve a definite time pattern of requirements which is to be met and which extends over a specifically prescribed period of time. They may consist of a terminal objective, like a point which is required to be met by travel. Typically, the prescribed requirement would be met with the least effort, with maximal contribution to some effective junction. Infinite horizons involve a repetitive process of decision that extends indefinitely into the future. An example of such problems would be a continuing pattern of demand for an item, or improving the capacity of the specified piece of equipment.

Some of the more obvious applications to logistical problems are in the various areas of inventory management. Transportation routing has also received substantial attention.

1. It can treat problems at both continuous and discrete values.
2. It can employ non-linear as well as linear objective functions with constraints.
3. The approach is suited for problems with interrelated sequential decisions made over successive time periods.
4. The approach provides a contingency plan. Optimal paths from future states are calculated so that even if the predicted state is not achieved in the next stage, the actual optimal path is still provided.

---

[1]Kuester and Mize, p. 155.

There are two primary disadvantages to dynamic programming.
The first is that some problems are simply too large computationally
for present generation computers. Unfortunately, it is difficult
to determine how complex the problem may be until a substantial
time investment is made. Second, there is no standard mathematical
formulation for all types of dynamic programming problems. Each
problem and objective function must be considered individually.

Linear Programming

In the mid 1950s, linear programming appeared as a mathematical solution to various kinds of optimizing problems. The
method was developed for use by the military forces, but industry
recognized the potential value of linear programming to many types
of its problems. Linear programming problems tend to be associated
with complex situations, many interacting variables, and competing
objectives. The variables may be of a diverse nature, such as money,
time, man-hours, machine-hours, and other factors dependant on the
problem to be solved.

General Linear Programming Model

The general programming model usually consists of a function
which is to be maximized or minimized. The value of the object or
variable to be optimized is given the algebraic symbol Z. Z is a
scaler, a single real value such as total profit or total cost.

$$Z = C_1X_1 + C_2X_2 + C_3X_3 + \ldots + C_nY_n$$

where C_i (i = 1,2,3,4 . . . n) = a set of n constants that define
the profits (or costs) related to the corresponding X_i
element: that is, C_1 represents the profit (or cost) of
each unit of X_1; similarly, C_2 represents the "price" for
each unit of X_2 and so forth.

X_i (i = 1,2,3,4, . . . n) = a set of n unknown variables that are to be given values that maximize (or minimize) the value of Z. The set of X_i values that maximize (or minimize) the value of Z is called the optimum solution to the linear programming problem.

Simple linear programming problems can be solved or represented graphically. Figure 5.5 shows inputs of fertilizer used in producing wheat and corn. Each portion of each curve is linear, but the segmented curve represents a continuous function. The constraint of this example is the quantity of fertilizer. Activities that draw upon this constraining resource are wheat and corn production.

The only thing lacking for a solution to maximized profits (or contributions) of the fixed resource is the price of wheat and corn. The price line can be drawn in quadrant one to obtain a solution. The line which represents the price of wheat divided by the price of corm is drawn as a tangent to the function taken from the first quadrant, which represents production possibilities between output of corn and output of wheat. The point where the price line is tangent to the output function represents the optimal solution in this problem.

Problems with only one constraining resource or equation usually are trivial. Several resources are utilized in production and distribution problems. In the previous example, corn and wheat could have used land, labor, and fertilizer. Let us assume that there are available 85 acres of land, 400 hours of labor, and 240 pounds of fertilizer, in the following proportions: (1) land is equally divided with respect to corn and wheat; (2) four hours of labor per acre are required for corn and five hours of labor per acre for wheat; (3) 300 pounds of fertilizer per acre are required for corn; and (4) 200 pounds of fertilizer per acre for wheat.

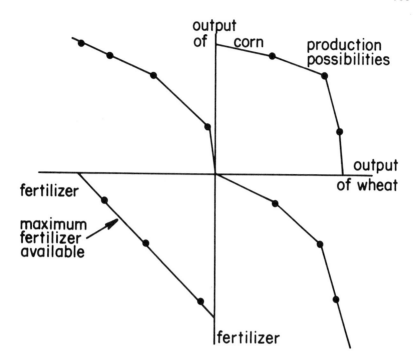

Figure 5.5.   Variables in a Linear Programming Problem Shown
              Graphically.

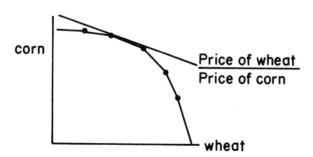

Figure 5.6.   Graphic Solution to a Linear Programming Problem.

	Sign	B_i	X_1	X_2		
C_j			35	20		
Land	$\leq$	85	1	1		
Labor	$\leq$	400	4	5		
Fertilizer	$\leq$	240	3	2		

The equations which reflect each of these are as follows:

$$X_1 + X_2 \leq 85$$
$$4X_1 + 5X_2 \leq 400$$
$$3X_1 + 2X_2 \leq 240$$

Since the optimizing equation requires that every input variable have a cost, every column must have a C_j value, even if the value is 0. In this illustration, cost for corn X_1 is $35, and the cost for wheat is $20. The maximizing equation would then be

$$Z = 35X_1 + 20X_2$$

The order of input of the equations into the computer program is important. Usually the order is the "less than" equations, the "equality" equations, and, the "greater than" equations. One must specify the sign for each equation.

A problem with "less than" and "greater than" constraints can be illustrated by showing that the solution is limited to points on the production possibilities curve above a certain level for one of the activities.

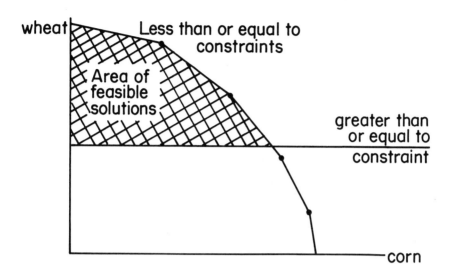

wheat | Less than or equal to constraints

Area of feasible solutions

greater than or equal to constraint

corn

Figure 5.7. Graphic Illustration of Area of Feasible Solution.

For example, in Figure 5.7 the area of feasible solutions is the cross-hatched area above the greater than, or equal to, constraint line, but between the vertical axis and the line indicated by the less than, or equal to, constraints. To include a constraint that wheat must be brought into a solution at 25 acres or more, a row would be added to the matrix as follows:

	Sign	B	X_1	X_2		
C_j						
	$\geq$	25	0	1		

Care must be taken that the greater than equation does not require more resources then are available. If this happens the area of possible solutions is reduced to zero; this would be an impracticable solution by linear programming.

Setting Up a Linear Programming Problem

Profit maximization and cost minimization are two typical problems handled by linear programming. While they are similar in the case of cost minimization, profits are negative (losses are minimized).

Cost minimization will be used to illustrate preparation of the problem for solution by computer. This problem compares direct shipments of total volume quantities to less than volume shipments through the concentration and dispersion terminals. In the problem, A and B are production points; M, N, O, and P are retail outlets. Shipments can be made directly from A to M or N, and from B to O or P; or, they may go to concentration point R from A and B, then to dispersion point S, and finally to the retail outlets M, N, O, and P. The plant capacities for A and B are as follows: plant A equals 600 units per month; plant B equals 400 units per month.

The retail outlet demand requirements are:

Retail Outlet M = 225 units per month
"   "   N = 175   "   "   "
"   "   O = 250   "   "   "
"   "   P = 250   "   "   "

The transportation costs and terminal costs are as indicated below:

Transportation Costs		Terminal Costs	
A-R =	$ .25	R =	$ .06
B-R =	.20	S =	.15
R-S =	.42		
S-M =	.18		
S-N =	.20		
S-O =	.15		

Transportation Costs (Cont.)
<pre>
  S-P =   .20
  A-M =   1.15
  A-N =   1.10
  B-O =   .95
  B-P =   1.05
</pre>

The problem is to minimize transportation and terminal costs
between production points and retail outlets. Initially, for a
problem of this type, a flow diagram would be helpful. A flow
diagram for this problem is presented in Figure 5.8.

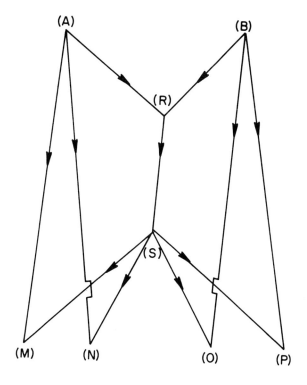

Figure 5.8.   Flow Diagram for the Problem.

We are concerned with the initial supply points and the
retail demand points. Following is a list of possible routes along
which the products could flow.

1. A to M
2. A to N
3. A to R to S to M
4. A to R to S to N
5. A to R to S to O
6. A to R to S to P
7. B to O
8. B to P
9. B to R to S to M
10. B to R to S to N
11. B to R to S to O
12. B to R to S to P

With the routes established, costs can be accumulated for
each. For the routes outlined above, the cost factors will be
accumulated as a total cost along the particular route. We will
assign an unknown X variable to each of the twelve routes, to
simplify writing out the equations for the objective function and
the constraints.

Route	Variable	Trans. Costs	Terminal Cost	Total
A-M	X_1	1.15	-0-	$1.15
A-N	X_2	1.10	-0-	1.10
A-R-S-M	X_3	.25,.42,.18	.06, .15	1.06
A-R-S-N	X_4	.25,.42,.20	.06, .15	1.08
A-R-S-O	X_5	.25,.42,.15	.06, .15	1.03
A-R-S-P	X_6	.25,.42,.20	.06, .15	1.08
B-O	X_7	.95	-0-	.95
B-P	X_8	1.05	-0-	1.05
B-R-S-M	X_9	.20,.42,.18	.06, .15	1.01
B-R-S-N	X_{10}	.20,.42,.20	.06, .15	1.03
B-R-S-O	X_{11}	.20,.42,.15	.06, .15	.98
B-R-S-P	X_{12}	.20,.42,.20	.06, .15	1.03

The objective function, which is to present the problem in
mathematical form, now can be formed. The object is to minimize
the total transportation and terminal costs for shipping products
from two plants to four retail outlets. The objective function
would be written as:

$$\text{Min } Z = 1.15X_1 + 1.10X_2 + 1.06X_3 + 1.08X_4 + 1.03X_5 + 1.08X_6$$
$$+ .95X_7 + 1.05X_8 + 1.01X_9 + 1.03X_{10} + .98X_{11} + 1.03X_{12}$$

The objective function provides the object of the problem.
It is necessary to state the constraints of the problem as well.
If there were no constraints on the problem, then the minimization
would be to produce absolutely nothing, because the cost would be
nothing. This problem has six constraints placed upon it--the
number of items produced at each plant, and the number of items
demanded by the retail outlets. The presentation of constraints
in this problem is one of many that satisfy the conditions of the
problem. Normally, the production constraint would be listed as
an equal to, or less than, constraint; since here the supply
exceeds demand, the constraints on production plants are shown
as equalities, to insure maximum production and to satisfy the
demand at lowest possible cost.

The constraints for production would be written as follows:

$$X_1 + X_2 + X_3 + X_4 + X_5 + X_6 = 600$$
$$X_7 + X_8 + X_9 + X_{10} + X_{11} + X_{12} = 400$$

By referring back to the route assignments, it can be seen
that X_1 through X_6 represent all the routes leading from plant A.
This means that all products flowing along these routes cannot
exceed 600 units, the capacity of plant A. The same analogy
applies to plant B. These two constraints take care of the production end of the problem. This insures in the solution that all
available production is utilized, but will not exceed the capacity
of either of the plants.

The constraints for the retail outlets are as follows:
$$X_1 + X_3 + X_9 = 225 \text{ for retail outlet M}$$

$$X_2 + X_4 + X_{10} = 175 \text{ for retail outlet N}$$

$$X_5 + X_7 + X_{11} = 250 \text{ for retail outlet O}$$

$$X_6 + X_8 + X_{12} = 250 \text{ for retail outlet P}$$

These constraints are written as equal to, or less than, equations because the supply exceeds the demand; therefore, one or more of the plants will not sell all the products it can produce. For each outlet there is a summation of all the routes feeding that outlet. Each outlet receives exactly its demands.

Integer Programming and Combinational Models

There are several, frequently occurring situations that lead to planning models which contain integer-valued variables. These situations include:

1. Equipment utilization
2. Setup costs
3. Batch sizes
4. "Go-No-Go" decisions
5. Sequencing, scheduling, and routing decisions

The integer model is of the general form.

$$\text{optimize } \sum_{j-1}^{n} = c_j x_j, \tag{1}$$

subject to

$$\sum_{j=1}^{n} a_{ij} x_j \leq bi \quad \text{for} \quad i = 1, 2, \ldots, m \tag{2}$$

$$x_j \geq o \quad \text{for} \quad j = 1, 2, \ldots, n \tag{3}$$

$$x_j \text{ integer-values} \quad \text{for} \quad j = 1, 2, \ldots, p \ (\leq n). \tag{4}$$

When p=n, so that every variable must be integer-valued, the model is called a pure integer programming problem. Otherwise, the problem would be a mixed integer programming problem.

The objective function (1) may be defined to either maximize or minimize. An integer programming problem may consider inequalities and equalities. The constraints (4) distinguish an integer from general linear programming problem.

All of the planning situations listed above are important for logistics systems planning. "Go-No-Go" decisions, also frequently referred to as capital budgeting decisions, include plant/warehouse location, sales territory analysis, and business acquisition. Sequencing, scheduling, and routing decisions include the traveling salesman problem, machine scheduling, line-balancing, critical path scheduling with resource constraints, preventive maintenance scheduling with constraints, and truck dispatching. Sequencing, scheduling, and routing problems are special cases of what are categorized as combinatorial models. A combinatorial optimization problem consists of finding the optimum value of the objective function from among a finite set of alternatives.

In the past, despite all of the articles written discussing the potential of applying integer programs to planning decisions, the actual utilization of such models has been limited. This is because the computational effort of solving real world planning situations has been too great. In addition, integer models frequently ignore critical considerations that exist in actual planning situations.

Recently, a computational technique that solves mixed integer problems by Bender's Decomposition method indicates a practical approach to an important class of logistics planning problems. The approach will be presented here using as an example a frequently occurring problem in logistics system design: optimal location of distribution centers for raw material and/or finished goods handling and storage.

174

Geoffrion and Graves[1] provide the most authoritative presentation:

> The simplest version of the problem to be modeled is this. There are several commodities produced at several plants with known production capacities. There is a known demand for each commodity at each of a number of customer zones. This demand is satisfied by shipping via regional distribution centers (abbreviated DC), with each customer zone being assigned exclusively to a single DC. There are lower as well as upper bounds on the allowable total annual throughput of each DC. The possible locations for the DC's are given, but the particular sites to be used are to be selected so as to result in the least total distribution cost. The DC costs are expressed as fixed charges (imposed for the sites actually used) plus a linear variable charge. Transportation costs are taken to be linear.
>
> Thus the problem is to determine which DC sites to use, what size DC to have at each selected site, what customer zones should be served by each DC, and what the pattern of transportation flows should be for all commodities. This is to be done so as to meet the given demands at minimum total distribution cost subject to the plant capacity and DC throughout constraints. There may also be additional constraints on the logical configuration of the distribution system.
>
> The mathematical formulation of the problem uses the following notation.
>
> i index for commodities,
>
> j index for plants,
>
> k index for possible distribution center (DC) sites,
>
> ℓ index for customer demand zones,
>
> S_{ij} supply (production capacity) for commodity i at plant j,
>
> D_i^ℓ demand for commodity i in customer zone ℓ
>
> $\underline{V}_k, \bar{V}_k^\ell$ minimum, maximum allowed total annual throughput for a dC at site k,
>
> f_k fixed portion of the annual possession and operating costs for a DC at site k,
>
> v_k variable unit cost of throughput for a DC at site k,
>
> $c_{ijk\ell}$ average unit cost of producing and shipping commodity i from plant j through DC k to customer zone ℓ
>
> $X_{ijk\ell}$ a variable denoting the amount of commodity i shipped from plant j through DC k to customer zone ℓ

[1]A. M. Geoffrion and G. W. Graves, "Multicommodity Distribution System Designed by Bender's Decomposition," Management Science, Vol. 20, No. 5, January 1974, pp. 822-844.

$Y_{k\ell}$ a 0-1 variable that will be 1 if DC k serves customer zone , and 0 otherwise

Z_k a 0-1 variable that will be 1 if a DC is acquired at site k, and 0 otherwise.

The problem can be written as the following mixed integer linear program

$$\text{Minimize } X\geq 0; y, Z=0,1 \quad \Sigma_{ijk\ell} C_{ijk\ell} X_{ijk\ell} + \Sigma_k [f_k Z_k + V_k \Sigma_{i\ell} D_{i\ell} y_{k\ell}]$$

subject to
$$\tag{1}$$

$$\Sigma_{k\ell} X_{ijk\ell} \leq S_{ij}, \qquad \text{all } ij \tag{2}$$

$$\Sigma_j X_{ijk\ell} = D_{i\ell} Y_{k\ell} \qquad \text{all } ik\ell \tag{3}$$

$$\Sigma_k Y_{k\ell} = 1, \qquad \text{all } \ell \tag{4}$$

$$\underline{V}_k Z_k \leq \Sigma_{i\ell} D_{i\ell} Y_{k\ell} \leq \overline{V}_k Z_k \qquad \text{all } k \tag{5}$$

Linear configuration constraints on y and/or z (6)

The quantity $\Sigma_{i\ell} D_{ij} Y_{k\ell}$ is the total throughput for period modeled of the kth DC. The constraints (2) $\Sigma_{k\ell} X_{ijk\ell} \leq S_{ij}$, all ij are the supply constraints, and (3) requires that both demand must be filled when $Y_{k\ell} = 1$, and that $Y_{ijk\ell}$ must be 0 for all ij when $Y_{k\ell} = 0$. The requirement that a customer zone must be served by only a single DC is defined by constraints (4) $\Sigma_k Y_{k\ell} = 1$.

Besides keeping the total annual throughput between $\underline{V}_k$ and $\overline{V}_k$ or at 0 according to whether or not a DC is open, (5) also enforces the correct logical relationship between y and z (i.e., $z_k = 1 \leftrightarrow Y_{k\ell} = 1$ for some ℓ). Constraints (6) are deliberately not spelled out in detail for the sake of notational simplicity. The only requirement is that they be linear and do not involve any X-variables.

The arbitrary configuration constraints (6) give the model quite a lot of flexibility to incorporate many of the complexities and idiosyncrasies found in most real applications. For instance, (6) permits:
- upper and/or lower bounds on the total number of open DC's allowed;
- specification of subsets of DC's among which at most one, at least one, exactly two, etc., are required to be open;

- precedence relations pertaining to the open DC's (not A unless B, etc.);
- mandatory service area constraints (if DC A is open, it must serve customer zone B);
- more detailed capacity constraints on the size of DC than (5) permits, as by weighting the capacity consumption characteristics of each commodity differently or by writing separate constraints for individual or subsets of commodities;
- constraints on the joint capacity of several DC's if they share common resources or facilities;
- customer service constraints like

$$(\Sigma_{k\ell} \, t_{ik\ell} \, D_{i\ell} Y_{k\ell})/\Sigma_\ell \, D_{i\ell} \leq T_i,$$

where $t_{ik\ell}$ is the average time to make a delivery of commodity i to customer zone ℓ after receiving an order at DC k, and T_i is a desired bound on the average delivery delay for commodity i.

The technique noted herein specializes Benders' well-known partitioning procedure to the problem described so that the multicommodity LP subproblem decomposes into as many independent classical transportation problems as there are commodities. This decomposition technique makes it possible to solve problems with an almost unlimited number of commodities. Geoffrion and Graves continue:

An elaborate all-FORTRAN implementation has been carried out for the variant of Benders Decomposition . . . . The objective of solving large problems in moderate computing times required the use of efficient algorithms for solving the master problems and subproblems, and careful data management techniques. These matters are discussed briefly in this section.

Master Problem

The master problems, of the form (8_a), are pure 0-1 integer linear programs with a variable for every allowable DC-customer zone combination $(Y_{k\ell})$ and for every possible DC site (Z_k). Typically this leads to at least several hundred binary variables. Thus it was necessary to devise a specialized method which exploits the special structure of (8_a). The method we employ is a hybrid branch-and-bound/cutting-plane approach with numerous special features.

The cuts employed are the original mixed integer cuts proposed by Gomory in 1960, and are applied to each node problem in order to strengthen the LP bounds and to drive variables toward integer values in preparation for the choice of a branching variable. Absolute priority is given to z-variables over y-variables in branching. Reversal bounds are calculated for variables which are branched upon using relaxed versions which drop the integrality requirements on y (while keeping the integrality requirements on (z) and transfer a linear combination of all constants except (5) and individual variable bounds up into the objective function. The multipliers which determine the linear combination are the appropriate dual variables of a node problem solved as a linear program (ignoring the integrality requirements on both y and z).

The linear programming subroutine takes full advantage of the generalized upper bounding constraints (4), and also exploits certain other aspects of the problem structure. It economizes on the use of core storage by generating columns as needed from compactified data arrays.

Finally, it should be mentioned that a number of logical relationships between the variables are built in at various points of the master problem algorithm so as to detect several kinds of infeasibility and "fix" the free variables when this is justified.

Subproblem

The transportation subproblems are solved using a new primal simplex-based algorithm with factorization. Contrary to the conventional wisdom, such methods are superior to out-of-kilter type algorithms for most network flow applications. This is certainly true for the present application, where only the costs of the transportation subproblems change between successive solutions. An earlier implementation using an out-of-kilter algorithm was an order of magnitude slower on the average.

Data Input and Storage

Core storage requirements are economized by extensive use of overlay, cumulative indexing, and the creation of compact data sets from which model coefficients can be generated conveniently as needed. Most of the larger of these data sets are kept on disk. Raw problem data pertaining to permissible $ijk\ell$ combinations, transportation costs, and customer demands are input from tape to a preprocessor problem which creates the appropriate data sets on disk. These are then accessed directly by the main program, which receives the rest of the problem data (S_{ij}, $\underline{V}_k$, $\overline{V}_k$, f_k, V_k and configuration data for (6) from direct keyboard input using the URSA conversational

CRT-display remote job entry system at UCLA. The editing and scope display facilities of URSA make this an ideal means of entering and revising all but bulk data. Matrix generation and similar chores are accomplished entirely by the preprocessor and main programs.

The specific types of configuration constraints (6) accommodated in the current program include: fixing selected $Y_{k\ell}$ and Z_k variables at specific values to set up regional or otherwise reduced versions of the full problem; mutual exclusivity constraints on DC sites; mandatory service area constraints for each DC; and a limit on the maximum number of DC's that may be open.

Newly generated cuts are stored on disk for use in the reoptimization mode. The last primal transportation solution is also stored on disk to serve as an advanced start in subsequent runs for which it is still feasible.

Criteria[1] to evaluate the realism of linear programming models and the effectiveness of computational methods tend to conflict with each other; the more realistic the model, the more difficult it is to devise an effective computational solution method. Geoffrion describes and evaluates the capabilities of selected major model methods presently available from the published literature and from various consulting firms and software vendors.

Other Types of Linear Programming Techniques

There are other types of linear programming techniques: trans-shipment, separable programming, quadratic programming, and polyperiod programming.

The trans-shipment approach is used when there are many origin points, intermediate distribution points, and multiple destination points. If the usual technique were applied, separate paths would have to be drawn from each origin through the distribution

---

[1]A. M. Geoffrion, "A Guide to Computer-Assisted Methods for Distribution Systems Planning," Sloan Management Review, M.I.T., Winter 1975, Vol. 16, No. 2, pp. 17-4.

point to each destination. In more complex models, this becomes tedious. Instead, transfer rows are used to keep track of the amounts in each distribution point. This is useful in simplifying linear programming for complex problems where many paths are involved.

Separable linear programming is used when the relationship of the activity level and the cost or profit is not constant. The C_j values need to be changed every time the activity level changes. Separable problems must be set up using total cost and total quantity rather than on a per unit basis. Each quantity and total cost combination would enter as an activity.

Quadratic programming can also be used to reflect changing price-quantity relationships. The relationship of price to quantity must still be linear; price must change as a linear function of quantity. When price is multiplied by quantity to get total cost, a quadratic equation results. The derivative of this equation is used in the quadratic maintenance.

Polyperiod programming is designed to handle shifts of resources from one period to another. Transfer columns are used, rather than transfer rows. Each activity is broken up to apply to a single period. The solution is not necessarily sequential, but can move forward or backward in the solution. There are other linear programming routines that account for several periods with feed forward only, as in dynamic programming.

Basic Assumptions in Linear Programming

Several basic assumptions should be understood in order to use linear programming techniques. Although the following list may seem somewhat formidable, it nevertheless is necessary in order to properly use this technique.

1. The problem must be quantifiable. Linear programming is completely mathematical in nature and can only deal with numbers.

2. The problem must contain alternative courses of action. There is no decision required if there is only one choice to be made. An example of unacceptable linear programming would be only one path from an origin to the destination. An acceptable problem would be two or more alternatives with the accompanying costs and restrictions on those paths.

3. The feasible choices must have some sort of restrictions on them. If you were trying to minimize time on the paths between origins and destinations, acceptable restrictions would be the maximum speed of conveyances and distance of the routes utilized.

4. The relationship between the activity levels and the use of resources must be linear. For example, if a cost is assumed for a given path between an origin and a destination, that particular cost can be the only one used for the problem. Alternative costs involve alternative paths. There are two ways in common use of overcoming this limitation. One is separable programming, where a nonlinear curve is divided into several separate parts. The routines for solving quadratic programs are sometimes costly and may not be generally available.

5. The inputs and outputs must be sufficiently divisible in order to arrive at a solution. For example, a solution may suggest the use of half the container or .79 of a ship. Depending on the problem and the kind of resource constraints, this assumption may be limiting. It may not be too difficult if the individual using the technique understands that he may or may not have to move up to the next size in order to implement the solution.

6. The inputs and outputs should be additive and independent. For example, the profits of one activity or the amounts of resources used by it are not affected by the levels of other activities.

7. Units of input and output should be homogeneous. The resources must be similar enough to be added together. If they are not, then each must be used as a separate constraint. This can be cumbersome, as in the case where the time of engineers for different projects cannot be added or grouped in some way; each engineer's time must be considered separately.

8. An objective solution within the feasible alternatives and restrictions must be capable of providing the best possible solution. This condition can be either minimal or maximal in nature. It assumes that trade-offs between two or more variables sometimes need to

be considered; this ratio of tradeoff must be decided
at the outset. The ratio cannot vary with the level
of activities.
9. Sometimes it is required that the variables may not
be negative in nature. Although technically this is
true, this particular assumption does not cause any
major difficulties. For example, it is necessary in
a transportation problem to assume that there are costs
in moving a ton or some other unit from A to B. If
the activity could come into solution at a negative
level, the cost of shipping from B to A would be minus
$5. This sum would be gained every time a reverse
shipment is made. To avoid this, but to allow for
reverse shipments, another activity must be put into
the tableau representing shipments from B to A at an
appropriate cost.
10. The prices or other indicator of the value of inputs
and outputs must remain constant throughout the problem.
This basic assumption can be overcome through the use
of separable and quadratic programming.

Although this list is not intended to be all inclusive,
it serves as a good bench mark for the care to be maintained in
the use of linear programming. It is a powerful and useful tool
with proper use.

CHAPTER 6

SYSTEMS NETWORK THEORY

Systems network theory takes the graph of a network, models
the characteristics, and states these characteristics in the form of
flow and force variables, so as to determine the interrelationships
of the parameters introduced in the modeling process.[1]

The use of systems network theory in the description and
development of electrical networks is generally recognized. Electrical networks, telephone networks, power systems, and some traffic
flow applications have been completed utilizing the theory's principles. The theory has been applied as well in the production and
transportation areas.

The development of suitable force variables, consistent
with known economic principles and their proper use in network
analysis, has been a problem in previous applications. Systems
network problems have been solved using propensity variables--a
term interchangeable with force, but which does not properly convey
the relationship in the economic and business context--such as rate
of production, cost of commodity,[2] marginal cost of movement,[3] and
mass-energy costs.[4]

---

[1]H. Koenig, Y. Tokad, and H. Kesavan, Analysis of Discrete
Physical Systems (New York: McGraw-Hill, 1967), Chs. 2-3.

[2]F. Mossman and J. Hynes, Systems Network Theory: Applications to Distribution Problems (Braintree, Mass.: D. H. Mark, 1968),
Chapter 3.

[3]J. P. Hynes, Motor Carrier Rates in a Normative Spatial
Environment (Unpublished Ph.D. Dissertation, Michigan State University, 1971).

[4]H. Koenig, W. Cooper, and J. Falvey, "Engineering for
Ecological, Sociological, and Edonomic Compatibility," IEEE

These applications have not satisfactorily expressed the demand, push, or "force" which initiates, relays, or terminates flows along branches. Because of the difficulty of stating a satisfactory force variable, the use of systems network theory has not been widespread; in fact, it has been limited to academic applications in business. Such techniques as dynamic programming, which use only flow variables, are more widely used and accepted, but cannot state any measure of force or demand, thereby limiting their application.

Simulation techniques, which substitute heuristic or probabilistic techniques in lieu of the determination of usable demand factors, is another level of programming. It should be noted that all these techniques are accommodations for an inability to characterize and portray the demand factors of the system being examined.

The Problem

Characterizing a suitable "force" function is the greatest hurdle in the development and use of systems network theory in the socio-economic discipline. The force variable in the electrical network applications is well defined by a series of laws defining the relationships of flows and forces, just as they are in the other physical science applications.[1] The use of systems network theory as an analytical tool in the study of economic processes therefore has not been investigated extensively because of the

---

Transactions on Systems, Man, and Cybernetics, Vol. SMC-2, July 1972, pp. 319-331.

[1]T. C. Koopmans and S. Reiter, "A Model of Transportation," Activity Analysis of Production and Allocation, ed. by T. C. Koopmans (New York: John Wiley & Sons, Inc., 1951), pp. 222-59.

184

difficulty of operationalizing the features of the technique, and applying them to actual business and governmental problems.[1]

Review of previous works in the field do not yield evidence of full use of the technique except in very restricted situations, although there have been several excellent efforts. The prime reference is written by Koenig;[2] this laid the initial base for the work of Mossman and Hynes,[3,4] who have applied the theory and established some basic methodology to the problems of transportation networks.

Applications in the field of transportation appear to offer opportunities for development because of the similarities of flows along transportation links and terminal throughput capabilities to the same applications in electrical circuit theory. The transportation problem is well known in linear programming models; the applications of Mossman and Hynes have utilized linear programming to implement systems network theory. This approach limits the problem to static solutions, and thus fails to provide adequate temporal sensitivity. Transportation problem solutions accomplished by the works of Mossman and Hynes have focused on the flow aspects

---

[1]Other linear graph applications within socio-economic systems are described in contemporary literature. For example, see H. Koenig and T. Manetsch, Systems Analysis of the Social Sciences (East Lansing, Mi.: College of Engineering, Michigan State University, 1966). (Mimeographed.) also; M. Beckman, D. Christ, and M. Nerlove, Scientific Papers of Tjallings C. Koopmans (New York: Springer-Verlag, 1970), pp. 184-209.

[2]H. Koenig, Y. Tokad, and H. Kesavan, Analysis of Discrete Physical Systems (New York: McGraw-Hill, 1967), pp. 343-421.

[3]F. Mossman and J. Hynes, Systems Network Theory: Applications to Distribution Problems (Braintree, Mass.: 1968), pp. 18-37.

[4]J. Hynes, Motor Carrier Rates in a Normative Spatial Environment (Unpublished Ph. D. Dissertation, Michigan State University, 1971).

of the transportation network. Though considerable work was done
attempting to establish a propensity (force) variable suitable
for expression of the demands within the system, the studies
focused on marginal movement costs, which were not entirely
satisfactory, especially in the operational sense.

Systems network theory has the ability to move from time
period to time period in the technique. It is in this area that
the research will develop and demonstrate a suitable technique
for the derivation of the "force" variable so critical to socio-
economic applications. As Baumol points out, "No matter how
ingenious the economists' circumlocutions that have been employed,
there has been no substitute devised to replace the demand
function."[1]

Other applications of the propensity (force) variable
have attempted to express this parameter as a finite number, as
derived in the accounting sense. Accounting values, such as cost
per unit, have not been usable general statements of propensity.
Index numbers or ratios are more adaptable to the general case
and are freed of some constraints such as magnitude differences,
scale problems, and quality or time differences.

Systems Network Theory Considerations

The use of systems network theory is based on the ability
to model and characterize the behavior of individual entities and
their environment and to assemble these behavior traits into
systems. A system in our context is defined as "a coordinated
collection of physical elements and conceptual linkages intended
to serve a common purpose."[2] While the physical sciences were

[1]W. J. Baumol, Economic Theory and Operations Analysis
(2nd ed.; Englewood Cliffs, N.J.: Prentice-Hall, 1965), pp. 210-230.

[2]A. M. Lee, Systems Analysis Frameworks (New York: Wiley
& Sons, 1970), p. 18.

first to utilize the systems approach to problems, the social sciences also have developed considerable experience in the approach. From the definition and recognition of economic systems, the procession to use of physical science techniques in certain aspects of economic inquiry, such as this dissertation, is a natural and evolutionary step. Systems network theory builds on the definition and is particularly suited for those economic applications seeking to maximize benefits gained from the use of scarce resources.[1]

The Axiom and Postulates of Systems Network Theory

Systems network theory is a body of knowledge that proceeds from the elementary laws of electrical circuits developed by Kirchoff,[2] and specifies that there are two considerations in a circuit--voltage and current--which are complementary in nature. Flows and flow variables are analogous to electric current; "force" is analogous to voltage and electrical pressure. The electric power system depends on the complementary nature of voltage and current, just as flows of goods and funds are dependent on demand or "force" in a business firm. Therefore, systems network theory is more suitable than other programming techniques for those applications where "force" must be considered.

---

[1]R. Handy and P. Kurtz entitled A Current Appraisal of the Behavioral Sciences (Great Barrington, Mass.: 1964, Behavioral Research Council), for an excellent overview of the challenges to application of systems sciences to the behavioral science.

[2]G. Kirchoff, Uber die Auflosung der Gleichungen, auf welche man bei der Unter-suchungen der Linearn Verteilung Galvanischer Strome gerfuhrt wird (English translation, Transaction of the Institute of Radio engineers, CT-5), March 1958, pp. 4-7.

Limitations in the ability to define the "force" variable are obstacles in the use of the theory, but also provide the key to future applications.

The components of a system, as utilized in systems network theory, is the linear graph.[1] It is possible to model the system, assemble the linkages, derive component equations to mathematically express the linkages and, finally, to control the system so as to measure performance and auxiliary effects.[2] Components may then be stabilized and redesigned to provide for optimized performance.

The fundamental axiom of systems network theory states that a mathematical model of a closed system characterizes the behavior of the system as an entity, and independently of how the component is interconnected with other components to form a system.[3] This is further defined by a series of postulates which characterize the system:

Postulate I: The pertinent behavior of characteristics of each n-terminal as an identified system structure is completely identified by a set of n-1 equations in n-1 pairs of oriented complementary variables, identified by an arbitrarily chosen terminal graph.[4]

Postulate II: The systems graph is defined operationally as the collection of edges and vertices obtained by coalescing the vertices of the component terminal graph in a one-to-one correspondence with the way in which the terminals of corresponding components are united to form the system.[5]

---

[1]H. Frank and I. Frisch, Communication, Transmission, and Transportation Networks (Reading, Mass.: Addison-Wesley, 1971), Ch. 2.

[2]H. Koenig, Y. Todad, and H. Kesavan, Analysis of Discrete Physical Systems (New York: McGraw-Hill, 1967), Ch. 1.

[3]Ibid., p. 3.

[4]Ibid., p. 5.

[5]Ibid., p. 6.

<u>Postulate III</u>: The algebraic sum of the "force" variables implied
by the oriented edges of any circuit in the systems graph
is zero.[1]

<u>Postulate IV</u>: The algebraic sum of the flow variables around a
vertex form a cut-set sum to zero. (A cut-set of a connected
graph is a set of edges which, when removed, divide the
graph into two unconnected parts; no sub-set has the first
property).[2]

When limits to use of such techniques as linear and dynamic
programming were reached, the use simulation models and heuristic
decision techniques were introduced to overcome defects in application of multi-period decision problems inherent in these methodologies. Methodologies which are based on network and graph theory
offer solutions for the analysis of systems through multiple periods
of operations. As the higher order control systems previously
described are capable of learning, the graphic methods are also
capable of being controlled through multiple time periods, as is
the second order system previously mentioned.

Graph and Network Definitions

We have developed a set of definitions and terminology for
standard use in the text. From the brief description in Chapter 1,
the following terms will be used throughout the remainder of this
chapter, and are keyed to Figure 6.1.

Edges: the line segments oriented in the direction of the
arrows and numbered 1 through 6, and their respective end points
(two on each line segment). The end points a and b and the line
segment 1 is called edge 1.

---

[1]Ibid., p. 111.

[2]Ibid., p. 113.

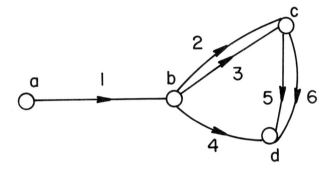

Figure 6.1. A Simple Systems Graph.

Vertices: the end points of the edges. The vertices in the graph in Figure 6.1 are a, b, c, and d.

End Vertex: a vertex with only one edge incident to it. Vertex a has only one edge incident to it.

End Edge: the edge incident to an end vertex; a vertex with only one edge incident to it. Edge 1 is an end edge; and vertex a is an end vertex.

Sub-Graph: a subset of edges in a graph; edges 1, 3, and 5 form a sub-graph. In our subsequent determinations a sub-graph must contain at least one edge.

Path: formed by edges 1, 3 and 5, linking all vertices in the graph. By following the path, one can move sequentially from vertex a to vertex d. Generally, a graph can have many paths. For example, in the graph in Figure 6.1, the sub-graphs 1, 2, and 5 form paths, as do 1, 4, and 6. If there is a path between every pair of vertices in a graph, then the graph is said to be connected.

Circuit: when each of the vertices in a graph has exactly two edges incident to it. A circuit forms a closed path in the graph set of vertices. Additionally, a circuit in a connected graph means there are two distinct paths between any pair of vertices in the graph. The circuit in the sub-graph b, c is formed by edges 2 and 3.

Graph Organization

A tree is an important factor in the analysis of the movement in a graph. In a connected graph, a tree is a set of edges which are connected, containing all the vertices in the graph, but not forming circuits. In Figure 6.1, the heavy lines 1, 3, and 5 form a tree; all the vertices are connected and there are no circuits (no vertices in tandem have more than one path between them). An important property of a tree in graph is that it has exactly $v-1$ edges. Inspection of the graph in Figure 6.1 for possible trees in the graph will substantiate this fact.

The edges in a tree are called branches. Those edges not in the tree form what is called a co-tree; the edges within the co-tree are called chords. Unlike the edges in a tree, the co-tree's edges need not be connected. They are particularly significant because the addition of a chord establishes a circuit. Since a tree contains exactly $v-1$ edges, the number of chords in a co-tree (within a graph of e edges), is $e-(v-1)$ or $e-v+1$. In a graph of e edges and v vertices, with a co-tree of $e-v+1$ chords, there are $e-v+1$ circuits, none of which are identical. The set of $e-v+1$ circuits is called a set of fundamental circuits. The orientation of each fundamental circuit is determined by the defining chord; in Figure 6.1, in the tree (1, 4, 5) the defining chord (2) orients the fundamental circuit in a clockwise direction. The orientation establishes the constraints on the across variables in the system component--whether they possess positive or negative values.

The next property of systems network theory is the concept of the cut-set. A cut-set of a systems graph is a set of edges which, when removed from the graph, is in exactly two parts; no sub-set of the original set of edges has the property of separating the graph into two parts.

Concomitantly, the removal of a branch from the tree will separate the graph into two parts; there is only one path between any pair of vertices in the tree. If there were more than one path, then a circuit would result.

The separation of the graph into exactly two parts allows a further definition of the system being analyzed. The concept of a tree provides us with an operational procedure for selecting a cut-set of edges. In a tree, only one path can be selected between any pair of vertices. Consequently, the removal of a branch separates the graph into two parts. In Figure 6.2, the broken line cuts across edge 6, a branch in the tree (2,3,6,9)

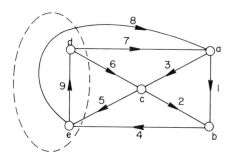

Figure 6.2. An Illustration of a Cut-Set.

and chords 4, 5, 7, and 8 to form a cut-set. The orientation of the graph, now in two parts, is determined by the defining branch. The number of fundamental cut-sets is equal to v-1 in a graph; the number of fundamental cut-sets in a graph is identical to the number of edges in a tree. If an edge is present in the cut-set, then a 1 is entered when the edge orientation is the same as that

of the defining branch; a -1 is noted if the edge orientation is
opposite to that of the defining branch; a zero is entered if the
edge is not in the cut-set. For the cut-set shown in Figure 6.2,
this vector would be written as follows:

$$1 \quad 2 \quad 3 \quad 4 \quad 5 \quad 6 \quad 7 \quad 8 \quad 9$$

$$(0 \quad 0 \quad 0 \ {-1} \ {-1} \quad 1 \quad 1 \quad 1 \quad 0)$$

(Cut-set 4, 5, 6, 7, 8)

This cut-set vector is generalized as:

any cut-set vector F and any arbitrary vector of through
variables Y identified by the e edges of the system
graph, or

$$FY = 0$$

This equation, called a cut-set equation of the graph of
the system, is one of the basic postulates of system network
theory. The complete set of cut-set equations composed of fundamental cut-sets form one segment of the characterization of the
system. By assembling the cut-set equations for the systems graph
into two column vectors, with the first v-1 edges corresponding
to the branches in each cut-set in the first column vector and
the remainder in the second column vector, a coefficient matrix
is generated, as shown below:

$$
\begin{bmatrix}
1 & 0 & 0 & 0 \\
0 & 1 & 0 & 0 \\
0 & 0 & 1 & 0 \\
0 & 0 & 0 & 1
\end{bmatrix}
\begin{bmatrix}
Y9(t) \\
Y6(t) \\
Y3(t) \\
Y2(t)
\end{bmatrix}
+
\begin{bmatrix}
0 & -1 & -1 & 0 & 1 \\
0 & -1 & -1 & 1 & 1 \\
1 & 0 & 0 & -1 & -1 \\
1 & -1 & 0 & 0 & 0
\end{bmatrix}
\begin{bmatrix}
Y1(t) \\
Y(4)(t) \\
Y(5)(t) \\
Y7(t) \\
Y8(t)
\end{bmatrix}
= 0
$$

Figure 6.3. A Matrix of Cut-Set Equations for the Systems Graph.

The elements of the vectors have been rearranged to form
a unit matrix composed of the defining branches of each cut-set.
Similarly, the fundamental circuit equations can be generated to
form a set of circuit equations to form another of the basic
postulates of systems network theory. The circuit vector can
be generalized as:

> Any circuit vector G and any arbitrary vector X of across
> variables identified by the e edges of the system graph,
> or

$$GX = 0$$

This relationship forms another segment of the analysis of
the system. By assembling the circuit equations for the systems
graph into two column vectors, composed of branch variables in
the first column vector and the chord variables in the second,
a set of simultaneous equations of the form generalized above
are generated. A coefficient matrix is developed as shown below:

$$
\begin{bmatrix}
-1 & -1 & 1 & 0 \\
0 & -1 & 1 & 0 \\
1 & 1 & 0 & 0 \\
1 & 1 & 0 & 1 \\
0 & 0 & -1 & -1
\end{bmatrix}
\begin{bmatrix}
X_{9(t)} \\
Y_{6(t)} \\
X_{3(t)} \\
X_{2(t)}
\end{bmatrix}
+
\begin{bmatrix}
1 & 0 & 0 & 0 & 0 \\
0 & 1 & 0 & 0 & 0 \\
0 & 0 & 1 & 0 & 0 \\
0 & 0 & 0 & 1 & 0 \\
0 & 0 & 0 & 0 & 1
\end{bmatrix}
\begin{bmatrix}
X_{8(t)} \\
X_{7(t)} \\
X_{5(t)} \\
X_{4(t)} \\
X_{1(t)}
\end{bmatrix}
= 0
$$

Figure 6.4. A Matrix of Circuit Equations for the Systems Graph.

Here again, the elements of the chords have been rearranged
to form a unit matrix, just as the defining branches had been
arranged in the cut-set equations.

194

These coefficient matrices are significant because the negative transposition of either of the non-unit matrices is equal to the other. Taken as they are developed, the scalar product of these matrices equals zero. The power developed in the system is contained within, and the system can be considered closed. This property of orthogonality is important in the development of the remaining portions of the mathematical description of the system being analyzed.[1] The state models of systems derived from these coefficient matrices form the basis of the mathematical description and control of the complex systems found in engineering and socio-economic applications.

System Component State Model

To formulate a state model for a system, knowing the characteristics of the edges in the system, the procedures can be followed as shown below. Assume the system is graphed, as in Figure 6.5.

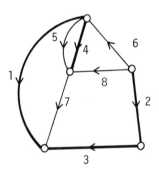

Figure 6.5. A Systems Graph with a Selected Tree of Edges.

---

[1]H. Koenig, Y. Tokad, H. Kesavan, and H. Hedges, Analysis of Discrete Physical Systems (New York: McGraw-Hill Book Co., 1967).

The tree for the systems graph is established as edges 1, 2, 3, and 4; and the co-tree, as edges 5, 6, 7, and 8.

In order to establish the state model equations, one can develop the coefficient matrices for the cut-set and circuit equations, as shown below:

$$
\begin{bmatrix} 1 & 0 & 0 & 0 \\ 0 & 1 & 0 & 0 \\ 0 & 0 & 1 & 0 \\ 0 & 0 & 0 & 1 \end{bmatrix}
\begin{bmatrix} y1(t) \\ y2(t) \\ y3(t) \\ y4(t) \end{bmatrix}
+
\begin{bmatrix} 0 & -1 & 1 & -1 \\ 0 & 1 & 0 & 1 \\ 0 & -1 & 0 & -1 \\ 1 & 0 & -1 & 1 \end{bmatrix}
\begin{bmatrix} y5(t) \\ y6(t) \\ y7(t) \\ y8(t) \end{bmatrix}
$$

Figure 6.6. Cut-Set Equations.

$$
\begin{bmatrix} 0 & 0 & 0 & -1 \\ 1 & -1 & -1 & 0 \\ -1 & 0 & 0 & 1 \\ 1 & -1 & -1 & -1 \end{bmatrix}
\begin{bmatrix} x_1(t) \\ x_2(t) \\ x_3(t) \\ x_4(t) \end{bmatrix}
+
\begin{bmatrix} 1 & 0 & 0 & 0 \\ 0 & 1 & 0 & 0 \\ 0 & 0 & 1 & 0 \\ 0 & 0 & 0 & 1 \end{bmatrix}
\begin{bmatrix} x_5(t) \\ x_6(t) \\ x_7(t) \\ x_8(t) \end{bmatrix}
$$

Figure 6.7. Circuit Equations.

Note that the fundamental cut-sets are:
6, 7, 8, 1
6, 8, 2
6, 8, 3
5, 7, 8, 4, and the fundamental circuit equations are:
4, 5
1, 2, 3, 6
1, 4, 7

1, 2, 3, 4, 8, and that they equal v-1 cut-sets and e-v+1 circuits. It should also be noted that the non-unit matrices in Figures 6.6 and 6.7 are the negative transpose of each other.

Let the equations for each edge of the system graph in Figure 6.5 be given as shown below.

a. $x_{1(n)} = f_1(n)$ (a known function of time)

b. $x_{2(n)} = q_2 y_2$

c. $y_{3(n+1)} = p_3 y_3(n) + q_3 x_3(n)$

d. $x_{4(n+1)} = p_4 x_4(n) + q_4 y_4(n)$

e. $x_{5(n)} = q_{5(n)}$

f. $y_6(n+1) = p_6 y_6(n) + q_6 x_6(n)$

g. $x_7(n+1) = p_7 x_7(n) + q_7 y_7(n)$

h. $y_8(n) = f_8(n)$ (a known function of time)

Referring back to the tree for the system graph, it should be noted that as the tree is selected, the state model equations should be explicit in the primary variables. The edges that correspond to branches should have their equations written in the primary variables, expressed in across variables. Those edges in the co-tree that correspond to chords should be written in through variables whenever possible. The equations above show as many of the dynamic equations in the state model that are included in the state variables as primary variables. (Edges 1 and 8 are expressed as known functions of time. A maximally selected tree would include the across (propensity) variable in the tree, Edge 1, and the co-tree would include the through (flow) variable in the co-tree, Edge 8. This is because these equations cannot be inverted. The terminal equations for the components (edges) can be written in the primary variables shown below:

$$\begin{bmatrix} x_4(n+1) \\ y_6(n+1) \end{bmatrix} = \begin{bmatrix} p_4 & 0 \\ 0 & p_6 \end{bmatrix} \begin{bmatrix} x_4(n) \\ y_6(n) \end{bmatrix} + \begin{bmatrix} y_4 & 0 \\ 0 & q_6 \end{bmatrix} \begin{matrix} y_4(n) \\ x_6(n) \end{matrix}$$

$$\begin{bmatrix} y_7 (n+1) \\ x_3 (n+1) \end{bmatrix} = \begin{bmatrix} -p_7/q_7 & 0 \\ 0 & -p_3/q_3 \end{bmatrix} \begin{matrix} x_7(n) \\ y_3(n) \end{matrix} + \begin{bmatrix} 1/q_7 & 0 \\ 0 & 1/q_3 \end{bmatrix} \begin{bmatrix} x_7(n+1) \\ y_3(n+1) \end{bmatrix}$$

$$\begin{bmatrix} x_2(n) \\ y_5(n) \end{bmatrix} = \begin{bmatrix} q_2 & 0 \\ 0 & q_5 \end{bmatrix} \begin{bmatrix} y_2(n) \\ x_5(n) \end{bmatrix}$$

$$x_1(n) = f_1(n)$$
$$y_8(n) = f_8(n)$$

By applying the fundamental cut-set and circuit equations to Figures 6.6 and 6.7 the secondary variables may be eliminated. The resulting equations are shown in the following illustration:

A.
$$\begin{bmatrix} x_4(n+1) \\ y_6(n+1) \end{bmatrix} = \begin{bmatrix} p_4 & 0 \\ 0 & p_6 \end{bmatrix} \begin{bmatrix} x_4(n) \\ y_6(n) \end{bmatrix} + \begin{bmatrix} q_4 & 0 & 0 & -q_4 \\ 0 & q_6 & 0 & 0 \end{bmatrix} \begin{bmatrix} y_7(n) \\ x_3(n) \\ x_2(n) \\ y_5(n) \end{bmatrix}$$

$$+ \begin{bmatrix} 0 & -q_4 \\ -q_6 & 0 \end{bmatrix} \begin{bmatrix} x_1(n) \\ y_8(n) \end{bmatrix}$$

B.
$$\begin{bmatrix} y_{7(n)} \\ x_{3(n)} \\ x_{2(n)} \\ y_{5(n)} \end{bmatrix} = \begin{bmatrix} P_7/q_7 & 0 \\ 0 & P_3/q_3 \\ 0 & -q_2 \\ 1/q_5 & 0 \end{bmatrix} \begin{bmatrix} x_{4(n)} \\ y_{6(n)} \end{bmatrix} + \begin{bmatrix} -P_7/q_7 & 0 \\ 0 & P_3/q_3 \\ 0 & -q_2 \\ 0 & 0 \end{bmatrix} \begin{bmatrix} x_{1(n)} \\ y_{8(n)} \end{bmatrix}$$

$$+ \begin{bmatrix} -1/q_7 & 0 \\ 0 & -1/q_3 \\ 0 & 0 \end{bmatrix} \begin{bmatrix} x_{4(n+1)} \\ y_{6(n+1)} \end{bmatrix} + \begin{bmatrix} 1/q_7 & 0 \\ 0 & -1/q_3 \\ 0 & 0 \end{bmatrix} \begin{bmatrix} x_{1(n+1)} \\ y_{8(n+1)} \end{bmatrix}$$

Substituting equation B into equation A results in the final state model equation for the system graph and component equations we have developed.

The final state model equations are

$$\begin{bmatrix} x_{4(n+1)} \\ y_{6(n+1)} \end{bmatrix} = \begin{bmatrix} P_3 & 0 \\ 0 & P_4 \end{bmatrix} \begin{bmatrix} x_{9(n)} \\ y_{6(n)} \end{bmatrix} + \begin{bmatrix} P_5 & P_7 \\ P_6 & P_8 \end{bmatrix} \begin{bmatrix} x_1(n) \\ y_{8(n)} \end{bmatrix} + \begin{bmatrix} P_9 & 0 \\ 0 & P_{10} \end{bmatrix} \begin{bmatrix} x_{1(n+1)} \\ y_{8(n+1)} \end{bmatrix}$$

where
$$P_1 = \left[P_x + P_7 \left(\frac{q_4}{q_7} - \frac{q_4}{q_5} \right) \right]$$

$$P_2 = \left(P_6 - \frac{q_6}{q_3} \right)$$

$$P_3 = \left[P_1 \left(\frac{q_7}{q_4+q_7} \right) \right]$$

$$P_4 = \left[P_2 \left(\frac{q_3}{q_3+q_6} \right) \right]$$

$$P_5 = \left[\left(\frac{q_7}{q_4+q_7} \right) \left(-P_7 \ \frac{q_4}{q_7} \right) \right]$$

$$P_6 = \left[-p_6 \left(\frac{q_3}{q_3+q_6} \right) \right]$$

$$P_7 = \left(\frac{-q4q7}{q4+q7}\right)$$

$$P_8 = \left[\left(\frac{q3}{q3+qb}\right)\left(\frac{p3q6}{q3} - (p3q6q2)\right)\right]$$

$$P_9 = \left(\frac{q4}{q4+q7}\right)$$

$$P_{10} = \frac{q6}{(q3+q6)}\;^1$$

Component equations for flows through variables have been expressed in other network techniques such as linear programming, PERT analysis, quadratic and integer programming.

Characterization of the Force Variable

The determination of the across variable in systems network theory application for problems other than engineering has been very limited. The following segments relate to the development of what has been called the across, propensity, or pressure variable.[2] The authors selected the term "force" variable as being closest to the socio-economic sense of demand. The "force" with which goods, people, or communications flow through the network is precisely the demand factor which economists portray in the classic supply and demand relationship. The following description of an actual application of systems network theory to an airport planning problem depicts a methodology for constructing a suitable complementary force variable to accompany flow data and forecast future demands and flow patterns.

[1] For 2 differential equation equivalent solutions of problems the reader may refer to H. Koenig, et al., p. 137.

[2] H. Koenig, Y. Tokad, and H. Kesavan, Analysis of Discrete Physical Systems, p. 7.

200

This portion of the chapter is concerned with the development of the "force" variable function used to characterize the demand for air travel in an airport planning study of several base cities in Michigan. The three base cities--Lansing, Flint, and Bay City-Saginaw--with Detroit--the hub city--form an excellent example of the "hub and spoke" airline transportation plan in the United States. Trunk line service is provided between high density (hub) airports, and is characterized by use of aircraft like the Boeing 707 and 747, McDonnell-Douglas DC-8 and DC-10, and Lockheed Tri-Star. Feeder service is provided by airlines between hub airports and medium and low density airports, characterized by aircraft like the Boeing 727, McDonnell-Douglas DC-9, and Convair 440 aircraft.

This system is designed to provide air service to cities which could not support full trunk line service to and from major population centers. By providing feeder service, larger population centers then perform the assembly function of pooling small groups of passengers from remote locations into groups of sufficient size to support trunk line service to major population centers. The Federal Aviation Administration (FAA) plan, for the period 1971 through 1980, shows development and funding for 30 hub airports and 149 medium density air carrier airports.[1] The three base cities in this study all qualify as medium density airports; Detroit is classed as a high density hub airport.

Since the hub airports perform the assembly and disassembly function within the system, the number of origin-destination

_____

[1]High density (hub) airports are those that enplane over one million passengers annually, while medium density airports are those that will enplane from 50,000 to one million passengers annually. For an excellent description of the planning funding of the national airport system, see The National Aviation System Plan, Ten Year Plan, 1971-1980, Department of Transportation, Federal Aviation Administration (Washington, 1970).

passengers per capita is higher than that seen at the spoke cities, reflecting the numbers of passengers moving through the hub city for further movement to other destinations.

A graphic display of this arrangement is depicted in Figure 6.8. It shows that actual origin-destination traffic for large centers of population exceeds the national average while smaller cities show lower than average traffic per capita. Figure 6.8 is constructed so that the same scale depicts both the actual amount of air travel per capita originating at cities of various population levels shown on the ordinate, and the forecast amount of air travel shown on the horizontal line.

Any city which has a level of air passenger traffic equal to the national average forecast would be shown on the 45° line. The 45° line represents the indicated forecast level of air travel, measured by the vertical distance of the point from the horizontal axis, as exactly equal to 100 per cent of its actual level of air travel on a national basis, as measured by the horizontal distance of the point from the vertical axis. In 1968, for example, 6,823,960 origin-destination passengers moved through the Detroit air terminal. During that year, the national average of air travelers was 1.07 per capita. The Detroit facility averaged 1.34 origin-destination passengers per capita.[1] Detroit would be located in the hub city section of Figure 6.8. Conversely, the Michigan cities which provided transfer passengers to the Detroit air terminal recorded levels of passengers per capita listed in Figure 6.9. This may be due, in large part, to travelers within the system who elect to drive to the hub city rather than utilize the local air service.

It is apparent that the base cities analyzed in this study and shown in Figure 6.9 handled a lower than average number of

---

[1]Origin-Destination Survey of Domestic Airline Passenger Traffic, 1968, Civil Aeronautics Board, Washington, D.C.

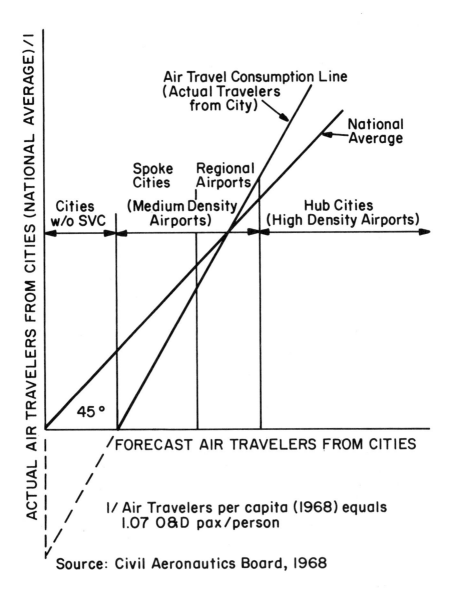

Figure 6.8. Typical Airline Service Offered at Cities.

City	Population (000's)	O & D Passengers per capita	O & D Passengers
Jackson	149	.09	14,616
Flint	487	.33	158,954
Lansing	361	.71	254,511
Bay City-Saginaw	372	.75	268,805
Grand Rapids	514	.83	424,255
Detroit	5,015	1.34	6,823,960

Source: Michigan Department of Commerce, State Aeronautics Commission, 1968 Data.

Figure 6.9. Origin and Destination Passengers Per Capita for Selected Michigan Cities.

airline passengers per capita than the national average of 1.07 for 1968. The table shows that as city size increases, the rate of airline travel increases. This supports the information in Figure 6.8. It also shows that there is a range of city size that should have a level of service equal to the national average (regional airports). It would seem then that at this particular city size, the economies of airline service which provide access to the city are such that a sufficient number of passengers are generated, thereby making feasible trunk line operations to hub cities.

This exact relationship is limited, of course, to the cities depicted in the system being analyzed. The element of distance is not considered in the graph, but will be shown as a vital element in the relationship of demand for the modes of travel. The intersection of the air travel demanded at the Michigan system cities is an indication of the number of travelers and combined cities sizes that are required at a single facility

to ensure a supply of air service equal to the national average--
the level of service which would enable trunk line service direct
to and from major hub cities. The total system demand is balanced
by the increased demand at the hub city, because of those travelers
who elected to use surface travel for the first leg of their
journey rather than utilize local air service.

Demand Factors for Air Travel

Several investigators have attempted to develop the
empirical relationships of demand for air travel.[1] One such
effort considered and determined the effects of distance as it
concerned the attraction between two cities.[2] The authors
related three considerations of the distance factor, which they
called the primary reason for utilizing air travel:

1. The distance between two people may be related to the
   probability that an occasion for communication between
   them will arise. As we move out from any point in the
   economy, the variety of demands that can be satisfied
   rises as the distance from the point increases; the
   self-sufficiency of larger areas, other things being
   equal, is greater than that of smaller areas.

2. Distance is related to price and may be taken as proxy
   for the cost of the trip.

---

[1]Some examples of work accomplished in the area are given
below. P. Cherington, "The Domestic Market for Air Transportation,"
Flight Forum (sponsored by Connecticut General Life Insurance
Company), July 1962, pp. 1-10. "Benefits from a National Air
Service Guide," an excerpt from testimony by G. Burnard before
the U.S. Senate, Committee on Commerce, Review of the Local Air
Carrier Industry, Washington, D.C., USGPO, 1966, pp. 335-337.
"The Economics of Convenient Airline Service," Tijdschrift voor
Vervoerswetenschap, No. 3, 1966, Netherlands Institute of Transport,
pp. 217-233 (reprinted in Passenger Transport Michigan State Uni-
versity Business Studies, 1968).

[2]J. Lansing, J. Liu, and D. Suits, "An Analysis of Inter-
urban Air Travel," Quarterly Journal of Economics (February 1961),
pp. 87-95.

3. Distance is related to the competitive position of
   different modes of travel; in particular, there is
   likely to be no advantage in traveling by air instead
   of by some other means of transportation if the distance
   is less than some minimum number of miles. Beyond that
   distance, the time saved by air over the other modes
   may be expected to be roughly proportional to the number
   of miles to be covered. There is reason to suppose
   that the proportion of all travel which is by air will
   be close to zero for very short distances and tend to
   increase with distance.[1]

These three factors--distance-mass attraction, distance-cost,
distance-modal choice--constitute the source of demand for airline
travel; in fact, for all travel. They also form the basis for
the derivation of the "force" variable utilized in this analysis.

Distance-Mass Attraction

The attraction of population masses for retail sales is
well known, and is generally so widely accepted as a measure of
the power of trading area that it has been granted the cognomen
of "law." First propounded by Reilly over 40 years ago, the
"law of retail gravitation" expresses the relationships of city
size and distance as they pertain to the ability of trading
centers to attract patrons.[2] The relationship is a linear one,
with attraction of a direct function of the ratio of population
and an inverse relationship of the square of the distance separating the two cities. This relationship is also expressed in
the distance-mass attraction statement. Our statement also says
that as the size of the city increases, the self-sufficiency
increases, and that smaller cities are less able to support
themselves and provide necessary service. This implies something

---

[1]Op. cit., p. 89.

[2]W. Reilly, The Law of Retail Gravitation (New York:
William J. Reilly, 1931).

other than a straight line relationship, possibly some curvilinear
increasing function as city size increases. A revision of
Reilly's original formulae by Converse substantiated the inability to express a straight line relationship when city size
differences exceeded multiples of 20, and the predictive power
of the original statement is reduced.[1] There are limits,
then, which must be observed in the application of the Reilly-
Converse formulae; the comparison of retail power must be used
only for cities of similar sizes. This would obviate the use
of such a model for use in this "force" variable determination,
since there is such a large disparity in the sizes of Detroit
and the three base cities. We must search further for a suitable
determinant.

Distance-Cost

Distance and cost relations are well established in the
field of transportation where, as in the statement of the cost
and price relationship, there is a direct correlation. As
distance increases, the cost of moving that distance increases
directly, though there are instances where there are discounts,
called rate tapering, for trips of extended lengths.[2] While in
the traditional depiction of demand, price is the determinant
of quantity, the demand for travel must contend with competitive
modes, time, convenience, service, accessibility, safety, and
price. For these reasons, the factor of price or cost does not
lead us nearer to a suitable measure of "force" without considerable adjustment for the aforementioned factors and for the

---

[1]P. Converse, A Study of Retail Trade Areas in East Central
Illinois, Business Studies Number 2 (Urbana, Illinois: The University of Illinois, 1943).

[2]D. Pergrum, Transportation: Economics and Public Policy
(Homewood, Ill.: Richard D. Irwin, Inc., 1968).

heterogeneity of the individual traveler and his utility-preference values. In addition, because of the prevailing differences in average fares per mile for different city-pairs—principally because of the availability of lower priced coach service on some routes—there are other possible abattoirs which trap the investigator who uses price alone as a measure of demand for air travel. The differences in city-pair markets, population, income, and tastes in these markets also mitigate against the use of price alone.[1] In addition, where different types of carriers (trunk, local, or third level) operate on the same route segment or within the system being analyzed, the apparent differences of equipment, times, and connections, along with price, may very well consist of the full aspects of what could be called the cost-price aspect of the "force" variable. Because of the incalculability of the price aspect, this phase of the typical demand function was not selected for use directly in the "force" variable construction.

Distance-Modal Choice

While the price factor is not directly utilized in the analysis for the derivation of the elements of the demand function, the modal-choice factor contains as one of its elements the factor of price or cost. The traveler, in making his choice of mode, takes into account the elements of time, cost, and distance prior to initiating travel. An important element is travel time differences, and the traveler attaches a value of this time, just as he measures the value of accessibility to the

[1]For an example of a study of the elasticity of air fares and demand for air travel on a national basis see S. Brown, and W. Watkins, "The Demand for Air Travel: A Regression Study of Time-Series and Cross-Sectional Data in the U.S. Domestic Market," Paper—47th Annual Meeting, Highway Research Council, Washington, D.C., January 16, 1968.

terminal for each mode, the schedule convenience, vehicle delay at the terminal, and average station wait. This time-value concept forms the basis for measuring the total cost of the block-times for each mode of transportation utilized in reaching his destination. A comparison, planned or unconscious, is made by the traveler regarding the mode options to be utilized in traveling. It would seem that travelers are willing to accept certain penalty costs in order to save time; when these penalty costs exceed a certain level, the less expensive mode is selected. One study on the time-value coverage principle states that most air travelers are willing to accept a $2 to $3 penalty cost just to save one hour traveling by air, over and above a slower but cheaper means on the surface.[1]

Modal Choice in the Research Cities

The aspects of modal choice decisions in the research cities for air travel required to move through the Detroit facility from the base cities was clearly demonstrated in a 1968 study of land use in the Detroit metropolitan area. This study, which measured the anticipated land requirements for various industrial needs, services, highways, and population, estimated the composition of air travelers moving through the Detroit air terminal facility. A passenger survey was conducted by all the airlines serving the city.[2] This sub-study of the Detroit Regional Transportation and Land Use Study (TALUS) provided much valuable

---

[1]R. Rice, "Time and Cost in Carrier Competition," Pas-senger Transportation, ed. by S. C. Hollander (East Lansing, Michigan: MSU Business Studies, 1968), pp. 114-117.

[2]Travel Patterns & Characteristics of Airline Passengers, Detroit Metropolitan Airport, 1968, Wayne County Road Commission (Detroit, Michigan, 1969).

input for the data used in this study.[1] Passenger information taken from respondents originating at the three base cities substantiated the modal choice factor previously stated.

The travelers' choice of modes to move to the Detroit facility was in general agreement with the statement that there was some minimum distance at which almost no demand for air travel could be generated for the local air terminal. This distance effect on modal choice is shown in Figure 6.10. The graph shows that at a distance of 40 miles, almost all travelers elected to utilize surface transport rather than the available airline service connecting the city of Jackson and the Detroit air terminal facility. The effect of distance at greater ranges is shown by the proportion of travelers choosing to fly from Grand Rapids rather than drive to the Detroit airport. From this information, one can infer that the distance of 40 miles constitutes the indifference point at which the time-value of air service is overcome by the less expensive means of driving to the hub air terminal facility. There is, of course, the long distance end of the spectrum, which shows that almost no one would choose to drive to the hub air terminal facility when the distance exceeds 180 miles. This modal choice on the part of the traveler constitutes an important factor in the demand for air travel.

From Figure 6.10 one may also infer that there is some fixed waiting time (the distance of 40 miles) associated with air travel which the traveler can save by using surface transportation to get to the hub facility. This waiting time, when equated to an automobile driving speed of 60 miles per hour, is approximately

---

[1] Detroit Regional Transportation and Land Use Study, Southeast Michigan Council of Governments (Detroit, Mich., 1969). The survey referenced in 1 above was accomplished by a joint effort of the two agencies listed and was not included in the TALUS publication.

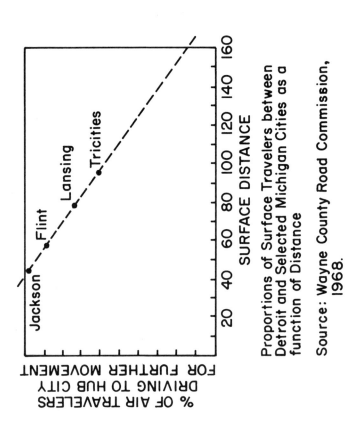

Figure 6.10. Percent of Air Travelers Driving to Hub City for Further Movement.

equal to the time to park the car, be ticketed, and wait the 30
minutes requested by airlines.

If this is the case, the traveler then must decide if
savings is afforded by air travel; as the distance to the hub
airport increases, a greater proportion elect to travel by air.
Not all the travelers attach the same value to time, but the
relationship in Figure 6.10 is linear; the same proportion elect
to change modes per mile of distance. This is not surprising,
since it reflects the changing elasticity of demand for airline
travel as distance increases. The demand becomes inelastic
since the largest proportion of travelers have already been
switched over to the airline mode. Thus, it takes a larger time
savings to cause the last numbers to move into the air travel mode.

This time ratio (surface driving time over air travel
time) is critically important to the demand for air travel because
of the higher cost of air travel as compared to the perceived
cost of driving an owned automobile. Since the traveler already
possesses the vehicle, the additional cost of air travel over
and above the cost of surface movement must be accompanied by a
real time savings. As the time ratio in favor of air travel
increases, the number of travelers choosing the air travel mode
increases after the 40-mile distance and out to the 180-mile
distance. This travel time ratio rather than the utilization of
either cost, time, or convenience alone shows the demand for air
travel, since it embodies all the elements as perceived by the
traveler. It also depicts the relationship shown in the distance-
modal choice factor. The distance-modal choice factor also affects
the first two distance factors of mass and cost, as described
through the proportionality of travel assigned to each mode by
the fixed time and speed difference of air to surface travel. In
the city combinations being investigated, the travel time ratio,
surface travel time divided by air travel time, ranges from a

factor of 2.40 to a factor of 3.31. This ratio is derived from highway travel times from the center of the spoke city to the Detroit airport for the surface mode and equated to a speed of 60 miles per hour, and from the actual flight time from the spoke city airport to the Detroit airport as published in the airline schedules. The surface travel time becomes the numerator of the ratio, the flight time, the denominator. Thus, the ratio can express technological changes in either of the two modes. Improved highways would lower surface travel times, but would adversely affect the demand for air travel, while improved flight times would increase the demand for air travel. In the relatively short distance included in this system, the fixed component of the air travel mode (the 40-mile minimum distance) as perceived by the traveler represents the greatest area for improvement since to the traveler it represents the greatest single time factor. This factor is depicted in the portrayal of the demand factor selected for this systems problem, and thus is considered automatically when stating the relative demands for the surface and air travel modes, as used in the determination of systems flows and "forces."

The Service Level Ratio Effect

The actual service levels at the spoke cities reflect the relative demand between the several cities and the national system airline. Service level is stated by the Civil Aeronautics Board (CAB) as the number of origin-destination passengers per capita. An origin-destination passenger is defined as a single boarding and disembarkation with no immediate stops enumerated. As distance increases the demand for airline service increases, because of the time-value savings accrued by the traveler when using air transport. This is manifested by a greater demand per capita at greater distances and a lower demand at short travel distances, due to the higher proportion of travelers electing to fly rather than

drive at the longer distances. This effect is reflected in the
service level offered at the local spoke city air terminal
facility, not in the number of aircraft arrivals and departures,
but in the actual passenger boardings; these, in the long run,
depict the actual service level. The total system demand is
balanced in this case by increased demand at the hub city,
resulting from the origination of air travel at the hub city
by those travelers who elected to use surface travel for the
first leg of their journey rather than local air service. This
shows the individual preference and time-value associated with
the distance between the originating spoke city and the hub city.
In order to establish a reference point, the national average
for the year being considered is utilized as a base value and
the service levels at the air terminal facilities being studied
are computed as a percentage of that value. In the case of
Detroit in 1968, the value assigned to the service is equal to
1.34, while that associated with Lansing is .71. From these two
values, a service level ratio has been constructed using the hub
city (Detroit) value as a denominator and the spoke city (Lansing)
value as the numerator. The resulting service level ratio is a
number less than one for all Detroit/spoke city combinations, i.e.,
Lansing-Detroit within the "hub and spoke" system of Detroit and
its spoke cities. An additional constraint on this value is that
it be less than 1.00/1.34; the city being considered, then, has
an associated service level equal to the national average. This
would indicate that it is capable of being independent of the
air terminal facility located in Detroit, since it does not need
the assembly function accomplished by the Detroit facility for
its spoke cities. This service level ratio comprises the second
element of the "force" function utilized in the system study. It
relates the "force" function that is equal to the demand for air
travel at the base cities being considered to the travel time
ratio as perceived by the traveler.

The "Force" Function

The two elements of travel time ratio and service level ratio comprise the "force" function as developed for use in this application of systems network theory. Together, they express the relationships of demand or "force" between the system base cities and Detroit. The "force" function is shown in Figure 6.11. The service level required at a spoke airport in the system is related to the travel time ratio by the following relationship:

$$F = a + b + CT^2$$

F = Service Level Ratio (Spoke city/
Detroit) (Force Value)

T = Travel Time Ratio (Surface Driving
Time/Air Flight Time)

In this form the "force" equation is:

$$F = -3.089 + 1.819T - .209T^2$$

The equation shows that demand for air travel is equal to zero at travel time ratios less than 2.0, increasing rapidly, then increasing at a decreasing rate as the service level ratio approaches .75 (the ratio of 1.00/1.34). This is the ratio of independence from use of the Detroit air terminal facility.

From the graph, one can ascertain that the area to the right of and below the "force" curve contains the feasible area for service at spoke airports. This is a level lower than that offered presently, but within the modal choice possibility constrained by the travel time ratio which fixes the limit of traveler decisions.

215

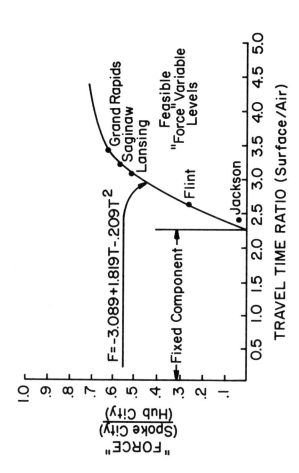

Figure 6.11.   Air Travel System "Force" Variable.

Changes in the travel time ratio will cause the "force" curve to shift either to the left or right. Improvements in air service through reduced travel times causes a shift to the left, reducing the fixed component of the air travel demand--minimum distance at which the traveler first begins to choose air travel. Likewise, improvements in surface transportation which enable the traveler to reach the air terminal facility more quickly will cause the "force" curve to move to the right, thus reducing demand for air travel at the affected spoke city.

For the purposes of this analysis, it is assumed that there will be no improvements in the travel time ratio; there will be no high magnitude changes in the other mode. This allows only a vertical shift in the "force" curve due to changes in the relative growth rates at the various spoke cities over the period being considered. Rather, forseen changes in technology will be incremental improvements in both the surface and air travel modes, resulting in only slight travel time changes and little or no ratio value changes.

Projecting the "Force" Function

The "force" or demand function values in the "hub and spoke" system are based on the relative values of the local demand for air travel and compared to the national average per capita. In the closed system design of the systems network technique, each edge possesses unique "force" and flow variable values. The "force" variable is directionally oriented on the basis of passenger flow, in order to fulfill Postulate IV of systems network theory, requiring flows around circuits to sum to zero.

The "force" function that drives the systems model is the air travel demand generated at each city in the system. This "force" value is based on the forecast growth in population and personal income during the period being considered, 1968 to 2000.

These factors are the same used by the CAB to estimate the number of passenger-miles per capita on a national basis.[1] Adapting the general formulation to the local system, the forecast measures the passengers' per capita growth rate as a function of time, based on the changes in personal income and population. In addition, the formulation provides for growth in acceptance of air travel. The formula developed is:

$$PPC_i = PPC_{i-1} + .0725(1.3Per_i + 1.1 \ PI_i + .3AR)$$

PPC_i = Passengers per capita

Per_i = Population Growth Rates per annum

PI_i = Personal Income Growth Rate per annum

Ar = Growth in acceptance of air travel (equals .3 per annum)

i = Forecast year

The factors in this formulation were applied to the research cities and a forecast of air traveler rates was constructed for the years 1970, 1980, 1990, and 2000. These forecasts are used to establish the particular "force" value for each city in the systems model, shown in Figure 6.12.

City	1970	1980	1990	2000
Flint	1.09	1.36	1.41	1.46
Lansing	1.06	1.31	1.36	1.40
Tri-Cities	1.06	1.28	1.35	1.39
Detroit	1.37	1.46	1.53	1.57

Figure 6.12. Passengers Per Capita Forecast for Selected Michigan Cities.

---

[1]See footnote 1 on page 31 (Brown and Watkins). The authors develop the rationale for this formulation for passenger-miles on a national basis using regression analysis.

Application of Systems Network Methodology

This section is concerned with the systems model of the traffic flows and system forces in the airport system formed by the research cities. The model provides a view of the air travel system and establishes the interrelationship of the flows and forces within the system for all origins and destinations outside the four-city system being analyzed.

Structure of the System

The system has two sectors: (1) the currently operating airline system; and (2) the proposed regional airport system. The present system is composed of the local airports and the air routes and highways links with the Detroit facility. The proposed regional airport system consists of the highway links between the research cities and the regional airport, and the air link with the Detroit terminal. Each of the systems has its interfaces with the national airport system.

The base cities are considered to generate a force or demand for air travel, stated and measured in passengers per capita. Through this demand, a flow of air passengers from the city is produced. This flow is measured in passengers per year. The model differentiates between travelers who drive from the local city to the Detroit hub airport and those who utilize the local air service. This is shown in the model by one path (edge) for surface travel and one path (edge) for air travel between the spoke city and the hub city, e.g., Flint and Detroit.

Each of the airports in the system has an interface with the national airport system, evidenced by the airline connections with destinations other than Detroit.

The proposed regional airport is included in the system and is joined to the three base cities and Detroit by a similar set of edges linking the base cities. The force or demand for this vertex (airport) is considered to be a function of the three base cities.

The demand generated at the base cities is transferred from the local air terminal facilities to the new regional airport, leaving the local airport without airline service. This transfer is affected when the relative demand for airline service at the three base cities reaches a critical level.

The systems model, as designed, operates on an iterative basis--being a state sequential mixed-parameter type. This model is characterized by its ability to provide successive time period information based on prior system states. Mixed-parameter refers to a hybrid state equation utilized to describe the actions of the system. The state equation uses both force and flow information to describe the action of the model. The state equation in this study is a discrete-time type; the variables are linear functions of time-dependent functions and current systems variables.

The state equations for this model take the form:

$$S(n+1) = P \cdot S(n) + Q \cdot E(n)$$

where

>n is an integer representing discrete points in time,
>$S(n)$ is a vector of system variables at time n,
>P & Q are constant matrices containing system values, and
>$E(n)$ is a vector of variables dependent on time.

Discrete points in time, in our case, is on a yearly basis. The output as the state vector at time n becomes a portion of the inputs to the system for the ensuing time period. This recursive cycling is dependent also on the force and flow of the present time period. In this way, the model represents the actual system in operation, where forecast system states in one time period depend

to some degree on the conditions prevailing in the previous time
period.

The systems model also incorporates an output equation
system which contains the system outputs at time n in order to
more closely observe the interactions and changing conditions
within the model structure. This output vector takes the form:

$$R(n) = M \cdot S(n) + N \cdot E(n)$$

where

> R(n) is the output vector containing variables of interest
> in the systems model at time n, and

> M & N are constant matrices containing system values.

Both the state equation section of the model and the output
vector section of the model utilize identical inputs. This provision
allows the lateration of a minimum set of input variables in order
to change internal conditions within the model and to simplify the
simulation of changing economic conditions external to the system.

The equations for both the state and output sections of
the systems model are derived from the characteristics of the
linkage between each of the system graph vertices. The systems
graph utilized in this study differs slightly from the general
systems graph shown in Figure 1.2. The systems graph of the air-
port-city linkages is shown in Figure 6.13. The model consists
of 28 separate edges, each represented by complementary force and
flow. The state equations provide primary information on the
system conditions. The model developed in this study utilizes
all system outputs in the response equations for inspection and
determination of the intrasystem relationships.

The Mathematical Relationships

Each of the cities in this study possesses different force
and flow characteristics. The complementary relationship between

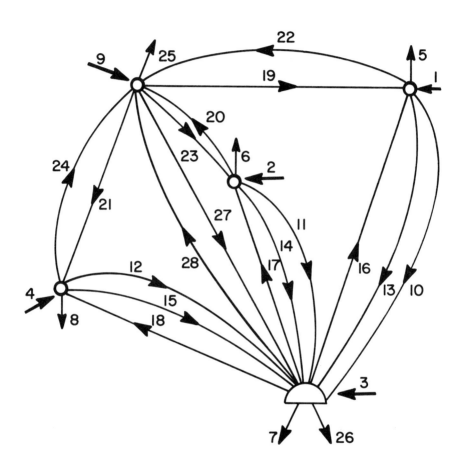

Figure 6.13. Systems Graph for the Component Model.

force and flow variables allows us to specify one of the variables if the other is known or can be calculated.

There are two types of equations in the systems model: (1) dissipative components and (2) dynamic components. The dissipative type are considered passive relationships within the model; they do not provide for changing relationships within the characterization of the edge being modeled. These dissipative equations are:

$$Y(n) = aX(n)$$

where

$Y(n)$ is the flow value at time n,

$X(n)$ is the "force" value at time n, and

a is a constant parameter indicating the relationship between Y and X.

The equation for edge 10 in the systems graph is:

$$Y_{10}(n) = 943 \, X_1(n),$$

where

Y_{10} equals the number of air travelers driving from SGN to Detroit,

X_1 equals the "force" value for SGN, and

943 equals the transformation coefficient for the edge.

The equation states that the annual flow of passengers along the edge is equal to 943 times the force value developed at SGN in the time period.

The a parameter indicates the linear relationship between the flow and force variables describing the edge in the model. It is equal to the slope of the line measuring the characteristics

of the flow and force variable. This can be considered to be
true within a limited range.

In this type of equation, a change in sign of one variable
signals a change in sign of the other variable. In the case of
the model, changes in sign of the force variable would amount to
the change in direction of flow between the cities being analyzed.

The dynamic equation is characterized by the time aspect;
the flow variable is dependent, at subsequent time states, on
the values of the force and flow component values in previous
time stages. This type of equation is of the form:

$$Y(n+1) = PY(n) + QX(n)$$

where

Y is the flow variable, and

X is the "force" variable.

In the above equation, the flow variable assumes the values of the
flow and force variables of the previous time period; the flow
variable of that time period is dependent on the values in preceding
periods. The equation for edge 5 in the systems graph is:

$$Y_5(n + 1) = .07 \ Y \ (n) + 4913 \ X_1(n) + 71.5$$
$$X_3(n),$$

where

Y_5 equals the number of air travelers who depart the SGN
airport for destinations other than DET,

X_1 equals the "force" value for SGN,

X_3 equals the "force" value for DET, and

.07, 4913, and 71.5 are the transformation coefficients
for the edge.

The equation states that the passenger flow in the next time period is equal to .07 times the flow in this period, plus 4913 times the force value at SGN, and 71.5 times the force value developed at DET in the present time period.

Component Equations

The component equations for the systems model in this study may be grouped into three like sets. They differ only in the coefficients used to determine the relationship of the force and flow variables. Each of the three base cities utilizes the same pattern of edges to describe its relationship within the airport system. The equation matrix shown in Figure 6.14 summarizes the systems graph shown in Figure 6.13.

Edges 1, 2, 3, and 4 prescribe the external force values for each of the cities in the system. The complementary flow variable is equal to the number of passengers moving into the system. These edges correspond to the drivers of the system providing energy for system operation. These equations take the form:

$$S_{1, 2, 3, 4}(n) = F(n)$$

These system force variables are taken as known functions of time and are derived from economic forecasts of air passenger traffic, as developed in the previous chapter.

The edges 5, 6, 7, and 8 are the edges which represent the air travelers leaving the system at the base cities. The equation for these edges take the form:

$$Y_i(n + 1) = PY_i(n) + QX_i(n) \text{ where}$$

$$i = 5, 6, 7, \text{ and } 8.$$

EDGE	Flint	Lansing	Tri-Cities	Detroit
Passengers driving to Hub	10	11	12	–
Passengers flying to Hub	13	15	14	–
Passengers from Hub	16	17	18	–
Passengers driving to MID	20	24	22	–
Passengers driving from MID	23	21	19	–
Passengers leaving system	6	8	5	7,26
"Force" for air travel	2	4	1	3
Passengers transferring to Hub from MID	–	–	–	28
Passengers transferring from Hub to MID	–	–	–	27

CITIES

Edge 26 collects and separates those flows which originate in the three base cities.

Figure 6.14. Component Equation Matrix.

These edges form a portion of the state equation system and provide the recursive sector of the model. These equations state that the flow in the subsequent time period is a function of the flow in this time period and the force in this time period. In this type of equation, the (differential) demand or force is utilized to reflect changes in growth patterns.

Edges 10, 11, and 12 represent the travelers who choose to drive to the hub city rather than utilize available local air service. The proportion of travelers who elect to use this mode at any given distance in the system is shown in Figure 6.14. The edges represent the difference in the force function value and the actual demand for air travel originating at the city to which the edge pertains. These edges take the form:

$$Y_i = G \cdot X_j$$

where

i = 10, 11, 12,

j = 1, 2, or 4, dependent on the city from which the edge originates, and

G = constant parameter relating the "force" at city j times the proportion driving to the hub airport. This value may be unique on each edge.

These edges are of the dissipative type, and indicate the direct transfer of force and flow within a single time period.

Edges 13, 14, and 15 correspond to the travelers who fly between the base city and Detroit. The force values on these edges are the system force values derived in the previous chapter. These edges are of the same type as edges 10, 11, and 12, and have the same mathematical relationships. They transmit the force developed at the base cities to the Detroit terminal facility for further movement into the national airport system.

Edges 16, 17, and 18 correspond to the return flow of travelers from the Detroit terminal facility to the base cities. These edges combine the travelers who drive and fly to the hub. It is assumed that the proportions of these travelers returning to the base city are the same as those who moved to the Detroit facility. These edges are of the same type as the outbound edges from the base cities (10, 11, 12, 13, 14 and 15), and possess the same property of transmitting the flows without any loss of force.

Edges 19, 21, and 23 are those which correspond to the travelers who will drive from the proposed regional airport to the base cities. These edges are also dissipative, directly transmitting the forces and flows generated at the base cities and returned through the regional airport.

Edges 20, 22, and 24 are those which correspond to the travelers who drive to the proposed regional airport; they are dissipative. These edges directly transmit the flows of passengers from the base cities. When the regional airport (MID) is activated, these edges will accomplish the same activities as the combination of the edges which radiate from the base cities during the time the local air service is in action. For example, at the FNT facility edges 11, 14, and 6 account for the outbound flow of travelers from the city while the local airport is in operation. When the regional facility is activated, local service will be terminated and all airline service will be offered at the regional facility for the city; edge 20 will perform the function of moving travelers outbound from the Flint area by surface to the regional facility.

Edges 27 and 28 correspond to the travelers who will utilize the MID facility as a transfer point to and from the Detroit facility. It is assumed here that if the level of service offered at the MID facility can be increased to a critical level,

there will be some trade-off of service between the Detroit
facility and the proposed MID terminal; there may be some transfer
of passengers between the facilities for further movement in the
national airport system.

Edge 26 in the systems graph is designed to total the
travelers moving through the Detroit facility and those who
originate at the base cities. The equation for this edge is
dissipative.

The two remaining edges--9 and 25--are of primary interest
in the system and are included in the state equations of the
systems model. These edges correspond to the travelers who will
enter and leave the three-city complex formed by the establishment
of a regional airport serving these cities. The equations for
these edges are of the dynamic type, and are expressed as follows:

$$Y_{25}(n+1) = PY_{25}(n) + QX_1 + QX_2 + QX_3 + QX_4$$

$$X_9(n+1) = PX_9(n) + QX_1 + QX_2 + QX_3 + QX_4$$

where

> Q is a constant value relating the flow variables to
> systems "forces."

These equations are combined into the systems interface
model, the state equation sector and the output vector as functions
of the systems input vector; they are capable of solution by conventional mathematical methods. The set of component equations
are shown in Figure 6.15.

Characteristics of the Model

The system of equations, depicted in Figure 6.15, have
certain standard characteristics that are of interest for possible
applications in the socio-economic environment. The transition

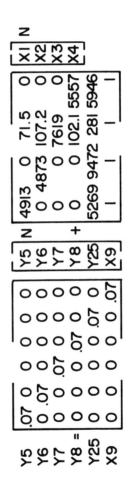

Figure 6.15. Systems Component Equations.

$$
\begin{bmatrix}
Y_{10} \\
Y_{11} \\
Y_{12} \\
Y_{13} \\
Y_{14} \\
Y_{15} \\
Y_{16} \\
Y_{17} = \\
Y_{18} \\
Y_{19} \\
Y_{20} \\
Y_{21} \\
Y_{22} \\
Y_{23} \\
Y_{24} \\
Y_{26} \\
Y_{27} \\
Y_{28}
\end{bmatrix}
=
\begin{bmatrix}
0 & 0 & 0 & 0 & 0 & 0 \\
0 & 0 & 0 & 0 & 0 & 0 \\
0 & 0 & 0 & 0 & 0 & 0 \\
0 & 0 & 0 & 0 & 0 & 0 \\
0 & 0 & 0 & 0 & 0 & 0 \\
0 & 0 & 0 & 0 & 0 & 0 \\
0 & 0 & 0 & 0 & 0 & 0 \\
0 & 0 & 0 & 0 & 0 & 0 \\
0 & 0 & 0 & 0 & 0 & 0 \\
0 & 0 & 0 & 0 & 0 & 0 \\
0 & 0 & 0 & 0 & 0 & 0 \\
0 & 0 & 0 & 0 & 0 & 0 \\
0 & 0 & 0 & 0 & 0 & 0 \\
0 & 0 & 0 & 0 & 0 & 0 \\
0 & 0 & 0 & 0 & 0 & 0 \\
0 & 0 & 0 & 0 & 0 & 0 \\
588 & 0 & 0 & 0 & 0 & 0 \\
0 & 0 & 0 & 0 & 0 & 0
\end{bmatrix}
\begin{bmatrix}
Y_5 \\
Y_6 \\
Y_7 \\
Y_8 \\
Y_{25} \\
X_9
\end{bmatrix}
+
\begin{bmatrix}
943 & 0 & 0 & 0 \\
0 & 3716 & 0 & 0 \\
0 & 0 & 0 & 1738 \\
941 & 0 & 0 & 0 \\
0 & 580 & 0 & 0 \\
0 & 0 & 0 & 538 \\
1140 & 0 & 71.5 & 0 \\
0 & 3960 & 107.2 & 0 \\
0 & 0 & 102 & 1985 \\
372 & 0 & 0 & 0 \\
0 & 487 & 0 & 0 \\
0 & 0 & 0 & 361 \\
372 & 0 & 0 & 0 \\
0 & 487 & 0 & 0 \\
0 & 0 & 0 & 361 \\
1140 & 3960 & 281 & 1905 \\
0 & 0 & 0 & 0 \\
0 & 0 & 421 & 0
\end{bmatrix}
\begin{bmatrix}
X_1 \\
X_2 \\
X_3 \\
X_4
\end{bmatrix}
$$

Figure 6.15. Systems Component Equations (Continued).

matrix (labeled P in the example of the state matrix shown earlier), if the connectivity of the system allows, may be raised
to the poser of the number of time periods in the iteration to
arrive at a solution for the state equation. If there are 20
time periods to be considered in the problem solution, the
transition matrix may be raised directly to the twentieth power
by matrix algebra to arrive at an immediate solution.

The model developed in this study does not have that
capability, since it is an identity matrix whose value, when
raised to any power, is still one, or equal to the original value.
This is due to the fact that there is no feasible air linkage
between the three base cities. The force function developed for
the system shows that at the distances encountered in the system
between the base there is no feasible level of air service that
can be developed to overcome the time ratios for surface and air
travel. However, this characteristic of the transition matrix is
an important feature, despite the fact that there was no usable
way to utilize this feature in the present model.

Additionally, only one edge in the output vector is stated
in terms of the state variables. This edge (27) provides the
energy for increasing the transfer of travelers to and from the
MID facility, based on the changing force levels of the system
when the MID facility is activated.

Activation of the MID facility was of concern in the study;
the switching of the system from the hub and spoke mode to the
regional mode was accomplished through the use of an external
constraint equation. Switching to the regional mode occurs when
the combined force values of the three base cities equalled the
force generated at the Detroit terminal.

This external decision equation accomplishes the switching
of the systems state and output equations, and is of the "on or off"
type. The decision equation is written in the following manner:

If $X_3 \geq X_1 + X_2 + X_4$ then Y_{20}, Y_{22}, and Y_{24} equal 0, but if $X_3 < X_1 + X_2 + X_4$ then Y_{10}, Y_{13}, Y_{11}, Y_{14}, Y_{12}, and Y_{15} equal 0.

The switching is accomplished by transferring the flows on the edges which correspond to the travelers leaving the system (5, 6, and 8), and those which correspond to the travelers driving to the regional facility (20, 22, and 24).

The use of the external switching constraint allows freedom in the analysis of the system to determine the time for activation of the regional facility. After activation, the analyst can observe the flow patterns within the system and is free to provide different force inputs to the system so as to produce desired system changes.

CHAPTER 7

LOGISTICS SYSTEMS PLANNING FOR THE FIRM

WITH SIMULATION

Introduction

Logistical planning can be classified in three categories: strategical, tactical, and operational. The basic criteria for delineation are the time duration involved in the decision, and the likelihood that the expected events will actually occur. Generally, strategic planning refers to the process of determining the major objectives of the logistics function and of resources, to achieve the required objectives; this usually involves system evaluation and redesign.

Tactical and operational planning concern the detailed deployment of resources to achieve the objectives of the strategic plan. In these two categories, the impact of any management decision is likely to be of shorter duration, and the probability that the expected events will occur is likely to be higher, than for strategic planning.

This chapter will present a review of a strategic planning simulator and a tactical/operational planning simulator. Emphasis will be on a dynamic model for an operational planning simulator, since less has been published on the utilization of dynamic simulation for operational logistics planning for the firm. The chapter consists of two major sections which present, respectively,

Appreciation is given to David Closs, Ph.D. candidate in the Michigan State University Graduate School of Business, for his assistance on the LREPS manuscript in Chapter 7.

strategic logistics planning with static simulation, and tactical/
operational logistics planning with dynamic simulation.[1]

Strategic Logistics Planning With
Static Simulation Models

This section reviews several early models and presents a
recently developed static model to be utilized in conjunction with
a dynamic model. The static models selected for review include:
a planning model to determine the geographical pattern of warehouse locations, by A. A. Kuehn and M. J. Hamburger;[2] a multicomponent physical distribution model, by H. N. Shycon and R. B.
Maffei;[3] and a distribution planning model, developed by Systems
Research Incorporated, to be utilized either separately or in
conjunction with the dynamic LREPS model.[4]

Kuehn and Hamburger Model

Kuehn and Hamburger developed a planning model to determine
the geographical pattern of warehouse locations which would be most
profitable to a company.[5] Figure 7.1 defines the model in terms of
a general flow diagram.

---

[1]Allan D. Schuster and B. J. LaLonde, "Twenty Years of
Distribution Modeling," a working paper (Columbus, Ohio: Division
of Research, College of Administrative Science, Ohio State University).

[2]A. A. Kuehn and M. J. Hamburger, "A Heuristic Program for
Locating Warehouses," Management Science 9, July 1963, pp. 543-666.

[3]H. H. Shycon and R. B. Maffei, "Simulation--Tool for
Better Distribution," Readings in Physical Distribution Management,
ed. by D. J. Bowersox, B. J. LaLonde, and E. W. Smykay (New York:
The MacMillan Company, 1969), pp. 243-260.

[4]Donald J. Bowersox, et al., "Dynamic Simulation of Physical
Distribution Systems" (East Lansing, Mi.: MSU Business Studies,
Division of Research, 1972).

[5]Kuehn and Hamburger.

1. Read in:
   a) The factory locations
   b) The M potential warehouse sites
   c) The number of warehouse sites (N) evaluated in detail on each cycle, i.e., the size of the buffer
   d) Shipping costs between factories, potential warehouses, and customers
   e) Expected sales volume for each customer
   f) Cost functions associated with the operation of each warehouse
   g) Opportunity costs associated with shipping delays, or alternatively, the effect of such delays on demand

2. Determine and place in the buffer the N potential warehouse sites which, considering only their local demand, would produce the greatest cost savings if supplied by local warehouses rather than by the warehouses currently servicing them.

3. Evaluate the cost savings that would result for the total system for each of the distribution patterns resulting from the addition of the next warehouse at each of the N locations in the buffer.

4. Eliminate from further consideration any of the N sites which do not offer cost savings in excess of fixed costs.

5. Do any of the N sites offer cost savings in excess of fixed costs?

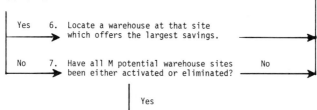

Yes   6. Locate a warehouse at that site which offers the largest savings.

No   7. Have all M potential warehouse sites been either activated or eliminated?   No

Yes

8. Bump-Shift Routine

   a) Eliminate those warehouses which have become uneconomical as a result of the placement of subsequent warehouses. Each customer formerly serviced by such a warehouse will now be supplied by that remaining warehouse which can perform the service at the lowest cost.

   b) Evaluate the economics of shifting each warehouse located above to other potential sites whose local concentrations of demand are now serviced by that warehouse.

9. Stop

Source: A. A. Kuehn and M. J. Hamburger, "A Heuristic Program for Locating Warehouses," Management Science 9 (July 1963).

Figure 7.1. A Heuristics Program for Locating Warehouses.

236

In the model, marginal cost of warehouse operation is
equated with transportation cost savings and incremental profits
resulting from more rapid delivery. The problem includes screen-
ing and evaluation of alternative warehouse locations for a fixed
set of exogenous inputs, which define transportation costs as
proportional to distance. Warehouse operating costs and opportunity costs associated with shipping delays are then used to
estimate cost savings for addition of warehouses. The primary
physical distribution components not considered are inventory
and communications.

The model is spatially, rather than time, oriented, since
it does not allow the development of the total order cycle and a
measure of the consistency of service.

The system behavior is static rather than dynamic, since
the model does not include information feedback control loops.
The model simulates, at a point in time, the activity that has
occurred during a total previous operating period. There is no
simulated calendar or passage of time within the model; therefore,
feedback control loops cannot be developed.

The environmental or exogenous inputs are fixed for each
simulated year. These inputs could be modified to simulate a
different point in calendar time for a future year. Thus, the
model could be helpful as a long-range planning tool.

Shycon and Maffei

In the multicomponent model developed by Shycon and Maffei,
the problem is to combine the best features of direct plant-to-
customer distribution with those of a national warehousing network.[1]
Analysis is made to determine the number, size, and location of
warehouses and processing locations which would properly serve

---

[1]Shycon and Maffei.

customers at a minimum cost nationally. The flow of the Shycon
and Maffei model is illustrated in Figure 7.2.

As in the Kuehn and Hamburger model, this model includes
elements of the transportation-warehouse operations and location
components. The authors state:

> It takes into account each of the important factors involved
> in the operation of a distribution system: transportation
> rate structure, warehouse operating costs, the characteristics
> of customers, demand for products, buying patterns of customers,
> costs of labor and construction, factor locations, product
> mix and production capacities, and all other significant
> elements. The factors, taken together, make up the distri-
> bution system.[1]

The model, however, does not include the inventory control or communications components of the physical distribution system.

According to the authors, it was designed to represent a
complex, high-volume, national distribution system with thousands
of customers. They state that the model makes provision for:

1. Each customer's order sizes, ordering patterns, the
   various types of shipments he receives, and his product
   mix.

2. Handling the costs of the various kinds of shipments made,
   such as carload, less-than-carload, truckload, less-than-
   truckload, and various shipment sizes within the lower
   classifications.

3. Variation in warehouse operating costs, such as labor
   costs, rentals, and taxes for different geographic areas.

4. The many different classifications of products which the
   company manufactures, the alternative factory source
   points for each of these products, and the factory capacity
   limitations on each.

5. The knowledge of where these relationships differ, so that
   adjustments to cost and volume estimates might be made.[2]

Initially, the model was developed for short-range planning,
but as the authors have stated, the customers' demand data, product

---

[1] Ibid., p. 244.

[2] Ibid., p. 249.

238

Preprocessing Run

(To eliminate the volume of shipments that go directly from factories to customers and hence will not effect the warehouse distribution system)

1. The computer is programmed for the preprocessing run. It is given detailed instruction as to what it should do with the customer information that it will receive.

2. Information on every customer in the national Heinz distribution system is fed into the computer.

3. The computer tests each customer to determine whether his volume of purchase is sufficient to justify direct shipments from factories.

4. A. If a customer's volume justifies shipments directly from the factory, the computer lists each such customer separately, according to the type of product he orders and the volume of his orders.

Test Run

(To determine the costs of distribution under various warehouse location configurations)

B. At this point the computer retains the volume of customer orders which are not shipped directly and must go through the warehousing system.

5. First, the computer has fed into it a new program which tells how to compute costs on the basis of the information which it will receive in step no. 6.

6. Next, the following information is processed by the programmed computer.

A. The results from the preprocessing run (i.e., the customer volume that flows through the warehousing system) which were retained in the computer in step no. 4.

B. The particular warehouse location configuration that is to be tested.

C. The freight rates, warehouse operating costs, taxes, etc. that make up the costs of the particular geographical areas in which the proposed warehouses are located.

7. The Computer Issues the Results:

The costs of distribution for the Heinz company under the tested warehouse location configuration.

Source: H. H. Shycon and R. B. Maffei, "Simulation--Tool for Better Distribution," in Readings in Physical Distribution Management, edited by D. J. Bowersox, B. J. LaLonde, and E. W. Smykay (New York: The Macmillan Company, 1969), pp. 243-60.

Figure 7.2. Simulation Test of a Particular Warehouse.

data, cost data, and the like could be changed to reflect long-range effects in the environment. Some of the possible uses of the model for long-range planning given by the authors include: (1) distribution cost studies for different combinations of customer classification schemes; (2) locational studies to determine the effect of shifts in customer type or location, factor relocation; (3) studies related to changes in product mix, customer consumption patterns, product capacity at factory locations; and (4) studies related to changes over time in annual volume or product line.

The Shycon and Maffei model does not develop a measure of the total order cycle and service dependability; it is spatially oriented, rather than time oriented. The behavior of their model is static rather than dynamic, since there is no simulator passage of time in the model; therefore, recursive equations or information feedback control loops are not possible. The environmental inputs are fixed for a given simulation run for one year. Thus, the major emphasis of the model is not to test the effects of a changing environment over a long-range planning horizon. However, as previously stated, various changes in environmental inputs do make the model suitable for testing the effect of any assumptions for a given future year.

Systems Research Incorporated-- Distribution Planning Model

The objective of this section is to describe the Distribution Planning Model (DPM) developed by Systems Research Incorporated to provide a rapid and effective tool for logistical configuration and strategic distribution planning and analysis. A description of the capabilities of DPM is presented in Appendix A. An example of the utilization of DPM for an actual strategic planning situation is presented in Chapter 8.

DPM Concept

The primary objective of the DPM simulator is to assist the project team test and evaluate various logistical system strategies, and to obtain accurate cost and service characteristics of each system. Typical problems in which DPM has assisted include questions involving recommendation of the best configuration, size, inventory stock policy, and customer assignment for local and regional distribution centers, manufacturing plants, pool centers, and terminal locations. DPM has also been utilized for transportation policy analyses.

The model has several attributes which are helpful for strategic planning. First, the impact of changes in the configuration can be measured and observed through the output of the model. All costs which would affect the configuration of the system are maintained by the model. These include transportation, inventory, warehousing, and production. In addition to the cost characteristics of the system, the service attributes are provided in terms of the percentage and dollar amount of sales satisfied within specified mileage radii. The tradeoffs between the various cost and service attributes can be evaluated to determine the best configuration which will meet the objectives of the firm.

Second, DPM, like the LREP-Operational model, is general enough to represent a wide range of logistics systems. The current limits of the model are 10,000 customers, 300 facility locations, and 99 echelons. The echelons are the number of levels in the system between the manufacturing plant and the ultimate customer. Currently, the model has the capability of tracking in detail 100 product groups. Based on research in over 40 projects, 100 product groups can represent statistically almost any number of product items or stock keeping units (SKUs) for strategic planning. These limits can be expanded if necessary.

Third, DPM provides four algorithms which may be used in making customer assignments during the simulation. These algorithms select the best configuration of facilities based on one or a combination of the following rules:

1. Least cost
2. Maximum service
3. Least cost while satisfying the desired service level
4. Fixed assignment

As a part of all four algorithms, each customer is assigned a list of possible sources. Each algorithm will evaluate the locations on the list when selecting a source for a particular customer.

The least cost algorithm attempts to minimize total system costs by assigning each customer to the source that can supply it at the lowest total variable cost. This variable cost includes transportation--both inbound and outbound, handling and storage, production functions, and inventory (if desired) for all levels in the configuration from the manufacturing plant down to the individual customer.

The maximum service algorithm assigns each customer to the location in the configuration which is nearest in a geographical sense. This assignment technique is used to analyze and explore the best service configuration.

The third algorithm combines attributes of the first two. Using this technique, each customer is assigned to the lowest total cost source within a designated service radius. This assignment method is generally used to determine the minimum cost configuration while maintaining a specified service level.

The fixed assignment algorithm is used to determine the cost and service characteristics of a configuration which has been given to the simulator externally. This method is used to validate cost functions, and when costing base systems. Combinations of the above algorithms may be used during simulations.

The <u>fourth</u> feature of DPM which is helpful for configuration analysis is its deletion algorithm. Using this mechanism, it is possible to begin a simulation with any number of locations and then systematically "sort down" by deleting locations, one at a time, until any desired number of locations remain in the system. The deletion technique is applied by taking out of the configuration the location which will cause the maximum decrease in the total system cost. This location choice is based on the variable and fixed costs associated with a specific location, along with the increased costs that would be incurred through the reassignment of the customers who were assigned to that location.

<u>Fifth,</u> the simulator is computationally efficient. For a typical run, in which it evaluated least cost assignments for 300 customers "sorting down" from 60 distribution centers, the CPU time required was about 30 minutes on a Burroughs 3500, or approximately 10 minutes on an IBM 370/145. Figure 7.3 presents a general block diagram of the simulator system.

<u>DPM Data Analysis Subsystem</u>

The data analysis subsystem for DPM is similar in design to and compatible with that of the LREPS model, which is presented later in this chapter. The data input requirements are of the same general categories as LREPS including:

1. Demand
2. Supply System
3. Manufacturing System
4. Distribution/Warehouse Systems
5. Transportation Network
6. Inventory System

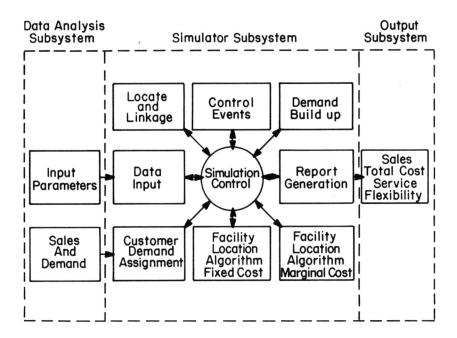

Figure 7.3. Systems Research Incorporated Distribution Planning
Model DPM Simulator System.

   7. Order Processing
   8. Cost Functions
   9. Customer Service
  10. Management Assumptions/Parameters.

DPM Report Subsystem

The DPM Report Generator Subsystem is similar to and compatible with that of the LREPS model. The standard reports for DPM include:
   1. Sales Report
   2. DC Transfer Report
   3. Cost Report
   4. Service Report
   5. DC Product Report
   6. Customer Area Report
   7. Other Reports.
*Report formats for DPM are presented in Appendix A.

DPM Operation

The DPM model is flow oriented and static in nature. It processes all activities for a discrete period; however, the effects of one period can be input into the data base before a future period is run. A location process is performed at the beginning of each run, and every time there is a configuration change to make facility location and customer assignments. The process can be divided into the distribution center (DC) location process and the customer location process.

The DC location process uses a set of possible links to configure a distribution network. This network may be multi-echeloned, with partial stocking capabilities at each level. The input for this process consists of the locations which are to be put into solution, their levels, a list of products which they may stock, and a list of sources from which they may obtain any products which the specific DC does not produce. The location process begins at the highest echelon and builds down. The aim is to find the minimum cost source for each product at every DC, based on variable handling costs and the transportation cost, using several classes of handling and inbound freight-cost. This process enables the model to obtain the total variable cost of supplying a particular product at a given location. When product sources have been established for all DCs, the DC location process is completed. There are some rules regarding levels and sources to facilitate the processing. In general, these restrictions force sources to be in a higher or equal echelon with a sequence number less than the current DC; alternatively, the source can be a producer. These rules follow the same restrictions as does the current LREPS model.

When the variable cost of supplying every DC with its products has been determined, an iteration is made through the customers to make DC assignments. Each customer has a string of up to 25 locations for each product from which he may choose the lowest cost source for the present configuration, based on the variable cost of supplying the product at a specific location and the transportation cost of shipping the goods from the DC to the customer. There are multiple freight and weight class capabilities in the transportation rates. These rates are generated externally to the model; thus, there is the capability to use piece-wise linear regression and/or point-to-point rates. The customer assignment is based on any one of the following rules: (1) fixed assignment (or fixed in combination with one of the other three), (2) least variable cost, (3) maximum service, or (4) least variable cost which also satisfies the desired service constraint.

All sales and demand information are processed as units or cases but conversions are used to compute retail sales. In order to facilitate the data preparation for this model, the data analysis subsystem is the same as the one used in LREPS. External to the actual simulation model, but with the capability of interacting with it, is the ability to factor the demand of all customers by product. This may be used for sensitivity analysis as well as to change forecasts.

After all customers have determined the best source for their products, the flow of demand is traced up the entire echelon structure. The demand at the warehouses is placed against the distribution centers and eventually against the production points. As the demand is traced through the system, the various demands and costs on the network are computed by each inter-facility link.

The final network configuration has the capability of up to 99 echelons, 300 DCs, and several thousand customers in the network.

Following the assignment and flow activities of the period, two types of report data are generated for all flow, cost, and service information for the period. The model produces two types of outputs. The more detailed is a compatible report file, which can be used with the standard report generation system. The second type of output is a much less detailed report, which would be suitable for usage from a terminal. This report gives the basic essentials of sales, cost, and service for each node and for the system as a whole. As a part of the report function, pseudo inventory costs and levels are developed. There are two options for computing this level. The first uses a "standard error of the forecast" factor, while the second employs the "square of n" rule.

Since this is not a temporal simulation, the service level reports are given in distance. For each DC, the service report shows the cumulative percentage of demand which has been delivered within a specified mileage radius. In the detail reports, this report is given by weight break.

The final module of the model is the deletion algorithm, the use of which is optional for any given run. There are two deletion algorithms available to the user.

The first considers for deletion all locations which have been flagged as "deletable" in the input, deleting the DC which will show the greatest reduction in total system cost. Total system cost includes fixed cost of the DC and variable costs associated with operation of the DC. The location chosen for deletion is then taken out of the solution by the algorithm. Following this deletion algorithm, another pass is made through the locating, assignment, and reporting modules. This deletion and costing iteration continues until there is the desired number of locations left or until a specified cost or service criteria is no longer satisfied.

The second algorithm does not actually delete any locations but changes the variable costs associated with a DC. A new variable cost is computed by summing the total fixed and variable costs and then dividing by the throughput at the DC.[1] Another pass is made through the locating and reporting modules to test the new variable costs. The user may schedule as many passes as desired through the process.

In summary, this strategic planning simulator, referred to as DPM, is the tool for structure analysis of a part or of the total distribution system. While it lacks the operational detail of LREPS, it provides the user with an efficient model to narrow the planning decisions. Because it is totally compatible with LREPS, the operational analysis can be obtained if the problem requires it.

---

[1]This new quantity is used as the variable cost for another pass. It is possible to re-compute the new variable cost selectively by location.

Tactical/Operational Logistics Planning
With Dynamic Simulation Models

This section initially provides an overview of two dynamic simulation models: industrial dynamics (ID) by J. W. Forrester,[1] and the distribution system simulator (DSS) developed by IBM.[2] The remainder of the chapter is devoted to the LREPS Operational Simulator with emphasis on the second generation LREPS model which is utilized primarily for operational logistics planning. This current model is based on the research at Michigan State University under a grant by Johnson and Johnson.[3,4]

Industrial Dynamics Model

Forrester's model attempts to match production rate to rate of final consumer sales. The process of production and distribution, according to Forrester, is the central core of many industrial companies. A recurring problem is to match the production rate to the rate of final consumer sales. Forrester states that, "It has often been observed that a distribution system of cascaded inventories and ordering procedures seems to amplify small disturbances that occur at the retail level."[5]

---

[1]J. W. Forrester, Industrial Dynamics (Cambridge, Mass.: The M.I.T. Press, Massachusetts Institute of Technology, 1961).

[2]M. M. Connors, C. Coray, C. J. Cuccaro, W. K. Green, D. W. Low, and H. M. Markowitz, "The Distribution System Simulator," Management Science, Vol. 18, No. 8, April 1972.

[3]Bowersox, et al., Dynamic Simulation of Physical Distribution Systems.

[4]D. J. Bowersox, Logistical Management (New York: The Macmillan Company, 1974).

[5]Forrester, p. 22.

The model, shown in Figure 7.4, deals with the structure and policies within a multiechelon distribution system. Flows of information, order, and materials are required to define the model. Three types of information are required: the organizational structure, delays in decisions and actions, and the policies governing purchases and inventories.

The organizational structure includes the nodes or echelons at which inventory exists: factory, distributor, retailer. Delays in flows of orders (information) and flow of goods are necessary to determine the dynamic characteristics of the system. Three principal components are defined by Forrester: orders to replace goods sold, orders to adjust inventories upward or downward as the level of business activity changes, and orders to fill the supply pipelines with in-process orders and shipments.

The physical distribution components in the industrial dynamics production-distribution simulator are: transportation, inventory, communications delays, a fixed set of locations, and warehouse or utilization.

The organization structure is a single factory, a single factory warehouse, and multidistributors and multiretailers. Each of the distributors and retailers are represented by a single location in the model. Aggregate increases and decreases in sales are assumed. Therefore, this model should be considered a single product type model. The problem as stated is one of total physical distribution system components for a single channel, single supply source, with multiechelon inventory nodes.

The model as developed is a "closed" system. Inputs are initialized as rate equations. Since the model is not presented as a decision-making tool, there is no reference to a planning period horizon for decision making. The response of simulation runs to various changes in inputs is measured for dynamic effects on system variables in terms of one to three years. The

period of influence therefore could be considered short range or
long range. The objective is to examine possible fluctuating or
unstable behavior arising from the principal structural relationships and policies over time.

The general solution approach used by Forrester is
heuristic. He makes the point that mathematical analysis is not
powerful enough to yield general analytical solutions to situations as complex as the total physical distribution system.
Forrester constructs a mathematical model of the industrial
system that tells how the conditions at one point in time lead
to subsequent conditions at future points in time. The behavior
of the model is observed, and experiments are conducted to answer
specific questions about the system, which is represented by the
mathematical model. The name simulation often is applied to this
process of conducting experiments on a model rather than attempting the experiments with the real system. Forrester states
that simulation consists of "tracing through, step by step, the
actual flows of orders, goods, and information, and observing the
series of new decisions that take place."[1]

Time is the unifying dimension in the model. As stated
by Forrester, in order "to be able to determine the dynamic
characteristics of this system, we must know the delays in the
flows of orders and goods."[2] The behavior of the model is
dynamic, in the sense that it consists of information-control
loops and deals with time-varying interaction.

The Distribution System Simulator

The Distribution System Simulator is a modeling tool which
produces a mathematical representation of a firm's distribution

---

[1] Ibid., p. 23.

[2] Ibid., p. 23.

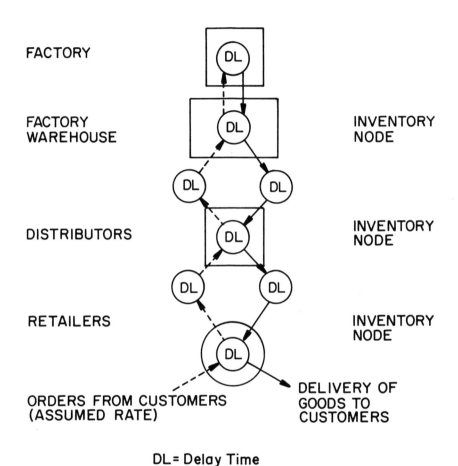

FACTORY

FACTORY
WAREHOUSE

INVENTORY
NODE

DISTRIBUTORS

INVENTORY
NODE

RETAILERS

INVENTORY
NODE

ORDERS FROM CUSTOMERS
(ASSUMED RATE)

DELIVERY OF
GOODS TO
CUSTOMERS

DL = Delay Time

Figure 7.4. Organization of a Production-Distribution System.

system.[1] The DSS user responds to a questionnaire which contains the options that he can use to develop a model of his distribution system. The user specifies the characteristics of the desired model by answering true or false. The options allow the analyst to take into account each of the major factors involved in the operation of a distribution system: the characteristics of customers' demand for products; buying patterns of customers; order filling policies; replenishment policies; emergency replenishment policies; redistribution policies; transportation policies; distribution channels; factory locations; production capabilities; other significant elements. Essentially, these options are inventory and product movement oriented--beyond this, DSS provides the capability, through user functions, to incorporate other vehicle scheduling algorithms, forecasting techniques, production schedules, and pricing mechanisms which are outside the scope of the existing options.

Since DSS emulates the essential parts of the actual distribution system, it permits the distribution system to be modeled so that a "total system approach" can be taken to the problem by OR personnel as well as by executives.

DSS is more than a distribution system model generator. It also generates the computer program for running the model on a computer. As indicated above, the DSS user specifies the characteristics of the desired model by answering a questionnaire. These answers are submitted to a computer, along with the DSS program. The result is: (1) the generation of PL/I program, whose logic is described by the options chosen on the questionnaire; (2) a complete specification of the data required by the simulation program generated; and (3) a complete specification of the information required for the output analysis available for

---

[1]Connors, et al.

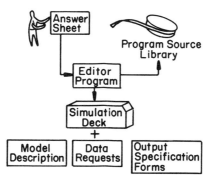

ORGANIZATION OF DSS

Figure 7.5.   Organization of a Distribution System Simulator.

the simulation generated.   The user need not be familiar with any
elements of computer programming in order to obtain the simulator,
instructions for its use, and output analyses; however, the
requirements of a thorough understanding of distribution systems,
modeling, and management science are imposed on the user.

Generating a distribution system simulation with DSS is
a multiple step procedure.   The process is shown schematically
in Figure 7.5.   The distribution executive or the operations
research analyst is assumed to be familiar with the distribution
system he seeks to model.   The analyst describes the environment
as well as the operating characteristics of his distribution
system by responding "true" or "false" to questions--about 450
of them--on the 10 DSS Answer Sheets.   The responses to the DSS
Answer Sheets are punched on computer cards, one Answer Sheet
per card, with the rows on the Answer Sheet corresponding to
columns on the card.   The resulting deck of cards is processed
by the Editor Program, which configures the desired simulator and
produces the input request forms on which the requisite data input

is to be entered 'nto the simulator. In addition to the data
requests, the Editor Program documents the model generated and
produces the forms upon which the specifications for the output
analysis are provided. The data requests, model documentation,
and output analysis forms are all particularized to the simulator
configured on the Answer Sheets and are mostly self-explanatory.
The user need only fill out the forms produced by the Editor
Program. Upon providing the required data, the user has completed
the process of building a simulator and specifying the output
analysis for his particular distribution system. The simulation
deck produced by DSS, together with the data input formatted
according to the instructions produced by the Editor Program,
can then be run on a computer.

A large number of different distribution system models--
over 12 feasible models--can be generated in this manner. It
should be emphasized that these are all functionally different
models; they are not merely parametrically different.

The effort required to develop DSS was comparable to the
effort required to build several large models. The combinatorial
problem is avoided by bringing together a number of devices
which, taken together, form DSS. These components are:

1. the external Answer Sheet, which defines the scope
and structure of the distribution systems models available;

2. the internal Source Library, a set of PL/I statements
from which those needed in the construction of any particular
model are "automatically" chosen;

3. an internal set of Decision Tables that specify which
commands from the Source Library are to be included in the
generated program as a function of the Answer Sheets;

4. an internal Editor that processes the Answer Sheets,
the Source Library, and Decision Tables in order to build the
simulation program and to produce a specification of the input

information which the user must supply for the simulation and
the associated output analysis in order to use the program;

5. an internal Output Generator that transforms the
raw simulation output into management reports. These detail
all product movement, storage, and maintenance; all operations
analysis; and all cost information reported optionally in terms
of dollars invested or in terms of cost functions derived from
operating information.

The total DSS system is composed of about 50,000 computer
cards. A reasonably complex simulation consists of 10,000 to
20,000 cards and requires 10 to 15 minutes on an IBM 360/40. A
simulator generated for a 6 stocking point, 15 demand point, and
100 item distribution system requires about 256K bytes of memory--
the core storage requirement for a simulator increase linearly
with the product of the number of stocking points and the number
of items.

The Basic Structure of DSS

The Distribution System Simulator views distribution
systems as being composed of three structural entities: demand
points, stocking points, and production resources. Figure 7.6
shows how these entities might interrelate in a multi-location,
multi-echelon distribution system. The circles are demand points,
the rectangles are stocking points, the triangles are the production resources, and the directed arcs are channels of distribution.
The interrelationships of these entities are arbitrary in DSS:
the channels of distribution can be bi-directional, the stocking
points can all be connected to each other via channels, demand
can take place at any point in the system, and any stocking point
can have access to the production resource. The particular
relationships between these components of the system are entirely
at the discretion of the modeler.

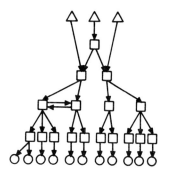

○ Demand Points
□ Stocking Points
△ Production Resources

Figure 7.6. Multi-Location, Multi-Echelon Distribution System.

      The part of DSS that is of most interest from the point of
view of improving the operation of the distribution system is the
collection of stocking points. The stocking points, usually
thought of as regionally distributed warehouses and echelons in
a distribution system but actually subject to a wide variety of
other interpretations, are the key modeling units because all of
the processes capable of analysis and optimization take place
there. Seven management activities are possible at each stocking
point: order queue reviews, backorder queue reviews, transportation reviews, normal replenishment reviews, emergency replenishment reviews, redistribution reviews, and history, forecasting
and parameter reviews. The inter-relationships among the first
six policy questions are presented in Figure 7.7. Figure 7.7
clarifies that DSS views inventory and product movement as the
key elements in structuring a distribution system. Ancillary

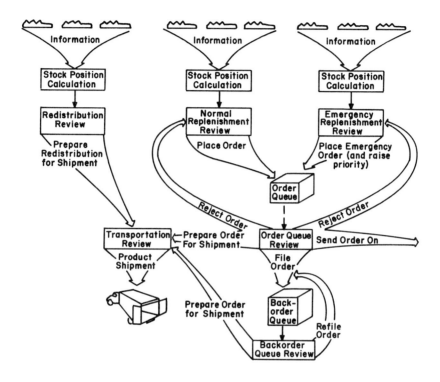

Figure 7.7. The Distribution System Simulator.

problems--facilities investment, plant location--are treated through
their implications for inventory and transportation management.
More detail or capability can be provided for existing options--
such as vehicle scheduling algorithms, production schedules,
allocation techniques and forecasting mechanisms--by employing
user functions.

It is important to note that the activities in Figure 7.4
are carried out in policy space--the policies may be implemented
simultaneously at the same or different stocking point(s). Each

258

of these reviews is characterized in terms of its own Answer
Sheet, which contains a wide variety of policy options which
can be used to implement the review.

The system is designed to respond to demands placed on
stocking points by demand points at either predetermined points
in time (as in a simulation of historical information) or at
random points in time (as in a simulation of forecasted information). The demand is of no concern to the system before it
takes place or after it is satisfied; information regarding it
is available only while it is in the system. Demands are not
all identical; they may be for different items, different
quantities, contain different priorities, have different backorder and partial shipment policies, and can be routed to
different stocking points within the system. Demand points are
a manifestation of the firm's customer environment. The firm
has no control over demands, although the analyst is still
responsible for modeling the demand processes; the objective
of DSS is to aid the user in finding better ways for the
distribution system to respond to the activity of the demand
points.

The production characterization specifies the interface
between the distribution system and the manufacturing environment. In DSS, the importance of the modeling detail and its
availability in the production characterization is minimal.
Production is modeled only at times at which quantities of goods
are delivered at stocking points.

System Evaluation with DSS

It is apparent in any discussion of the evaluation and
optimization of physical distribution systems that there are
trade offs present in any managerial decision concerning these
systems. The principal objective of DSS is to enable the analyst

to model and evaluate such trade offs as a continuum, rather than as a collection of discrete operating components. The goal of DSS is to enable the analyst to focus his attention on the operating problems of the system, rather than on the details of the tool itself.

While DSS focuses on the key distribution considerations-- inventory and product movement--it has utility for ancillary problems as well. Facilities location and investment, plant location, manpower studies and other factors can be treated by specifying alternative solutions to these problems and then simulating their effects on inventory and transportation. This, of course, requires a judgment on the part of the user as to whether inventory and product movement considerations are dominant or whether more specialized models are necessary.

As in the case with any simulator, DSS is a tool for evaluating rather than operating a distribution system. The end objective of the analysis is the ability to prescribe operating systems for large-scale physical distribution systems. The key is effective communication between the distribution executive and management scientist. DSS provides a vehicle for such com- munication by the executive's participation in the model building process through the questionnaire approach, thereby achieving more confidence in and understanding of the model. The team approach is enforced, however, because the management scientist is needed to build, understand, interpret, and exercise the models. DSS allows him to do this without being burdened with the details of the computerized implementation of his models and their modifi- cations.

LREPS Operational Planning Model

Introduction

The balance of this chapter is devoted to the LREPS model. First, the background and an overview of the LREPS model is presented. Second, the overall design concept and operation of the model are discussed. The third section describes the three basic modules of the current generation of LREPS, emphasizing several of the dynamic features that enable the model to be utilized for operational planning.

The tactical and operational logistics planning model, called LREPS-Operational, is a direct decendant of the LREPS model developed through the combined efforts of Johnson & Johnson and a team of researchers headed by D. J. Bowersox from the Graduate School of Business Administration at Michigan State University.[1,2] The latest implementation, completed by Systems Research Incorporated in 1973, places increased emphasis on tactical and operational planning rather than long range planning as in the original. The current LREPS Model's capabilities are presented in Appendix A.

From a user point of view, the current basic conceptual model is very similar to the first generation LREPS. However, the LREPS computer model and programs have been through two major redesigns since the original LREPS development in 1969. The first generation LREPS model was designed and programmed for the Control Data Corporation 6500 Computer, written in FORTRAN IV and GASP II-A. Approximately two years later, the model was reprogrammed in COBOL for the Burroughs 2500 Computer by Systems

---

[1]Bowersox, et al., _Dynamic Simulation of Physical Distribution Systems_.

[2]Bowersox, _Logistical Management_.

Research Incorporated, the firm with the marketing rights for the
LREPS model. A major redesign and second reprogramming effort
was completed by Systems Research Incorporated in 1973 to (1)
redesign LREPS as a more generalized network model; (2) improve
the efficiency of the computer programs to facilitate utilization
of the model for multiple runs required in logistics planning
studies; (3) incorporate and improve features to provide additional capability to simulate various transportation consolidation
and pooling policies, production schedule policies, inventory
policies etc. for operational planning; (4) develop more standard
COBOL programs to facilitate the model being implemented on
different computers; (5) increase the limit on the critical
variables; and (6) improve and standardize the input and output
subsystems.

The primary objective of the LREPS tactical/operational
planning simulation model is to assist in the development of
logistical operating plans. Given the objectives and a configuration of the logistics system, logistics costs, service and
profit trade offs may be simulated and analyzed. Typical problems
which LREPS-Operational has assisted in solving include questions
pertaining to inventory policies, shipping policies, and detailed
analysis of locational problems.

The model has several features which are invaluable in
tactical and operational planning. The model is dynamic, enabling
the simulated operations of customer service, costs, and profits.
Changes in the operating policy of transportation, production,
inventory, warehousing, and order processing can be evaluated to
assist in developing the best operating plan to meet the strategic
objectives of the enterprise. Third, the model is general enough
to represent a wide range of logistics systems, from the firm
with one major product line produced in one location, to the
business with many raw material vendors, multi-plants,

262

multi-warehouses, multi-customers, and multi-products. The output capability includes total logistics costs and several customer service measures, including customer and reorder cycle times, levels of stockout, backorders, and proximity to markets. Fifth, the output capability also enables the generation of profit and loss statements, customized to the needs of the user, to evaluate the impact of logistics operations in terms of profit contribution, gross margin, and/or net profit. Finally, the model has an algorithm to choose the best assignment for customer-product demand given the configuration of facilities to be tested.

LREPS-II: General Concept and Operation

LREPS is a distribution simulation model whose purpose is to assist management in evaluation of distribution operations' cost/service trade offs. The LREPS model is geared to replicate any firm's distribution system and its daily operating activities. It takes into account both location (spatial) and inventory (temporal) aspects of distribution, and measures customer service in terms of complete and individual components of order-cycle time, stock-out levels, order completeness, backorders, proportion of sales and orders receiving specified service levels, and total distribution cost.

The model works on the total system approach to distribution, thereby allowing the evaluation of trade offs between customer service and costs and the resulting profit contribution. With the model's present capabilities, transportation, DC[1] operations, inventory control, order communications, material handling, packaging, production planning and market forecasts are integrated into a single performance system for each distribution system alternative tested.

---

[1]The term DC in this chapter refers to plant, public, private, and/or leased warehousing, pool centers, break bulk terminals, distribution agents, freight consolidators, dealers, and other agents in the distribution channel.

LREPS, in operations research terminology, is a dynamic rather than a static model. This means it is capable of quanti- tatively analyzing and measuring the major variables influencing the distribution system, variables such as product, time, distance, flow, inventory accumulation, and demand characteristics. This, in turn, enables the model to simulate distribution activities on an order-by-order, day-by-day basis. Thus, each order, as it is placed, is traced from the customer to the DC, where it is processed and then shipped to the customer. As products are requisitioned from a DC, the inventory level is updated by product. When the DC reorder point is reached, an order is transmitted to plants for processing and shipping. At both DCs and plants, out-of-stocks can occur due to production scheduling, transportation, inventory control, and/or unexpected demand surges. During the tracing of an order in this multi-echeloned environment, customer service and distribution costs are cal- culated and reported.

The model automatically assigns market demand by customers and products to the lowest total cost source for a specified maximum service distance constraint and then determines the level of customer service provided in this assignment. Coupled with this capability, the model is unique in its ability to aid the distribution manager in testing any alternative's effectiveness with the passage of time.

The echelons in a multi-echeloned distribution system structure include: (1) raw material sources; (2) consolidation of inbound shipments; (3) processing or production; (4) plant warehouses; (5) regional distribution centers; (6) remote distri- bution centers; (7) customer wholesale warehouses; (8) distributors, (9) retail stores; (10) sales branches; (11) dealers. The final echelon represents demand units that have been represented by (1) individual key customer account; (2) county codes; (3) Standard

Metropolitan Statistical Area (SMSA); (4) economic trading areas (groups of customers); (5) Zip Code; (6) Zip Sectional Centers; (7) grids; (8) retailers; (9) wholesalers; (10) distributors; and (11) dealers.

Linkages between and within echelons are defined in terms of product and information flows. Product flow is treated in multi-product fashion. Information flow, related specifically to the order communication function, occurs between and within echelons.

Product flow is measured by standard units such as value, weight, cube, and density. Order-cycle time, the primary measure of customer service, is measured in terms of four elapsed time intervals: (1) order communication time, (2) order processing time, (3) transportation time, and (4) total penalty time accumulated under (1), (2), or (3), resulting from delay, deficiency, or queuing.

Orders and products are treated on a multi-channeled basis. Both information and product flows related to specific orders can be assigned specifically to alternative channel paths between manufacturing and point of demand. The system structure thus allows for the simulation of multi-product and information flow to occur in a multi-channel pattern through a multi-echeloned physical distribution system.

LREPS has three modes of operation. First, it may operate in a probabilistic or deterministic mode with regard to the total cycle-time relationship. Communication, order processing, and transportation times can be preset for any specified linkage, or discrete probability distributions may be specified.

Second, LREPS is oriented to variable time-planning horizons. The model operates on a time interval dependent basis (i.e. results achieved at the end of a time period are noted and influence operations during the next time period) and functions for some specified combination of days, quarters, or years.

Third, feedback loops are utilized to provide dynamic
behavior when desired. For example, sales of a product group
can be altered due to stockouts resulting from insufficient
inventory.

Three groupings of variables are defined in LREPS:
target variables, environment variables, controllable variables.
The major target variables are customer service and total cost.
Environmental variables are grouped into major categories of
demography, technology, and acts of nature. Each of these
categories is broken down into variables which are inter-active
with the model itself; i.e., demographic variables defined in
terms of cost-of-living indices, real estate value indices, and
demand determinants. The major controllable variables illustrated in Figure 7.8 structure the major physical distribution
and marketing overlap.

Distribution Cost Elements

The distribution cost centers most frequently included in
the utilization of LREPS to evaluate distribution alternatives
are:
1. Transportation to customers
2. Transportation to and between plants and DCs
3. Handling and storage
4. Order processing
5. Equipment, facilities, land, and overhead
6. Inventory
7. Production
8. Packaging

In evaluating the customer service levels provided by the present
and proposed distribution systems, both fixed and variable distribution costs are used for each of the above cost centers at all
locations. Transportation to customers represents freight charges
for either private, common, and/or contract accumulated by all
modes, weight intervals, and classes from plants and DCs.

	VARIABLE GROUPINGS	DESIGN OPTIONS
M	ORDER CHARACTERISTICS	ACTUAL OR PSEUDO
A O		
R R	PRODUCT MIX	ACTUAL OR PSEUDO
K I		
E E	NEW PRODUCTS	AS DESIRED
T N		
I T	CUSTOMER MIX	ACTUAL OR PSEUDO
N E		
G D	FACILITY STRUCTURE	ACTUAL OR PSEUDO BY ECHELON
	FACILITY CONNECTION	ACTUAL OR PSEUDO BETWEEN
D		ECHELONS
I		
S O	INVENTORY POLICY	REORDER POINT, REPLENISH-
T R		MENT, OR HYBRID BY
R I		ECHELON
I E		
B N	TRANSPORTATION	TRUCK, RAIL, AIR, PRIVATE
U T		AND CONTRACT TRUCK IN ANY
T E		COMBINATION BETWEEN ECHELONS
I D		
O	COMMUNICATION	COMPUTER, TELETYPE, MAIL,
N		TELEPHONE BETWEEN ECHELONS
	MATERIAL HANDLING	AUTOMATED OR MECHANIZED BY
		ENCELONS
	PRODUCTION	ACTUAL OR PSEUDO

Figure 7.8. LREPS Controllable System Variables.

Transportation to DCs is freight costs from plants and vendors. The handling and storage costs for the throughput volume are provided for each company, public, and/or leased facility. Order processing costs are assessed on each order at locations that process orders and/or reorders. Charges for equipment, land, and overhead are also allocated to each facility. Inventory carrying costs are developed by determining the inventory level for each

product and location and then assessing the appropriate inventory
carrying charge. Production cost is assigned by product and plant.
If products are obtained from an outside vendor, the purchase
price is used.

Other cost centers that have been included in the LREPS
applications include: raw materials, selling, marketing, administrative and corporate overhead, in-transit privileges, stop off
charges, and services to customer accounts. Other cost centers
can easily be added in the form of fixed and/or variable cost
functions.

Customer Service Elements

How does the distribution manager define and measure
customer service and associated costs of his distribution system?
Unfortunately, no single definition or measurement is being used
by all firms. However, a distribution manager must assess, either
formally or informally, the levels of service provided and the
relevant costs.

Within LREPS, customer service and the associated costs
and profit contribution are measured for detailed reporting.
The model currently measures the following distribution system
service elements by each plant and DC as applicable:

1. Complete customer order cycle
2. Complete DC reorder cycles
3. Individual components of customer order and DC
   reorder cycles
4. Proportion of sales and orders serviced within
   specified levels of order cycle time and/or miles
5. Stock out levels
6. Order completeness
7. Backorders

LREPS assesses the complete customer order cycle and the DC
replenishment or re-order cycle. The customer order cycle is
the elapsed time from the moment the customer submits his order

until the merchandise is received at his inbound shipping dock.
It accounts for the time used for transmitting orders from
customers to order entry, order processing, order transmittal
to DCs, order picking, and shipping of products to the customer.
Backorder time is also included if merchandise is not available.
The order replensihment cycle is the time required from the
moment the DC submits an order to its sourcing plant until the
merchandise is received for stocking.

While the complete customer and replenishment order cycles
are measured in total, components of each cycle are also evaluated.
These components include order transmission, order processing,
picking, out-of-stock, backorder, transportation, and production
times.

The model is capable of developing several other measures
for evaluating the degree of customer service. First, the model
reports the proportion of sales dollars and orders being served
within given increments of complete order cycle time and/or
distance. Second, the model reflects the ability to service
the customer with a stated inventory policy. This feature indicates the number of times stockouts occurred, (order completeness),
units stocked out, and backorders by location. Also, the backorders and stockout conditions are identified by specific product
and location. Third, customer pickup options can be evaluated
and reported by the model. Other customer service measures can
be utilized if desired by the user.

Reporting Capabilities

To successfully evaluate distribution alternatives, the
LREPS reporting system prints standard reports including, but
not limited to, the following:

1. Sales to customers
2. Distribution costs

3. Order cycle time
4. Normal order cycle time distribution--proportion of sales dollars and orders with given order cycle time increments
5. Inventory conditions
6. Service report by location and product
7. Shipments to other DCs
8. Receipts from other DCs
9. Inventory report by product
10. Customer sales report by product and source
11. Net profit and loss reports by customer region, DC, plant, and total company.

These standard reports are developed, as applicable, for each facility represented in the simulation. Any number of special reports by location can be developed, such as net profit and loss statements, customer pickup, and weight shipped by weight interval and class. The detailed P&L statements have been utilized by management to evaluate the impact of distribution service trade offs on company profits.

Design Configuration

The LREPS system is composed of three basic modules: data analysis, simulation, and report generation, as illustrated in Figure 7.9. The data analysis subsystem includes all of the LREPS support programs which are used to process client data for direct input into the simulation and report generation systems. The output of the data analysis system is composed of printed reports and specially designed files which describe the basic structure and flows of the physical distribution system.

The simulator, using as input the structured files generated in the data analysis subsystem and additional data describing various operational and control parameters, simulates the physical distribution system. LREPS is controlled and directed via the operational parameters; given the basic data analysis system, it can be supplied with many variable options to evaluate.

270

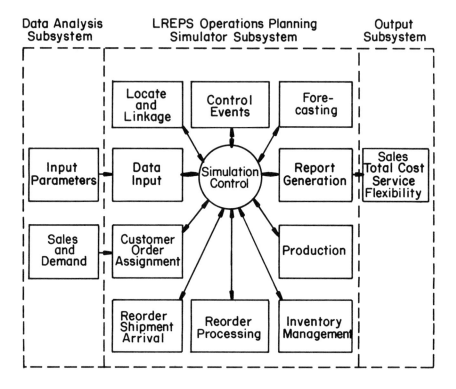

Figure 7.9. Systems Research Incorporated LREPS Operations
Planning Simulator System.

The output of the simulator includes a specially designed report file to be used by the report generation sybsystem. In addition, all files which were input can be retrieved and printed for the purpose of evaluating specific events.

The report generation system consists of two basic reporting modes. The first is the LREPS standard system, which provides operational and cost reports by location (distribution node), activity, and product. The second is a customized profit and loss type of report, which is easily prepared to reflect the client's standard cost reporting techniques.

The purpose of this section is to describe the three basic modules of the LREPS system. The discussion will include the relationships between the subsystems, the functions of each program within the subsystem, and the data requirements.

Data Analysis Subsystem

The data analysis subsystem can be categorized as follows: (1) demand analysis, (2) demand generation, (3) distribution node definition, and (4) demand node definition. The demand analysis is of primary importance, because it permits the LREPS user to visualize and manipulate the demand data structure and activities. The remaining analyses, involving the preparation of client data, ultimately produce all of the major files which describe the physical distribution system for LREPS.

The main purpose of the LREPS demand analysis system (LDAS) is to provide the user with the tools to analyze the demand structure, and to identify the nodes, products, internodal links, and the volume of customer sales. The emphasis is on customer activity, rather than the flow of product for distribution node replenishment. The major programs of the LDAS provide tape disk and report files, which are interpreted by the user and serve as input to most of the data and file preparation programs for both LREPS and the DPM models. The primary input for the LDAS is the client's record of demand or sales for the period. This input is most frequently a tape file of invoices.

Another option is a summary of the demand by period, such as month or year. The data specifies by period (date), the distribution node (DC), the demand node (called DU for demand unit), the product differentiation (such as line item code, product family), and the volume (dollars, weight, cube, and units or cases) of the transaction. Invoices are the most frequent option, as they inherently include the order characteristics of frequency and sizes and are therefore more easily applied to the LREPS system.

Given the record of customer demand, the LDAS programs generate tables summarizing activity of DC, DU, and product. These tables and a super matrix of all interactivity are extremely useful in analyzing the full customer distribution network and in modifying that structure.

Two major functions are performed in the demand generation system: generation of orders in the form and format used by LREPS, and development of a reference of product seasonability.

Generation of orders for the demand-driven LREPS can be handled in one of two ways. LREPS has the capability of internally generating orders based on demand for a specified period and specified order characteristics or statistics. This method is most frequently applied when the client data base does not maintain a record of invoices, or when some interval of time greater than a day is the simulation processing interval. The specifics and requirements related to using this option are referenced in the discussions of seasonality and distribution node definition.

The preferred method of order generation is the preparation of an order tape. The order tape is quite similar to the client invoice tape. Each transaction is represented with a summary of the total sales and a record of the individual line items being ordered. The format of the LREPS order differs from a client invoice in one major respect. The identifying numbers used by the client to indicate the shipping location, the customer, and the product have been replaced by the pseudo or referencing sequential numbers resulting from the LDAS.

Frequently, clients do not maintain all the necessary information LREPS requires on invoice records, like gross weight (shipping weight or product plus tare weight), cube, and occasionally the dollar value of the sale. The order tape may be massaged to provide all of the data. Provided weight/unit, cube/unit, dollar/unit or similar data, a program can be used to expand the data picked up from the invoice. Some of the information is optional. Depending on the types of cost functions to be used by the client, the minimum order volume descripters required are units (which may be cases or net weight) and shipping weight, although tare weight may be omitted if it is not significant. This program can also be used to increase order sizes of volumes ordered for sales growth averages.

The order generation programs ultimately provide an order tape with orders enumerated by date and indicating the product, demand, the customer to receive the shipment, the volume demanded, and the DC or shipper. The order tape thus prepared may be used for all options using LREPS.

The seasonality file is an optional LREPS file. Some industries are not seasonal, and hence order characteristics are customer oriented as opposed to product, monthly, or seasonally related. However, when product demand is seasonal, or when orders are generated internally by the model, the LREPS seasonality file is utilized to adjust forecasts, reorder points, and EOQs by product and period, to smooth the standard error of the product forecasts, and to generate internal orders.

A seasonality file can be developed in two ways. If the client-supplied demand data does not have sufficient representation, i.e., it is annual, seasonality factors can be input through card data to create a disc file. If invoices or weekly demand data is provided, the seasonality factors can be computed by a program based on historical frequencies.

The requirements for distribution node definition are threefold: descriptions of the functional characteristics of the node (DC); definitions of the intranodal links and freight costs primarily related to stock replenishments; and development of the production procedures for the manufacturing nodes.

The file which contains the DC characteristics related to order processing and stocking policies is most frequently called the DC file. Parameters in the DC file will define the attributes and functions of the node, which may represent a plant, warehouse, terminal, etc.

Given the functional role of each location, other parameters and variables are defined which describe the operation procedures. Depending on the function, the products manufactured and/or stocked are identified. While production schedules or cycles can be specified, it may be expedient or desirable to use the infinite production option. This option is frequently selected when production data is not available, or raw material availability is non-controllable, and so product availability cannot be a simulation concern, or if product availability is very high normally. In the DC file, the "infinite inventory" option may also be selected. In either case, the choice can be made for each location independently and, if selected, these options will result in unlimited product availability of all produced and/or stocked product at that location.

For the products handled at each location, more data items are specified in the DC file. The first describes the type of

inventory policy, whether a reorder point system with a fixed
EOQ or a replenishment system. In either case, standard safety
stock and EOQ data must be identified. There are four sets of
SS/EOQ values for each product. At each DC, a different set may
be chosen for all the products produced and all the products
stocked. If the products are only stocked at the location, the
replenishment sources must be specified.

The normal customer order processing procedures, such
as how to handle stockouts or backorders, are described in the
execution deck for LREPS. However, the distribution of order
processing time, its frequency and how long it takes to process
an order, exclusive of delays due to stockouts or shipping
procedures, is defined on the DC file. Additionally, procedures
in the event of stockouts, whether to ship partial lines,
backorder, etc., for replenishment reorders are defined. Stock
backorder allocation, when product becomes available, may also
be selected for reorders.

The DC file is a critical LREPS data bank. Since LREPS
projects frequently involve location analysis and stocking
policies, all of the policies related to the replenishment system
must be described.

Closely related to the DC file is the link file. As
indicated, the replenishment source for each product must be
specified in the DC file. The freight data relating to replenishment transactions is stored on the link file. Three types of data
are required for this file. The first is the description of the
link indicating the origin of ultimate shipper, the destination
of location initiating the reorder, and the circumstances under
which a transaction may occur. The latter is most significant
when locations are added or deleted from the system during a run.
The second relates to the normal order communication and lead
times involved in transactions across the replenishment link.

Data here includes the time it takes for the order to be placed
in the order processing system and most critically, the average
historical lead time--order submittal to order receipt. The
latter is used to initiate the inventory reorder points at the
destination.

The most substantial data on the link file is the freight
data including transit times and freight rates. Prior to pre-
paring the actual data, it is advisable to identify all of the
modes (truck, rail, piggyback, private, common carrier, etc.) and
the weight intervals required. To each condition--truck, 1,000-
2,000 lbs., boxcar, 40,000-70,000 lbs.--a freight condition number
from 1 to 99 is assigned. This number will reference parameters
describing the condition in the LREPS card input. Additional
attributes associated with the freight conditions are probabilities. Where consolidation of shipments to distribution nodes
may occur, firms frequently prefer to force truckload shipments
for less than truckload orders, using probabilities. Given a
freight condition, the weight interval and a probability must
be defined.

Once the freight conditions are identified, the link file
is readily completed. One program may be used to compute rates
and transit times based on linear regression equations or point
to point freight rates prepared by the firm or selected from
the motor freight guide; the distribution of and value of transit
times (variable also by mode and weight interval) can be coded
for the link file. When the link file is completed, all data
related to replenishment transactions are available for LREPS.

The last major file to be prepared to define the operating
procedures of the distribution nodes is the production file. The
layout of the production tape is quite similar to the order tape.
The data specifies the product, the producing location, the number
of units which will come off the production line, and the day when

the product will be available for stock. This is an optional
file to be used only if the other options, the production cycle
or infinite production, are not selected.

Input Requirements.--The process of using LREPS to evaluate
a physical distribution system does not begin with the execution
of the first data analysis subsystem program, but with a definition of a simulation subsystem (nodes, products, demand) of the
real world. The myriad and minute events occurring in the
logistical system, such as loading a pallet onto a fork lift
truck, delays at the unloading dock, can be simulated; in
evaluating the total distribution system, this would be impracti-
cal, as simulation time may approach real time. Hence, the first
process involves defining the limits of the simulated system.

The LREPS files can be generated with up to 9,989 demand
nodes, 989 distribution nodes, and 99 different "tracked" products.
These files can be expanded, but there are practicable limitations.
With fewer nodes, greater turnaround and flexibility in considering many options is improved. These usable limitations are
unique to each firm and best determined when the customer network and the user's requirements are known.

Simply stated, several basic questions must be answered:

1. What product categories should be defined from which
the user's full product line can be simulated representatively?
Can some line items be kept separate and others aggregated? What
are viable levels of aggregation: product families, physical
characteristics, fast-medium-slow mover categories? Would a
sample of line items be sufficiently representative for most
users?   With a large and diversified product line, some type
of analysis by product for the user is required to provide a
viable number of products to use in LREPS.

2. What aggregation unit will best represent the lowest
delivery echelon normally used by the firm?   The DU in the

model, frequently referred to as the demand node or unit, may represent the retail outlet, wholesale outlet, or an aggregation of these into geographically juxtaposed zones such as Standard Point Location, Zip Code section, market area, or some familiar category. The demand node in physical distribution planning is important as the ultimate source of the sale, as well as an important contributor to delivery freight costs. As is frequently the case, however, marketing strategy and response are quite similar in geographically defined areas, and freight rates differ minimally from town to town within a similarly defined market-tariff area. Hence, the customer must be defined as the unit from which orders and demand emanate for the purpose of simulation.

3. What and where are the distribution nodes? DCs may be plants, plant warehouses, public, private, regional, local, or customer consigned distribution centers. Existing locations, locations in process of development, and new potential sites for any function are included in this category. Also considered are sites which were closed, are being closed, or will be closed within the period to which the simulation is being applied.

4. What are the characteristics of the operating system? What types of inventories are maintained, and where? Is production (when, where, and how much) a contributing factor in the system? Is consolidation of freight, scheduled shipping, and pooling the important point to be considered? What are the operating costs? What freight costs are involved?

Evaluation of these and other questions reveals much about the type of data required for the model. The generalized data requirements presented below are the most frequently used. Some are optional, others expandable, depending on the complexity of the physical distribution system being evaluated and the length of the simulation period.

The general data requirements for the LREPS model are:

1. Demand
2. Supply system
3. Manufacturing system
4. Distribution/warehouse systems
5. Transportation network
6. Inventory system
7. Order processing
8. Cost functions
9. Customer service
10. Management assumptions/parameters

Report Generator Subsystem

The report generator subsystem consists of a series of subroutines that were designed to be utilized with LREPS and the strategic distribution planning model (DPM). These subroutines write the detailed results from the simulation runs to tape or disk. This feature permits summary reports and run status information to be obtained while the model is running, whereas the standard reports can be printed off-line at any time when the printers are available. The report programs are data cards to input titles and names, control report selection, frequency, and organization to input file selections.

The LREPS report generator subsystem prints various reports organized by time and/or location. Current standard reports include:

1. Distribution Center Reports
   -Sales to customers
   -Distribution costs, total and by individual function or cost center
   -Customer and replenishment order cycle times
   -Normal order cycle time distribution-proportion of sales dollars and orders with given order cycle time increments
   -Inventory conditions by location
   -Service report; number of stock-outs, number and percentage cases stocked out, average stock-out

time, number and percentage orders backordered,
lost sales due to stock-outs
-Shipments to other Distribution Centers and/or
plants
-Receipts from other distribution facilities or plants
-Weighted shipping distance
-Secondary sales to customers

2. Product Reports

-Product inventory and sales
-Product service report

3. Customer Sales Report

-Customer sales

4. Customer Freight Reports

-Weight shipped by customer, distribution center, and
freight condition
-Distribution center to customer freight cost

5. Customer Product Report

-Customer product report

These standard reports are developed, as applicable, for each
facility represented in the simulation, such as warehouse, plant,
distributor, and retail store. A large number of special reports
by facility location can also be developed, such as net profit
and loss statements by distributor and by warehouse, customer
pickups, and weight shipped by weight interval and class. In
some instances, clients have used the detailed P & L statements
to evaluate the impact of distribution service trade offs on
company net profit.

An example of the format for selected LREPS standard
reports is presented in Appendix A. The profit and loss programs
are designed to permit all costs of the total logistics system,
including corporate general overhead, corporate marketing, etc.,

, to be fully allocated to the lowest echelon in the system if requested by the user.

Simulator Subsystem

The LREPS simulator provides a means for simulating a distribution system without the disadvantages of reprogramming for every user. The present version of the simulator is written in American Standard COBOL for execution of the Burroughs medium scale computer line. However, there is no reason why the present version would not be able to be run on any machine which is at least its equivalent.

The LREPS simulator gives the modeler the capability of creating a network which will simulate his distribution system. The general network is defined as having nodes, demand points, and links. These give the system its spacial qualities. In order to integrate the fourth dimension of time into the system, the concept of an event is implemented. The basic simulator provides a driver for linking a simulation, in a time sense, from t_0 to $t_0 + n$, where n is the number of simulation periods. These time periods can represent any actual period of time. The various events can then be scheduled to occur in any of the various time periods. Some of these events can be controlled by the user; others are scheduled internally. The scheduling of an event causes one of the modules of the simulator to be executed. Each of the modules performs one of a number of distribution-related activities for the simulation. Some of these activities are order processing, inventory management, and shipment arrival. The simulator will perform all the events associated with a period and then advance to the next.

The LREPS spacial system is designed to allow for simulation of most distribution systems. The three primary entities in the system are nodes, demand points, and links. Any points in the system which stock inventory, produce product, or have demand placed against itself must be modeled as nodes. In the real world, this would include plants, regional warehouses, distribution centers, local warehouses, and sales branches.

The demand point represents the customer in the "real world" system. Actual demand points in the simulation could represent the user's individual customers or a geographical grouping of customers. Since a great amount of detail is usually not necessary at this level and, in some cases can be very detrimental to the purpose of the simulation, it is usually recommended that grouping of individual customers be used.

Links connect all the individual points in the system; DC-node reorders and customer-node orders travel over them. These provide both the communication and transit links. Of all the possible links in the network, a subset must be defined as being realistic and practical. These links have the temporal characteristics and costs associated with goods or information passing from one point in the network to another. A diagram of a typical distribution system with its associated links is given in Figure 7.10.

The LREPS temporal system is designed around its event structure. The events enable the model to perform distribution activities which give some meaning to the results of the simulation. There are three basic types of events: system, general, nodal. System events are those which affect the simulation itself. These control the length of the simulation, the reporting, and various controls within the simulator. The general events include activities which involve all of the nodes in the system, such as inventory management. Finally, nodal events are those which only affect a specific node. This would include events such as reorder processing and shipment arrival.

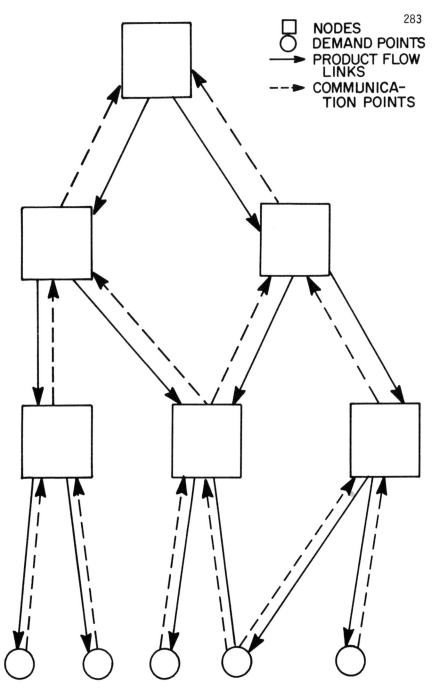

NODES
DEMAND POINTS
PRODUCT FLOW
LINKS
COMMUNICA-
TION POINTS

Figure 7.10.   Diagram of a Typical Physical Distribution System.

There are many subroutines or programs in the total LREPS Simulator. There will not be any attempt in this text to describe or even list all of them. However, there are a number of features that stress the dynamic capabilities of the model. The features selected for review are as follows:

1. LREPS event sequences
2. Production policy
3. Order processing policy
4. Inventory policy
5. Warehouse operating policy
6. Shipment policy
7. Customer service measurement

Brief descriptions of some of the capabilities of each of these features follow.

1. <u>LREPS Event Sequences</u>.--The LREPS event sequences provide the mechanism for the operation of the entire simulator. The simulator is organized as a set of events, which starts with a beginning of cycle event and finishes with the end of cycle event. Any type and any number of other events may be scheduled between these two. It is even possible to restart another simulation from the same place that a previous one stopped.

The types of events used by the simulator can be broken into three groups. These include: (a) the gateway routines, (b) the control routines, and (c) the operations routines. The individual routines that belong to each of these groups include:

a. Gateway routines

    1. Data read (input)

    2. Data out (report)

b. Control routines

    1. Locate (network initialization)

    2. Breakout (program stop)

    3. System control (utility functions)

    4. Switch set

c. Operations routines
   1. Forecast
   2. Invoice in (customer order processing)
   3. Production (read production file)
   4. Inventory management
   5. Customer order generation
   6. Reorder shipment arrival
   7. Check backorder queue
   8. Reorder processing
   9. Internal production (production generation)
   10. Pooling

These three groups of events make up the three subsystems of the simulator. Each routine makes up an event which may be scheduled independently of any other event processed by the simulator.

2. Production Policy.--Even though the LREPS simulator is not basically a production model, it can be used to model the interface between the production function and the physical distribution function. This can aid in simulating and studying the service and availability attributes which are occurring at the production point.

The LREPS simulator offers three different types of production modeling. Using one of these three events, it is generally possible to model almost any type of production policy that is currently being used or that might want to be tested. Combinations of all policies may be used where it is desired. The three forms of production are infinite production, scheduled production, and production generation. These routines provide a means of simulating the interface between the actual production function and the actual physical distribution function, rather than to actually simulate the production function.

The simplest production routine to use is infinite production. This routine is used primarily when production does not have an effect on the distribution function. It may be used when product availability at the plant is not a problem. The inventory at the production point can be preset to any arbitrary level when it is intialized at the beginning of the simulation run. Then, whenever any order or reorder is received, the following manipulation is performed:

$$IOH(ITP) = IOH(ITP) + ROQ(ITP)$$
$$IOH(ITP) = IOH(ITP) - ROQ(ITP)$$

where

IOH(ITP) - Inventory on hand for tracked product group ITP.

ROQ(ITP) - Quantity on order for tracked product group ITP.

It is obvious that the net effect of this operation results in no change in the inventory level at the production point, but the sales will be noted.

The second means of modeling the production function allows for the use of scheduled production. It provides the most control over the production activity of the model. To use this option, the production quantities and times are defined outside of the model and are read in. There is no feedback between the model and the production function, so the amount of production is not affected by the activities in the simulator. When the model is simulating the period that the production is to occur, the corresponding quantity is added to inventory on hand as follows:

$$IOH(ITP) = IOH(ITP) + PRODQ(ITP,IDAY)$$

where

IOH(ITP) - Inventory on hand for tracked product group IPT.

PRODQ(ITP,IDAY) - Production quantity for tracked product group ITP to be produced on day IDAY.

The third means of production provides the most dynamic capabilities within the model. This method can allow the production function to respond to the timing and level of demand. Within this method, there are two variations which allow for production to a P-level option or a produce-to-order option. In either case, the inventory situation is reviewed only when scheduled. However, this can be scheduled at any interval, from daily to weekly to monthly, or anything in between. At each review period, the inventory status is checked and the model determines whether or not product is required. The quantity that is produced is determined by one of the following rules, depending on the option being used. If the P-level option is being used, then this stocking level is determined by the simulator, using parameters supplied by the input in a manner similar to the way that the S-level and ROP are determined for the inventory management routing. For the produce-to-order option, the stocking levels are not used. The rules for determining if production should be scheduled and what quantity should be scheduled are as follows:

P-level

If $IOH(ITP) < ROQ(ITP)$

then

$PRODQ(ITP,IDAY) = P\text{-}LEV(ITP) - IOH(ITP)$

where

IOH(ITP) - Inventory-on-hand for tracked product group ITP.

ROP(ITP) - The point in number of units of inventory at which it is necessary to schedule production for tracked product group ITP.

PRODQ(ITP,IDAY) - Production quantity that is scheduled to be produced and available during period IDAY for tracked product group ITP.

P-LEV(ITP) - The quantity of tracked product group ITP that is produced up to level. This level is set through the input parameters.

Produce to Order

If BOQ(ITP) < 0

then

PRODQ(ITP,IDAY) = BOQ(ITP)

where

BOQ(ITP) - Quantity that is currently on the backorder queue for tracked product group ITP.

PRODQ(ITP,IDAY) - Production quantity that will be available during period IDAY for tracked product group ITP.

Note that the first option will place some amount of product into inventory on hand, while the second one produces only enough to fill the orders that are on the backorder queue. This final means of production is the most dynamic, in that it can provide a means of simulating the interface between the production and logistics functions. Either of these will allow the simulation to model stockouts at the production point and the associated service characteristics.

3. Order Processing.--The LREPS order processing module provides the physical equivalent to inventory availability checking and order picking for the LREPS simulator. The order processing for both customer orders and warehouse reorders is handled in essentially the same manner, so the modules will be discussed jointly.

First, when any order is received, the inventory must be checked to ascertain whether or not the inventory-on-hand is sufficient to satisfy the quantity on the order for that particular tracked product. The mathematical formulation for this would be:

$$IOH(ITP) > ROQ(ITP)$$

where

IOH(ITP) - Inventory-on-hand for tracked product group ITP.

ROQ(ITP) - Quantity on the order being processed for tracked product group ITP.

If this relationship holds for all of the items on the order, then the entire order is picked and the shipment is set up. The picking process is accomplished via the following calculation:

$$NIOH(ITP) = IOH(ITP) - ROQ(ITP)$$

where

NIOH(ITP) - New inventory-on-hand after the quantity on the order has been picked for tracked product group.

IOH(ITP) - Inventory-on-hand prior to picking the order for tracked product group ITP.

ROQ(ITP) - Quantity on the order for tracked product group ITP.

If the relationship does not hold for all of the items on the order, then the stockout processing module must be performed. The module will take appropriate action for items whose order quantities cannot be filled. For both customer orders and distribution center reorders there are different options available for handling stockouts. The particular option to be used at each DC must be specified by the user prior to running a simulation.

The first option states that the order can either be held until it can be filled in full, or it can be shipped with the stockout condition unsatisfied. If the first option is chosen, then the entire order will be saved on the backorder queue until all of the items can be filled. The orders on the queue are reviewed every time a restock shipment is received or product is produced at the DC or plant where the order is being processed.

As there is enough inventory found for each item, the line is
picked and held. When the entire order is filled, the order
continues with the remainder of the shipment processing module.
The second option will cause the incomplete order to be shipped
as is. The unfilled portion of the order will be treated as
either a backorder or a stockout, depending on which is desired
by the modeler. However, for warehouse reorders, the simulator
will not allow an item to be stocked out; it must be backordered.
This option may also be specified by location prior to running
the simulation. Either of these two options may also specify
that the entire item is dropped from the order, or only the
quantity that cannot be filled by the inventory on hand.

In general, there are four methods of handling unsatisfied
stockout conditions. These are as follows:

    a. Lost Sales--Ship full lines only

$$LS(ITP) = LS(ITP) + ROQ(ITP)$$

$$ROQ(ITP) = 0$$

where

    LS(ITP) - Lost sales for tracked product group ITP.

    ROQ(ITP) - Quantity on the order for tracked product
      group ITP. Note that the quantity is set to zero
      after it has been added to lost sales.

    b. Lost Sales--Ship partial lines

$$LS(ITP) = LS(ITP) + ROQ(ITP) - IOH(ITP)$$

$$ROQ(ITP) = IOH(ITP)$$

$$IOH(ITP) = 0$$

where

    LS(ITP) - Lost Sales for tracked product group ITP.

    ROQ(ITP) - Quantity on the order for tracked product group
      ITP. Note that this is reset to the inventory on hand
      after the stockout has been accounted for.

IOH(ITP) - Inventory on hand for tracked product group ITP.

c. Backorder--Ship full lines only

$$BOQ(ITP) = BOQ(ITP) + ROQ(ITP)$$
$$ROQ(ITP) = 0$$

where

BOQ(ITP) - Quantity on backorder for tracked product group ITP. Eventually this line will be filled and shipped in full as another order.

ROQ(ITP) - Quantity on the order for tracked product group ITP.

d. Backorder--Ship partial lines

$$BOQ(ITP) = BOQ(ITP) + ROQ(ITP) - IOH(ITP)$$
$$ROQ(ITP) = IOH(ITP)$$
$$IOH(ITP) = 0$$

where

BOQ(ITP) - Quantity on backorder for tracked product group ITP.

ROQ(ITP) - Quantity on the order for tracked product group ITP. Note that this is reset to the inventory on hand after the backorder has been accounted for.

IOH(ITP) - Inventory on hand for tracked product group ITP.

In both cases, where the backorder capability is used, the items on the order which have been backordered are eventually filled and shipped as another order. The time that elasped while the order was being filled is accumulated and reported as backorder time for a measure of customer service.

This is one of the unique capabilities offered by the LREPS model. Each order is processed independently, so stockout conditions can be detected and processed much like it is actually done in reality. This allows the modeler to simulate and obtain an accurate and realistic measure of customer service.

4. <u>Inventory policy</u>.--The LREPS inventory management
module allows the model user to select from replenishment options,
review period options, replenishment source options, and replenishment sizes.

The inventory replenishment rules available by product
and by location include a restock and/or infinite inventory
option. The restock option can be either fixed order quantity
or order up to S-level, as follows:

a. Fixed Order Quantity

$$ROQ(ITP) = EOQ(ITP)$$
$$\text{if } IOH(ITP) \; ROP(ITP)$$

where:

$ROQ(ITP)$ = reorder quantity of tracked product ITP;

$EOQ(ITP)$ = economic order quantity set by LREPS
for tracked product ITP;

$ROP(ITP)$ = reorder point set by LREPS for tracked
product ITP;

$IOH(ITP)$ = inventory-on-hand of tracked product ITP.

b. Order up to S-level

$$ROQ(ITP) = S(ITP) - IOH(ITP) - QOO(ITP) + QOBO(ITP)$$
$$\text{if } IOH(ITP) \; ROQ(ITP)$$

where:

$ROQ(ITP)$ = reorder quantity of tracked product ITP;

$S(ITP)$ = the replenishment level set by LREPS
for tracked product ITP. In the program the variable
$S(ITP)$ is represented by the sum of $EOQ(ITP)$ and $ROP(ITP)$:

$IOH(ITP)$ = inventory-on-hand for tracked product IPT;

$QOO(ITP)$ = quantity which is currently on reorder but has
not arrived yet for tracked product ITP;

$QOBO(ITP)$ = quantity which is currently on the backorder
queu for tracked product ITP;

ROP(ITP) = reorder point set by LREPS for tracked
product ITP;

Any location and any product may be defined as having infinite
inventory. To use this option, the LREPS defines IOH(ITP) at
the beginning of a simulation and this level is maintained. It
is not necessary for any reordering to be done for that product.
This option is most useful for production facilities where it is
not necessary or useful to simulate production.

The user may define the length of the review period for
each node location. Let the variable N represent the review
period in simulation time periods. The inventory review process
will only occur at the location once every N days.

$$NXTREVU(IDC) = TODAY + N(IDC);$$

where:

NXTREVU(IDC) = the next day on which an inventory is to
take place for location IDC;

TODAY = the current period of simulation;

N(IDC) = the review cycle in simulation periods for
location IDC;

The next review period is recomputed only at review time.

It is possible to allow two different sources for a
tracked product group from any location. When a reorder is
necessary, a choice will be made to select a source for replenishment. The selection is based on probabilities which are input
as part of the supporting data base. The mathematical formulation is as follows:

$$SOURCE(ITR) = SOURCE\ 1(ITR)$$
$$if\ R < P$$
$$SOURCE(ITR) = SOURCE\ 2(ITR)$$
$$otherwise$$

where:

> SOURCE(ITR) = the actual source that will be used for product group ITR for this replenishment;
>
> SOURCE 1(ITR) = the primary replenishment source for product group ITR;
>
> SOURCE 2(ITR) = the secondary replenishment source for product group ITR;
>
> R = a uniformly distributed random variable which may have a value > 0 and < 1;
>
> P = a value between 0 and 1, which specifies the proportion of times that SOURCE 1(ITR) should be chosen on a probabalistic basis; may be 1 but it may not be 0;

It is possible to force reorder quantities to be in pallet size increments. This option is useful only when the order up to S-level replenishment option is to be used. It is possible to round the reorder quantity either up to or down to the next multiple of a pallet size.

     5.   <u>Warehouse Operating Policy</u>.--The warehouse policy of the LREPS simulator is not an event itself, but is integrated into a group of other events. One of the unique features of the LREPS model is that it keeps an actual inventory for multiple products for multiple locations. This allows the model to be a very effective tool to study the effects of different warehousing strategies on the cost and service characteristics of a logistics system.

There are two basic attributes of warehousing in the LREPS model that make it ideal for testing warehousing policy. The model maintains an actual count of inventory on hand, and the temporal dimension of the model allows for time related cost and service characteristics of a policy. Even though these are two different attributes, their effect on the simulator is integrated, so their joint effect on the model will be discussed. The three primary areas that are affected by these attributes are costing, warehouse stocking, and service. These three areas are key producers of the dynamics of the LREPS model.

The two attributes affect costing by allowing time
dependent costing. This can provide an accurate measure of
storage costs, regardless of the manner in which they are calculated. This also allows inventory to be costed directly from
the average inventory in units by tracked product group. Using
corresponding report periods it is possible to compute the
inventory and storage costs on a monthly or even a bi-monthly
basis. For example, this would allow the stock to be charged
for an entire month if it arrived before the 15th, or for a half
of a month if it arrived later. This would allow various options
to be tested that might lower storage cost, such as scheduled
distribution. The costs may be based on the value, units, or
weight of the goods. Handling costs are computed on an in and
out basis as the goods are moved through each warehouse or plant.

The second area, warehouse stocking, can provide a tool
for testing various warehouse strategies. Besides the capability
of testing stocking policies, such as where products are stocked,
which static models may do, it is also possible to test more
involved operations problems, such as break-bulk, automated, or
across-the-dock operations. An inventory and stocking policy
can be developed which would simulate each of these options.
For example, a location which does not stock any products but
has the ability to backorder all of them is operating very
similarly to a break bulk point. Various lead time and inventory
level characteristics may be used to simulate other changes in
the logistics system, such as automation or central order processing. It is also possible to force pallet sized orders to
study their effect on handling cost. Since each order and
reorder is processed independently, and since the simulator has
a temporal dimension, the simulator provides a much better tool
than would a static model for testing operating procedures in a
warehouse.

The final area of interest which can be studied more readily through the use of a dynamic rather than a static simulation is service. Since the model does have a temporal as well as a spatial element, service can be measured within a time period. The service criteria measured here is whether or not the quantity desired is in stock. If it is not, service level will be affected adversely. Most static simulators do not confront this problem or, if they do, deal with it only on a probabalistic basis. However, for the LREPS simulator there is an inventory-on-hand available for each period; whenever the quantity desired is greater than this level, a stockout condition occurs and can be measured. The amount then can be treated either as a stockout or a backorder. A backorder will eventually be filled when stock is available and the out of stock time will be recorded. Using this capability, it is possible to study the effect of stockouts on system performance because of the dynamic nature of the model. For example, a stockout at the manufacturing level of the system may have a rippling effect on the remainder of the distribution system.

6. Shipment Policy.--Shipments to demand units and to other DCs are processed in a similar manner. For each order there are four factors which influence the selection of a shipment policy for replenishment as well as customer orders. The questions that these factors answer include: (a) are there any stockouts on the order; (b) can the shipment be pooled; (c) what is the weight of the shipment; and (d) are there any special flags that signal that special processing is required. The answers will determine the shipment policy and attributes of the order. These include whether or not the shipment will be pooled, the transit time required for the shipment to arrive at its destination, and the freight rate that will be used for the shipment.

Since the LREPS model is primarily an operations simulator,
the shipping policy decisions are made in a manner which is similar to how actual shipping decisions are made, on an order by
order basis. Each order is processed independently, and the
appropriate action is taken.

The first factor that affects the shipping policy is
whether or not any stockouts occurred on the order. If there
is no stockout, the processing continues. A stockout will cause
the line either to be dropped from the order or to be placed on
the backorder queue. The remainder of the order, if any, is
processed in the normal manner. After a replenishment is received
and the backorder is satisfied, the backordered position of the
order will be shipped out as another shipment.

Prior to actually shipping the order, the shipment policy
module will decide whether or not the shipment can be pooled
with other shipments. In order for a shipment to be pooled,
the source destination pair must belong to a pool group. All
pooling operations are done by this pool group. If the shipment
is to be pooled, the simulator will put the order on the queue
that is maintained for the pool group. The order will be removed
from the queue and shipped under one of two conditions: either
the maximum pooling weight has been obtained, or the allowable
pool time has elapsed, so all shipments must be cleared. The
above options will also allow the simulation of scheduled distribution.

In either case, the processing of the order will eventually
continue by selecting the weight break in which it will be shipped.
If the order is not pooled, then the weight of the order will be
used to select a weight break; if it is pooled, the total weight
of all of the shipments on the pool queue is used to select
the weight break. After the weight break has been chosen, the

appropriate rate for the DC-DC link or for the DC-DU link can be found. That portion of the shipment which is shipped across the link is costed at the rate which is applicable to the specific link. At the same time that the transportation rate is chosen, the simulated transit time is also determined. The transit time is obtained by using a Monte-Carlo technique, as follows:

Let t_1, t_2, t_3, t_4, and t_5 be five possible transit times in simulation periods, so that $t_i \leq t_{i+1}$. The cumulative probability function for these times are p_1 through p_5, with the following relationship holding $0 \leq p_1 \leq p_2 \leq p_3 \leq p_4 \leq p_5 = 1.0$. Whenever a transit time is required for the simulation, a random variable $r(0 \ r \ 1.0)$ is generated and is checked against each value of p in sequential order. When $r \leq p_i$, the process is terminated and the corresponding t_i is assigned as the transit time.

The fourth factor which can influence the shipping policy is an element which is only possible in simulation. This includes special cases, such as customer pickups or special stockout handling procedures. These are handled on a case by case basis, but they can add an additional degree of flexibility to solve the problem. The flags set in LREPS may specify that special freight rates should be used or the order should be handled in a particular way.

When all of these factors have been accounted for, the shipment may be simulated. The shipping weight of the order has been determined, so the rate and the time may be found. The order is placed in the event queue to be processed as a "shipment arrival" in "transit time" days.

7. Customer Service Measurement.--The customer service characteristics of the distribution system provides one of the primary areas where a dynamic simulator is more advantageous than a static model. The means of measurement of customer service include both order cycle times and out of stock conditions. Both

types of customer service characteristics are measured for
customer orders and warehouse restocks, and are reported independently.

One measure of customer service is the order cycle time.
This is the total time it takes from when the order leaves to
customer until the shipment arrives. The model divides the
total order cycle time into four categories, denoted by T1, T2,
T3, and T4. Each category is composed of one facet of the order
cycle time, and each can be reported independently so that the
modeler can determine the problem areas of his customer service.

The T1 component reflects the order communication time,
the time it takes for an order to be transmitted by the customer
until it is received by the company's order processing system.
This could reflect a telephone call, mail, or entry in a computer
terminal. The type of communications system will determine its
time and consistency. The T1 time can be different for each
customer-warehouse and each warehouse-plant link if necessary.
The method of computing T1 is as follows:

T1TIME is a base number of periods below which the communication time never gets. T1VAR is a pointer to one of the
internal probability distributions within the model. It is
a cumulative density function, so that $0 \leq p_1 \leq p_2 \leq p_3 \leq p_4 \leq p_5 = 1$.
Each time a value for T1 is desired, a uniformly distributed
random number r is generated with a value between 0 and 1,
and is compared against each value of p_i while i varies from
1 to 5. When $r \leq p_i$ the value of i is added to T1TIME to arrive
at the communication time that will be simulated for this
order. Thus the communication time has a possible value of
from T1TIME + 1 to T1TIME + 5.

The second component of the order cycle time group is T2,
or order processing time. This reflects the elapsed time for an
individual order to be processed through all necessary clerical

and computer channels, as well as the time necessary to pick the goods from inventory and pack them for shipment. This value can be different for each warehouse and plant location. The computation for T2, which is identical to that for T1, is as follows:

T2TIME is a base number of periods below which the processing time is never encountered. T2TIME may be zero. T2VAR is a pointer to one of the internal probability distributions within the model. It is a cumulative density function, so that $0 \leq p_1 \leq p_2 \leq p_3 \leq p_4 \leq p_5 = 1$. Each time a value for the corresponding T2 is desired, a uniformly distributed random number r is generated with a value between 0 and 1. This number r is compared against each value of p while i varies from 1 to 5. When $r \leq p_i$ the value of i is added to T2TIME. If T2VAR is zero the resulting value of i will be zero by definition. This would be the T2 as simulated for this order. So the order process time has the possible values of 0 or from T2TIME + 1 to T2TIME + 5.

The third component of the order cycle time is T3, or backorder time. This is the time that an order must wait on the backorder queue before the out of stock portion can be shipped. T3 is computed when an order is taken off the backorder queue by subtracting the date when the order was placed on the backorder queue from the current date. The measure of backorder time can give the modeler an idea of the effect of current inventory policy on customer service.

The final component of the order cycle time group is T4, or transportation time. This reflects the shipping time from the warehouse to the customer, or from the plant to the warehouse. There are different transit times for different links; within links there may be different times reflecting the use of different modes of transportation. The method for finding an appropriate

transit time for a shipment is different from the previous ones,
and will be explained further.

The input for the model allows for up to 5 different values
to be input for possible transit times. These times T_i may
have any integral value. A pointer T4VAR is also supplied
with each set of transit times. This also points to one of
the cumulative density functions defined within the model,
so that $0 \leq p_1 \leq p_2 \leq p_3 \leq p_4 \leq p_5 = 1$. Each time a value for T4 is
desired, a uniformly distributed random number r is generated
with a value between 0 and 1. The value of r is compared
against each value of p_i while i varies from 1 to 5. When
$r \leq p_i$, the corresponding value of T_i is chosen as the transit
time. So, the values of the T_i themselves are used as the
transit time.

The order cycle time, as simulated, is the sum of these
four variables. The standard output includes the average and
standard deviation of each of the components for each location.
Also available in the standard report system is a summary of
order cycle time within periods. For this report, up to eight
period values may be input prior to the simulation in ascending
order. The number of orders and the dollar value of the orders
are placed in the appropriate accumulator. The resulting reports
show the percentage of orders and dollars within n days, with n
being one of the service thresholds input. The result provides
an accurate means of looking at the customer service characteristics of the system being simulated.

The second measure of customer service views the out of
stock situation at each of the locations. This measure reflects
whether or not an out of stock condition occurred and, if it did,
whether it be treated as a stockout or a backorder. If the stockout option is used in the order processing routine, the occurrance
of the stockout along with the amount of the stockout is recorded.

It is then possible to report the number of stockouts, the volume of the stockouts, and the percentage of sales that were stocked out. When the backorder option is used in order processing, slightly more service information is made available. When a backorder occurs, the simulator records this, along with the amount of the backorder. When the order is taken off the queue, the backorder time is also accumulated. Finally, the average quantity on backorder is accumulated in a manner simular to the way the average inventory is developed. All of this information is available on the standard reports as well as the proportion of orders and quantity that is backordered. Both the backorder and stockout information are available by warehouse location and by product.

The above events are representative of the options offered by a dynamic simulator. These and other options of the LREPS model provide management with a powerful tool to assist in distribution operations planning.

CHAPTER VIII

APPLICATIONS TO LOGISTICS SYSTEMS ANALYSIS

Introduction

In this final chapter, the emphasis is on the application
of the analytical techniques to logistics systems analysis. The
first part of the chapter discusses the approach to logistics systems
design. Within this framework, applications are presented for
dynamic programming, mixed integer programming, and simulation. The
final portion of the chapter is devoted to general suggestions and
considerations which need to be considered in logistics systems
design.

Approach to Logistics Systems Design

The various approaches to business logistics systems design
are quite similar conceptually, although different in detail due to
experiences and background of the designers. Each approach should
include the basic steps of analysis or problem solving, with the
required detail to make the approach more specific for logistics
systems analysis.

All of the approaches have essentially the same objective--
to assist management in the continuous process of evaluation of
alternatives through implementation of logistic system design
improvements, in terms of cost and/or customer service (profit
contributions). In simplified terms, an approach can be defined
as three phases:[1]

---

[1] O. K. Helferich, "Working Paper--Logistics Systems Design
Manual" (Cleveland Consulting Associates, Lansing, Michigan, 1977).

Phase I: Project Definition and Organization
Phase II: Analysis and Recommendation
Phase III: Implementation

This approach has proven workable on many logistics systems design projects. Phase I provides management with a project work plan, including the estimate of required resources and expected benefits. Prior to committing major people-time, materials, and/or other dollars, management has the information to make a reasonable "go/no go" decision on proceeding to Phase II. This is important, since frequently Phase II requires a factor of five to ten times the resources of Phase I. The decision to proceed should be made only when Phase I output indicates acceptable cost/benefits will result from Phases II and III.

Although the specific tasks to achieve the objectives for Phase I will vary by project, the general approach to Phase I consists of the following tasks:

1. Review the present logistics situation to define costs, customer service levels, and logistics operations to provide a basis for evaluating alternate logistic systems alternatives (the logistics audit).

2. Interview key management personnel and each member of the project team to insure understanding of management objectives and to gain background for defining the specific questions and logistics systems alternatives to be evaluated in the study.

3. Develop a preliminary list of critical management study assumptions, logistic operating and marketing policies, and guidelines that are critical to the evaluation of the logistic alternatives and to the data collection effort.

4. Specify the required evaluation criteria and study outputs in terms of cost and customer service variables.

5. Select the solution technique (model) based on the appropriateness for the alternatives to be evaluated,

      ease of preparing input data, cost and time
estimates, and projected future utilization.

6. Define the specific data requirements, provide the
data formats, and assist in describing the data
collection procedures.

7. Outline any major manual analyses required to
supplement the computer model results to further
evaluate the impact on cost and customer service.

8. Conduct a working meeting with the project team to
review findings, conclusions, model selection
criteria, and preliminary project work plan.

9. Estimate the benefits in terms of cost reduction
(profit improvements) and/or customer service
improvements expected from the study.

10. Recommend, as appropriate, any suggestions for
immediate cost and/or customer service improvements
identified in Phase I by the joint project team.

11. Define project management procedures, including the
division of responsibilities between the user and
the technical staff, and assist in estimating the
manpower, computer, and other support requirements
for the study.

12. Develop a detailed work plan for Phase II.

13. Develop a final cost estimate for Phase II.

14. Prepare a brief report to communicate the results
of Phase I.

The joint effort of the user's staff and the technical
staff working together as a project team on Phase I improves the
probability of good communication throughout the study, and insures
that maximum effort will be placed on the critical issues and
variables.

The objective of Phase II is to define the best logistics
system improvements consistent with the cost and service objectives
established in Phase I. The general approach, assuming a computer

model is utilized as the primary solution technique, includes the following task groups:

1. Perform the data collection and preparation required for the model selected and the logistics alternatives to be evaluated.

2. Utilize the model to represent the existing logistics system for a previous operating period, to serve as a reference or comparison against all alternatives evaluated, and to develop credibility with management that the model selected can represent the user's logistics system.

3. Utilize the model results and supporting analyses to assist in defining the best logistics system for the selected planning horizon.

4. Conduct a series of work sessions involving the modeling or technical staff and user's staff (the total project team) to review model results, agree on conclusions and recommendations, and to develop a detailed implementation program.

The objective of Phase III is to implement the recommendations to achieve the expected cost/service improvements. The tasks of Phase III vary greatly, depending on the project and the logistics design (redesign) proposed. An example of these three phases for a typical project, where the objective is an evaluation of the business logistics system utilizing a computer model, is presented in Figure 8.1. Other approaches to systems design for specific logistics models such as computer simulation and optimization can be found in the literature.[1]

---

[1] D. J. Bowersox, Bernard J. LaLonde, and Edward W. Smykay, Readings in Physical Distribution Management (New York: The Macmillan Company, 1969), Chapter 13; D. J. Bowersox, Logistical Management (New York: The Macmillan Company, 1974), Chapter 11, p. 343; Benjamin S. Blanchard, Logistics Engineering and Management (Englewood Cliffs, N.J.: Prentice-Hall, Inc., 1974), Chapter 6, pp. 117-118; and Arnoldo C. Hax, "The Design of Large Scale Logistics Systems: A Survey and an Approach," Technical Report No. 106 (Cambridge, Mass.: M.I.T. Press, Operations Research Center, October, 1974).

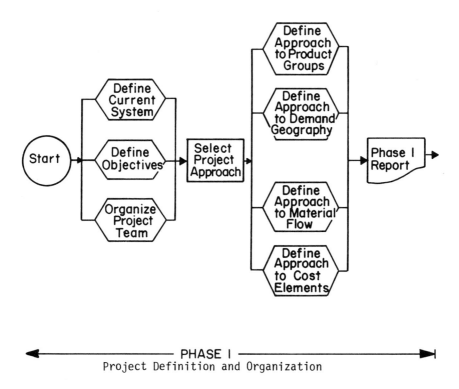

PHASE I
Project Definition and Organization

Figure 8.1. Distribution Strategy Study Task Flow Diagram.

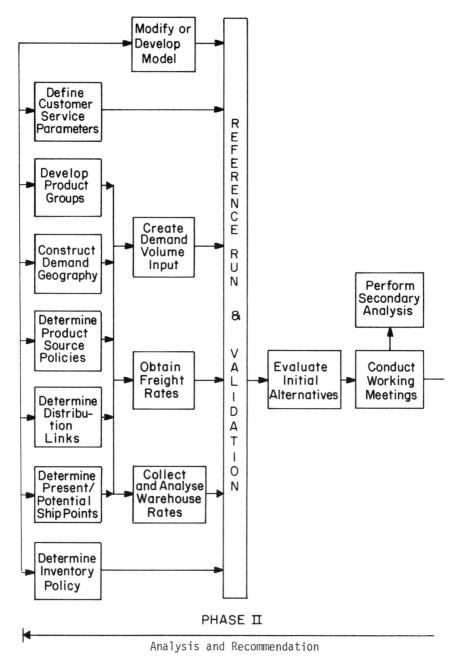

PHASE II

Analysis and Recommendation

Figure 8.1. Continued

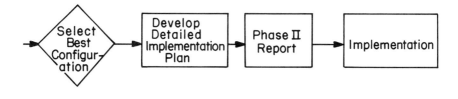

Figure 8.1. Continued.

Application of Logistics Systems
Design Techniques

This section consists of brief summaries of selected applied total logistics systems design techniques. The applications presented include:

1. Dynamic programming--a vehicle replacement study
2. Mixed integer linear programming--a food processor application
3. Static simulation model--a consumer product application
4. Dynamic simulation model--an industrial chemicals application and a small package consumer product application

A Dynamic Programming Model Application

Application of dynamic programming to problems in which all decision variables are known, either from experience or as determined by empirical methods, with uncertainty removed, is a simple recursive exercise. Computation for decisions (states) greater than three becomes very cumbersome, even when automated procedures are employed. As an illustration, the problem of deciding the least costly time to replace equipment will be solved using dynamic programming techniques.

Suppose a firm is concerned with finding the most cost advantageous time to replace vehicles in its truck fleet. Further, let us assume that the performance of the vehicle is unchanged during its lifetime, a result of more and more expenditures each year for maintenance as the vehicle ages. A new vehicle costs $18,000. Figure 8.2 shows the annual maintenance cost and trade in value for a period of six years. Additionally, time value of the money used in the out-years will not be considered. Then the notation for the objective function will be

$$f_N^{(n)} = \text{Total cost of N stages (given that the vehicle is (n) years old at the start).}$$

Year (n)	Operations and Maintenance Costs $M_o(n)$	Resale Values $R_s(h)$
1	3600	12000
2	4200	8000
3	4800	6000
4	5400	4500
5	6000	3000
6	7200	1800
7	9000	1000

Figure 8.2.   Vehicle Annual Costs and Resale Values ($).

Dynamic programming decomposes the decision process into a single stage problem followed by a problem of (N-1) stages, which are broken down successively into a series of single stages. Each year, therefore, comprises a single optimum decision, which is a requirement for minimizing the vehicle costs. The serial solution of the N stages, then the (n) states provides a tableaux of the various decision values for the manager.

Beginning the calculation process, the elements of the decision are whether to buy or to retain. The lower of the two values is the one the manager chooses. If the truck is replaced at the start of stage N, there will be an initial cost of $18,000 minus the resale value of the truck currently in the fleet, plus the operations and maintenance cost of the new truck during its first year of service. The sum of these costs, if the vehicle is replaced are

$$18000 - R_s(n) + M_o(n) + f(n - 1)^{(1)}$$

If the vehicle is not replaced, the costs incurred will be

$$M_o(n + 1) + f(n - 1)^{(n + 1)}$$

and the lesser cost of these two decisions should be the one
selected by a rational manager.

At the start of stage N, the best alternative is

$$fn^{(n)} = \min[(M_0 (n + 1) + f_{(n-1)}(n + 1))$$

$$18000 - R_s(n) + M_0(n) + f_{(n-1)}{}^{(1)}]$$

This selection shows how to compute $fn^{(n)}$ when you already know
$f_{(n-1)}{}^{(n)}$ beginning at N = 1. It also relates $f_1{}^{(n)}$ to $f_0{}^{(n)}$,
which is the cost of zero future stages when beginning with an
n-year old truck. It is the negative of the resale value of the
truck when it is no longer needed.

The equation for $f_1{}^{(n)}$ is:

$$f_1{}^{(n)} = \min[M_0{}^{(n+1)} - R_s{}^{(n+1)}, \; 18000 - R_s(n) + M_0(1) - R_s{}^{(1)}]$$

and $$f_1{}^{(1)} = \min[4200 - 8000, \; 18000 - 12000 + 3600 - 12000]$$

$$f_1{}^{(1)} = \min[-3800, -2400]$$

$$= -3800 \text{ (retain the vehicle)}$$

Performing this calculation for each of n years values
given provides the following decisions:

$$f_1{}^{(2)} = -1200 \text{ (retain)}$$

$$f_1{}^{(3)} = \quad 900 \text{ (retain)}$$

$$f_1{}^{(4)} = \quad 3000 \text{ (retain)}$$

$$f_1{}^{(5)} = \quad 5400 \text{ (retain)}$$

$$f_1{}^{(6)} = \quad 7800 \text{ (replace)}$$

A six-year-old truck would always be replaced, since the operating
costs continue to increase and resale values decrease. Our calculations stop at state 6.

The equation for stage 2 is

$$f_2^{(n)} = \min[(M_0^{(n+1)} + f_1^{(n+1)}, (18000 - R_s^{(n)} + M_0^{(1)} + f_1^{(1)})]$$

Since the decision maker knows $f_1^{(n)}$ (from our previous calculations), he can calculate $f_2^{(n)}$. These are as shown:

$$f_2^{(1)} = \min[M_0^{(2)} + f_1^{(2)}, 18000 - R_s^{(1)} + M_0^{(1)} + f_1^{(1)}]$$

$$= \min[4200 - (-1200), 18000 - 12000 + 3600 + (-3800)$$

$$= \min 3000, 5800$$

$$= 3000 \text{ (retain)}$$

Repeating the calculations as shown previously for the first stage, the decision values are as shown below:

$$f_2^{(2)} = 5700 \text{ (retain)}$$

$$f_2^{(3)} = 8400 \text{ (retain)}$$

$$f_2^{(4)} = 11400 \text{ (retain)}$$

$$f_2^{(5)} = 14800 \text{ (replace the vehicle)}$$

$$f_2^{(6)} = 16000 \text{ (replace the vehicle)}$$

The third stage can now be calculated as done for stage 2. These values are:

$$f_3^{(n)} = \min[M_0^{(n+1)} + f_2^{(n+1)}, 18000 - R_s^{(n)} + M_0^{(1)} + f_2^{(1)}]$$

Therefore f_3 is equal to

$$= \min[4200 + 5700, 18000 - 12000 + 3600 + 3000]$$
$$= \min (9900), (12600)$$
$$= 9900 \text{ (retain the vehicle)}$$

The remainder of the third stage values are:

$$f_3^{(2)} = 13200 \text{ (retain)}$$

$$f_3^{(3)} = 16800 \text{ (retain)}$$

$$f_3^{(4)} = 20100 \text{ (replace)}$$

$$f_3^{(5)} = 21600 \text{ (replace)}$$

$$f_3^{(6)} = 22800 \text{ (replace)}$$

Since each stage has two alternatives, the number of paths in the network is equal to 2^N; if the decision is made in 4 stages, there would be 16 decision paths at $N = 0$. Rather than constructing the network diagram, our method of calculation allows the construction of a table. If stages are added to the decision process, each addition doubles the number of paths in the diagram. The table, on the other hand, adds only one column to the table.

n	N=0	N=1	N=2	N=3	N=4	N=5
1	-12000	-3800	3000	9900	17400	25800
2	-8000	-1200	5700	13200	21600	30300
3	-6000	900	8400	16800	25500R	32400R
4	-4500	3000	11400	20100R	27000R	34500R
5	-3000	5400	14800R	21600R	28500R	36000R
6	-1800	7800R	16000R	22800R	29700R	32700R

Figure 8.3. Decision Values ($fn^{(n)}$).

R = Replace the Vehicle

The use of dynamic programming techniques develops the various optimal decisions for the firm. This example, of course, does not consider either rental or lease of vehicles, nor the purchase of used vehicles. Use of these options increases the number of paths in the network. The use of this technique for finite life resources provides a powerful tool for the decision maker.

A Mixed Integer Linear Programming Model Application

A mixed integer linear program[1,2] was applied to one of the nation's largest food canners and packers with several hundred product labels and annual sales over $450 million. The firm produced tomato products, cooking oil, matches, puddings, shortening, and many other products at 14 locations, and distributed nationally through 12 centers. Transportation was via common carrier rail, common carrier, and contract truck carriers, with extensive use of the storage-in-transit privilege for large rail-supplied customers.

The firm serviced each customer from a single distribution center for all products. This was a convenience for the customer through simplified accounting and communication systems and improved marketing functions. It permitted economics-of-scale in delivery, and consistency in order cycle.

The reason for the planning study was pressing distribution center expansion and relocation issues. The development of a computer-based model and its associated data required a coordinated team effort by personnel from accounting, data processing, marketing,

---

[1]A. M. Geoffrion, "A Guide to Computer-Assisted Methods for Distribution Systems Planning," Sloan Management Review, Winter, 1975, pp. 17-41.

[2]A. M. Geoffrion, "Working Paper No. 219: Distribution Systems Configuration Planning: Case Study in the Application of a New Computer-Based Method," Western Management Science Institute, Graduate School of Management, University of California, Los Angeles, CA.

316

operations research, production, traffic, and other functional
specialties. More than one man-year of work over six months was
required. Here is a simplified summary of facts and structural
assumptions on which the computer model was utilized:

1. Hundreds of products were aggregated into 17
    product groups by plant capability to make them,
    production technology, and gross-to-net shipping
    weight ratios.
2. The production capacity (CWT/yr.) of each of the
    14 plants is a given for each product group.
3. Distribution center locations were limited to a
    candidate list of 45 cities.
4. Operative distribution centers must be between
    stipulated lower and upper volume limits.
5. Thousands of customers were aggregated into 121
    customer zones by zip codes.
6. Annual demand for each product group by customer
    zone must be met.
7. All customers in a zone must continue to be
    serviced from a single distribution center for
    all products.
8. Distribution center locations must service a
    customer zone within a maximum number of days
    delivery time.
9. Differential production costs ($/CWT) are given
    when there is a significant difference between
    unit costs at different plants for a given product
    group.
10. The cost of each distribution center is expressed
    as a "fixed" charge if a location is used plus a
    "variable" cost ($/CWT) applied to the total
    annual throughout volume over all product groups
    (see Figure 8.2).

11. For each product group and possible plant-to-
distribution center transportation link, a freight
rate ($/CWT) is specified.

12. For each product group and possible distribution
center-to-customer zone line, a freight rate
($/CWT) is specified.

13. Transit rail rates are used when applicable.

Five changes were recommended in the firm's distribution
center locations involving the movement of existing facilities to
different cities and the opening of new facilities. The three
most urgent changes were implemented by the company. Improvements
in the assignment of customers to distribution center were also
implemented. The changes identified by the mixed integer linear
programming model cut annual logistics cost by $1 million.

A Static Simulation Model Application

The company used to illustrate the static model has a
broad line of consumer goods. Annual sales are approximately 30
million dollars; goods are sold through 100 market areas covering
the entire United States. Finished goods are processed in San
Francisco and Chicago. Each of these plants has a plant warehouse
that stocks a full line of products. The system utilizes 19
pre-finishing lines to supply the material for the final manufacturing processing. The existing system utilizes public warehouses
in Chicago and Memphis. Approximately 230 million pounds of
finished product are shipped annually. Shipments to customers
are made via rail and truck common carriers from the public and
plant warehouses.

The expected sales level for next year is $28,304,622.
Marketing believes that there is a high probability that sales
will increase from 15 to 25 per cent for the market areas in
the Eastern region. This is referred to as the Sales Level 2
forecast.

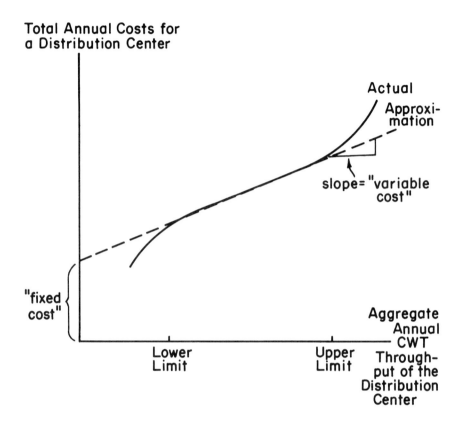

Figure 8.4. Hypothetical Approximation to Total Annual DC-Related
Costs as a Function of Aggregate Annual Throughput
(assuming that the most cost-effective design is
used at each level of throughput).

Management would like to identify the impact on volume
through the warehouses and the performance level for Sales Level 1
in terms of total cost and service for several alternative warehouse configurations. Likewise, they are interested in the same
evaluation for the Sales Level 2 forecast. In this case demonstra-
tion, the summary results of two simulation runs are presented in
Figures 8.5 and 8.6 to illustrate the capabilities of simulation
for logistics systems analysis, planning and design.

LOGISTICS COSTS

SYSTEM DESCRIPTION COST COMPONENT	EXISTING SYSTEM 2 PLANTS 2 PLANT WAREHOUSES 2 PUBLIC WAREHOUSES	ALTERNATIVE SYSTEM 2 PLANTS 2 PLANT WAREHOUSES 7 PUBLIC WAREHOUSES	COST DECREASE (INCREASE)
Production Costs	$19,849,925	$19,685,331	$ 164,594
Outbound Transportation Costs	2,741,482	1,693,200	1,048,282
Inbound Transportation Costs	981,608	759,132	222,476
Warehousing Operating Costs	416,839	464,349	(47,510)
Warehouse Fixed Costs	2,300,000	2,300,000	0
Inventory Costs	624,806	720,480	(95,674)
TOTAL LOGISTICS COSTS	$26,914,660	$25,622,492	$1,292,168

Figure 8.5. Consumer Product Logistics System. Performance Level: Sales Level 1.

CUSTOMER SERVICE
FRACTION OF SALES DOLLARS
WITHIN MILE INTERVALS

MILE INTERVALS	EXISTING SYSTEM	ALTERNATIVE SYSTEM	SERVICE INCREASE (DECREASE)
100 Miles	0.0607	0.1059	0.0452
200	0.1762	0.2962	0.1200
300	0.2564	0.3800	0.1236
500	0.4856	0.6368	0.1512
800	0.6428	0.7951	0.1523
1000	0.7777	0.8264	0.0487
1500	0.8736	0.8817	0.0081
2000 Miles	0.8941	0.9290	0.0349

Figure 8.5. Continued.

321

LOGISTICS COSTS

SYSTEM DESCRIPTION COST COMPONENT	EXISTING SYSTEM 2 PLANTS 2 PLANT WAREHOUSES 2 PUBLIC WAREHOUSES	ALTERNATIVE SYSTEM 2 PLANTS 2 PLANT WAREHOUSES 7 PUBLIC WAREHOUSES	COST DECREASE (INCREASE)
Production Costs	$20,841,564	$20,669,064	$ 172,500
Outbound Transportation Costs	2,920,387	1,782,683	1,137,704
Inbound Transportation Costs	1,040,177	817,046	223,131
Warehousing Operating Costs	437,353	487,623	(50,270)
Warehouse Fixed Costs	2,300,000	2,300,000	0
Inventory Costs	656,538	757,042	(100,504)
TOTAL LOGISTICS COSTS	$28,196,019	$26,813,458	$1,382,561

Figure 8.6. Consumer Product Logistics System. Performance Level: Sales Level 2.

CUSTOMER SERVICE
FRACTION OF SALES DOLLARS
WITHIN MILE INTERVALS

MILE INTERVALS	EXISTING SYSTEM	ALTERNATIVE SYSTEM	SERVICE INCREASE (DECREASE)
100 Miles	0.0578	0.1013	0.0435
200	0.1678	0.2964	0.1200
300	0.2466	0.3793	0.1327
500	0.4734	0.6350	0.1616
800	0.6346	0.7970	0.1624
1000	0.7817	0.8269	0.0452
1500	0.8750	0.8795	0.0045
2000 Miles	0.8947	0.9245	0.0298

Figure 8.6. Continued.

The results in this case study can be further summarized as follows:

	Existing System		Alternative		Change In	
	Total Costs (000)	Service %	Total Costs (000)	Service %	Total Costs (000)	Service %
Sales Level 1	$26,915	25.64	$25,623	38.00	-$1,292	+12.36
Sales Level 2	28,196	24.66	26,813	37.93	- 1,383	+13.27

As indicated by the results summary, the cost can be reduced while also achieving improvements in customer service at the critical 300-mile interval. This ideal situation does not always occur, but when it does, it eases the implementation decision.

A Dynamic Simulation Model
Application

The study objective in this industrial chemicals application was to evaluate the cost and service tradeoffs given different inventory levels for a logistics system with 20 warehouses and 2 manufacturing plants. The measure of customer service selected by the company was the in-stock rate, or the percentage of complete orders shipped. The current service level for the logistics system was an in-stock rate of 90% with a total logistics cost of $12,855,000. The specific goal was to define the costs for service levels substantially above the existing level of 91%. It was decided that the complete inventory cost versus service curve should be defined from the in-stock range of 89% to 98%.

The results for 89%, 91%, and 98% in-stock rates are presented in Figure 8.7. As expected, distribution center storage and inventory costs increase significantly with service level from the existing 91% to 98%, and decrease significantly from the 91%

Distribution Cost Centers

Customer Service Level Measured by Stock Availability
(Cost in Thousands [000] of Dollars)

	89% Alternative	91% Existing	95% Alternative	98% Alternative
Outbound Transportation	$ 4,080	$ 4,090	$ 4,100	$ 4,100
Inbound Transportation	1,980	1,960	1,970	1,920
DC Handling	2,340	2,340	2,340	2,310
DC Storage	260	325	440	690
Order Processing	2,390	2,390	2,390	2,370
Inventory Carrying	1,400	1,750	2,120	2,900
Total Distribution Costs	$12,450	$12,855	$13,360	$14,290

Total Cost Impact for Service Change from 91% Level

Cost Savings for reduction of service to 89% = $405,000
Cost Increase for increase of service to 95% = $505,000
Cost Increase for increase of service to 98% = $1,435,000

Incremental Cost Per Percentage of Service Change from 91% Level

Reduction from 91% to 89% = $(202,500)
Increase from 91% to 95% = $ 126,250
Increase from 91% to 98% = $ 205,000
Increase from 95% to 98% = $ 310,000

Incremental Sales for Breakeven Profits (000's of Dollars)

Net Profit as a % of Sales	89% Alternative	91% Existing	95% Alternative	98% Alternative
At 2% Net of Sales	(20,300)	0	25,300	71,800
At 4% Net of Sales	(10,100)	0	12,600	35,900
At 6% Net of Sales	(6,800)	0	8,400	23,900
At 8% Net of Sales	(5,100)	0	6,300	17,900
At 10% Net of Sales	(4,100)	0	5,100	14,400

Figure 8.7. Inventory Cost Versus Service.

to 89% level. The total annual cost increases to improve service
from 91% to 95% and 98% are $505,000 and $1,435,000, respectively.
The total annual cost savings possible if service is lowered to
89% is $405,000.

The plot of the inventory cost versus in-stock availability for many companies is a continuous smooth curve as shown
in Figure 8.8. The results in this study, shown in Figure 8.9,
were quite different from the theoretical curve of Figure 8.8.
The basic reason for the difference is the unusual demand pattern
for customer orders. The order frequency for this situation was
determined to be as follows:

PERCENT OF ORDERS	UNITS PER ORDER
25%	Less than 400
15%	Between 400 to 999
20%	Between 1,000 to 1,999
25%	Between 2,000 to 3,999
10%	Between 4,000 to 7,999
5%	Between 8,000 to 16,000
0%	Above 16,000

The curve illustrated in Figure 8.9 was substantiated by
numerous simulation runs and accepted by the company after a
detailed review. The relative slopes of the curve indicate that
it would be relatively inexpensive to increase service for each
one per cent between 91% to 95%, compared to the cost to increase
each one per cent between 95% to 98%. As shown in Figure 8.7,
the additional cost per each per cent of service increase between
91% to 95% is an average of $126,250; between 95% to 98%, the
additional cost per each per cent is an average of $310,000.
The additional cost for each percentage increment change was
developed in the study from the curve drawn by accurately
plotting results for various levels.

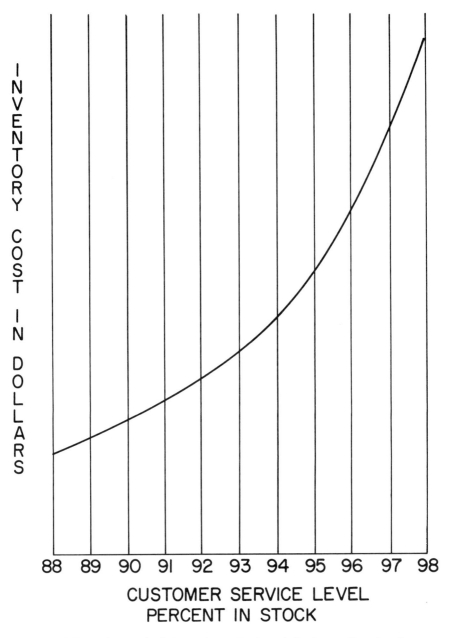

Figure 8.8. Theoretical Inventory Cost and Customer Service Curve.

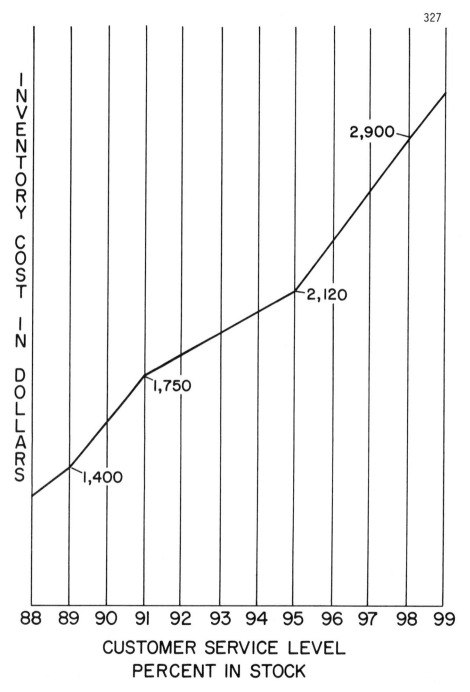

Figure 8.9.   Actual Inventory Cost and Customer Service Curve.

The results below 91% in-stock were also of interest to
the company, since a reduction of 2% to 89% could reduce costs by
$405,000. The distribution manager was concerned with marketing
management's desire to implement a 98% service level. Therefore,
a break-even profit analysis was developed. A summary, shown in
Figure 8.7, indicates the additional sales volume required to
achieve the current net profit, if inventory investment was
increased to provide 95% or 98% service. For example, at a net
profit of 6% on sales for 98% service, $23.9 million of additional
sales must be generated to achieve the same total net profit.
Likewise, if lower service of 89% is acceptable, sales could drop
$6.8 million before net profit would be less than the profits
achieved at 91%. If, on the other hand, it is assumed sales
would not drop for a reduction to a service level of 89%, the
increase in profit would be approximately $202,500, which would
be equivalent to an additional $6.8 million in sales. In this
situation, the company selected and implemented the 95% service
level.

The importance of this example is not the particular
values, but the fact that in-stock service level versus inventory
cost for a given firm does not necessarily follow the theoretical
curve illustrated in Figure 8.8. It also points out that knowledge of the actual curve for a distribution system definitely can
assist management in selecting the appropriate operating service
level to achieve greatest benefit from each dollar of inventory
investment.

A Second Dynamic Simulation
Model Application

In a study for a major consumer product merchandiser, the
objective was to improve service and possibly reduce costs for a
product line with an average retail store customer order size
of 40 pounds. The present system with 8 partial line distribution centers, had an operating cost of $1,256,500 and provided

an average customer order cycle time to 30 days, with a
standard deviation of 20 days. The order cycle time for the
customer's retail stores was found, after an extensive field
survey, to reach 50 days 30% of the time, and approximately
70 days 10% of the time.

After LREPS analysis and evaluation of the field test
data, one central full line DC and a revised order processing
system were recommended. The new distribution system provided
an average order cycle time of 14 days, with a standard
deviation of 4 days at an operation cost of $998,600 (Figure
8.10).

DISTRIBUTION COST CENTERS	8 PARTIAL LINE DCs	1 FULL LINE DC
Transportation Inbound to DCs	$ 233,400	$ 79,800
Warehouse Facilities and Equipment	150,000	84,000
Warehouse Handling and Storage	187,000	74,600
Order Processing	108,000	108,000
Transportation Outbound to Customer	163,600	398,200
Administration Overhead	180,000	80,000
Inventory Carrying Cost at 20%	234,500	174,000
TOTAL COST	$1,256,500	$998,600
CUSTOMER SERVICE Order cycle	30 days	14 days
Standard deviation of order cycle time	20 days	4 days

Figure 8.10. DC Configuration Versus Service Distribution Costs.

The cost savings for the revised system was $257,900, which is a 20.5% reduction in cost and a greater than twofold improvement in service based on order cycle time. Just as important was the reduction of the variation of order cycle time. The recommendations suggested by the LREPS analysis and the field survey were implemented, and after one year of actual experience, the expected improvements in performance were being achieved.

A Simulation Case Study Utilizing Both Static and Dynamic Models

The general approach to utilizing computer model(s) for strategic and tactical logistics systems analysis, planning and design, consists of the following phases:

Phase I: Problem Definition and Organization

Phase II: Analysis and Recommendation

Phase III: Implementation

This section presents appropriate comments on each task group, as related to an actual logistics planning situation.

Phase I: Problem Definition and Organization

The Phase I tasks discussed in this case study are situation analysis and model selection. The reader interested in tasks related to project timing, costs, work plan, etc, factors equally important in the conduct of a complex logistics study, is referred to another document.[1]

Situation Analysis.--This task consisted initially of performing an audit or situation analysis of the current logistical system. Based on the logistical audit, the scope of the problem, solution criteria and technique, strategic and operational planning horizons, data requirements and all other

---

[1] O. K. Helferich, "Working Paper--Logistics Systems Design Manual."

management assumptions and study parameters were defined. It was determined early in the logistical audit that the study would not require consideration of the raw materials subsystem or the production subsystem in the computer model. These subsystems of the logistics system were simple enough in this situation to evaluate manually. The distribution subsystem did require analysis utilizing the computer models. A summary of the situation analysis of the distribution subsystem is presented next.

The company distributes nationally approximately 100 product lines. Company sales are highly seasonal; they peak a few months in advance of the customer utilization period. The advance or early sales account for approximately 85% of annual sales. A price concession or incentive program of 5% to 10% is usually offered to customers who agree to purchase and accept early delivery. The advance sales are usually followed by a relatively moderate, but extremely important, period of highly profitable in-season sales which account for the remaining 15% of annual sales.

The advance or incentive ordering has resulted in two distinct patterns of logistical operations. First, during the incentive order program, products are not required immediately by customers. Thus, shipments are programmed at the convenience of the company to achieve the lowest possible total logistical cost. The incentive shipments are made from the closest possible manufacturing source. Product ordered on the incentive program must also be economically accessible through warehouses to facilitate customer order pickups. The delivery of incentive orders is accomplished on a scheduled basis to achieve full car and truck loads. Second, the logistical system must be very responsive to additional demand in-season. During this in-season period, sales generation is directly related to capability to deliver products within a short order cycle time; i.e., one day from order placement until delivery to customer.

Sales generally are highly concentrated in the Midwest, where 10 states represent 70% of annual sales. The customers are represented by 500 county groups selected as the ship-to demand points. A summary of the sales data for the reference year 1976 is as follows:

ANNUAL SALES - 1976
(000)

Dollars	$438,511.0	Cases	4,880.0
Weight lbs.	300,274.4	Lines	51.0
Cube ft^3	17,331.0	Orders	27.0

The logistical system consists of four basic types of facilities: 4 manufacturing plants, 6 in-transit warehouses, 20 full-line warehouses, and 4 partial-line warehouses. Prior to the study, these 34 locations were utilized to make customer shipments. The in-transit facilities serve two functions. First, storage is provided until customer demand justifies shipment. Second, the close proximity of in-transit facilities to manufacturing locations limits the risk of advanced shipment before the need occurs. All warehouses are public, with direct cost based on volume throughout and duration of storage.

The primary method of shipment from plants to field warehouses is via rail carload and some common carrier truckload. Shipments from field warehouses to customers normally move via truck. Approximately 30% of the volume is picked up by customers. Transportation accounts for approximately 45% of total logistics costs. Transit times were based upon the mode of transport and size of shipment. The transit times employed on LTL shipments were based upon a survey, whereas CL and TL transit times were derived from national service standards.

Orders are processed at a central office on a batch basis after entry via an order telecommunication network. The elapsed time from order entry to shipment release (in-transit status) from warehouse or plant location usually is not greater than 24 hours.

The company was concerned with two measures of customer service in the study. The first was the proximity of customers to a warehouse, based on distance (or transit time) from the customer to the nearest facility providing customer shipments. The second measure was the customer order cycle. Customer service requirements vary significantly between in-season and incentive order period. During the in-season period, customer orders are filled direct from warehouse stock in the field, thereby providing a high service level. During the incentive or advance order period, service time is secondary to realization of economy and routinization of logistical operations by achieving scheduled, minimum cost, volume shipments. Incentive order operations are not critical with respect to customer service, since the customer is ordering in advance of actual need.

These measures of customer service are significant because they provide a realistic estimate of the extent to which customers could engage in merchandise pickup if they desired. For example, assuming a customer would not travel overnight for a pickup, the total dollar sales within the 2-day period realistically represent the upper limit on potential customer pickups. The standard costs developed for the study included, but were not limited to, the following:

1. Order processing at a standard fixed cost per month with a variable cost per order.
2. Inventory at before tax cost of 18% per annum of average inventory per field warehouse location.
3. Handling and storage at the local rate applicable to each existing and potential facility, based on actual costs; appropriate storage rate applicable at in-transit warehouses.
4. Inbound transportation from plants and in-transit warehouses to field warehouses, based on point-to-point rates.

5. Transportation rates to customers based on a
combination of point-to-point and regression
equation rates.

6. Production costs.

The costs for the reference year 1976 were as follows:

ANNUAL DISTRIBUTION COSTS 1976
(000)

Transportation to warehouses	$3,867.8	
Transportation to customers	3,801.3	
Total Transportation		$7,669.1
Storage		1,463.0
Handling		739.0
Ordering		555.6
Inventory		6,301.2
TOTAL		$16,727.9

A list of several additional key assumptions for the study are
summarized in Exhibit 8.11.

   Model Selection and/or Development.--The Distribution
Planning Model (DPM),[1] a static simulator, was selected as the
solution technique to assist in developing the strategic plan
for the described logistics situation. The LREPS--Operations
Planning Model,[2] a dynamic simulator, was selected to assist in
evaluating various tactical operating plans to achieve the
strategic objectives. The major purpose of the remainder of
this paper is a discussion of how these two models were utilized
to assist in strategical and operations logistics planning for
the described problem situation.

---

[1] O. K. Helferich.

[2] O. K. Helferich

1. Existing configuration (number and location) of manufactur-
    ing plants and in-transit warehouses assumed fixed over the
    study planning horizon of 1976 through 1980.

2. Geographical distribution of customers and relative degree
    of market penetration assumed fixed over the study planning
    horizon. To accommodate anticipated changes in sales
    through 1980, order size distribution increased when net
    sales increased, when net sales decreased changes were
    made in aggregate quantity of order.

3. Production schedule at manufacturing plants based upon
    near equalized output across the year. No backorders or
    split orders permitted for customer distribution on
    validation runs, both permitted for all other simulations.

4. Inventory initialized on a base stock of 25% of forecasted
    annual demand per warehouse location. Subsequent replenish-
    ment based on a 90-day incentive order forecast and order
    frequency.

5. Field warehouses and customer assignments for validation
    replicated actual assignments, while for alternatives
    evaluated by simulations assignment was based upon least
    total logistical system cost for various specified customer
    service level(s). Total cost included production, trans-
    portation, inventory, and warehousing.

6. For purpose of simulated order processing and customer
    service measurement a standard time of 24 hours was
    adopted to replicate order receipt, processing, trans-
    mittal to warehouse location, warehouse order selection,
    loading and tender to transport mode. Outbound transit
    times based upon standard TL and CL time/distance per-
    formance with LTL transit times based upon a survey of
    actual experience.

7. Product replication based upon a stratified sample of 50
    products.

8. For all future projections forecasted sales provided by
    the company all cost computations based upon 1976 standard
    dollars.

Figure 8.11.   Examples of Management Assumptions and Guidelines
               for the Strategic and Operations Logistics Study.

Phase II: Analysis and Recommendation

The Phase II tasks covered are data collection, analysis and preparation, calibration and validation, selection of best logistics configuration, selection of best operating plan, and recommendations.

Data Collection, Analysis, and Preparation.--The task of data collection, analysis, and preparation is always critical for a logistical study. This was especially true for the comprehensive study that provided the basis for the case situation reported in this paper. The general categories of data included: (1) sales, (2) customer, (3) product, (4) manufacturing and warehouse system, (5) transportation network, (6) inventory management system, (7) order communications system, (8) logistical costs and service levels, and (9) all other management assumptions and parameters for the study.

The logistical audit and situation analysis defined the problem in the detail necessary to specify the data requirements. The audit also permitted the project team to develop a compromise as needed concerning the ideal data requirements, compared to the practical limits of data availability. Although some difficulty was encountered in obtaining existing service level facts-- such as transit times and customer pickup statistics--the company was able to provide the required data.

Calibration and Validation.--Several preliminary runs of the DPM--Strategic and LREPS--Operations Planning Models were made for the purposes of validation to provide credibility with the user and to demonstrate the following four aspects of the two simulators:

1. Overall validity of simulated results for a previous period compared to actual logistics system costs and service for the same period.

2. Capability of the simulators to generate accurate
   sales volume, based on the sample of products
   (simulated) in the study.
3. Time phasing capabilities of the LREPS--Operations
   Planning Model to handle production cycles coupled
   with incentive order allocation and in-season sales
   requirements.
4. Capability of the simulators to replicate customer
   pickup potential and practice.

For the purpose of basic model validation in the consecutive twelve month period, 1976 was selected for comparison of
simulated results to actual. The simulated to actual sales were
well within the ± 5% expected error due to data input. In fact,
the simulation results were 98.5% of expected sales. The 1.5%
error was due to incomplete data on the company's invoice
records. A comparison of the total distribution costs, including
inventory, showed that the simulated system was 1.1% lower than
the actual figures experienced for the year. The variances in
individual cost accounts from the actual cost were also either
negligible or explainable.

A final aspect of basic validation was concerned with
the capability of replicating customer pickup potential and
actual volume. The quantification of customer pickup potential
is highly correlated to sales within a 2-day total order cycle
time. In total, the simulator replicated customer pickups at
28%, compared to 29% as determined from an invoice analysis.

Utilization of DPM: Selection of Best Logistic System
Configuration.--The primary system variables evaluated in the
redesign of the logistics system were: the number of DCs, DC
locations, product stocking policies, and utilization of the
warehouses. A list of 50 potential warehouse sites was
generated by the project team for evaluation. The criteria for
selecting these potential warehouse locations included, but was

not limited to: location of customer demand; present warehouse locations; geographical variables of distribution costs (e.g., transit time, distance, order lead times, etc.).

The technique of utilizing DPM to determine the best system of warehouses consisted of the following steps:

1. Selecting from 50 potential warehouse locations the minimal total cost warehouse configuration for the incentive order program and the in-season demand periods for 1976, 1978, and 1980.

2. Selecting the warehouses that will achieve minimum cost with customer service approximating the current level.

3. Evaluating full product line stocking policies versus partial line stocking.

4. Developing the system of warehouses with consideration for additional service constraints of transit time and customer pickups.

5. Selecting a best set of regional warehouses.

This procedure provided the quantitative information necessary to evaluate the effect of the variability of demand, both through the period of forecast years and by marketing periods. The testing of alternate product stocking policies compared with system service constraints of order delivery time and customer order pickups also assisted in determining the best set of warehouses for the distribution system.

The techniques of selecting minimum cost warehouse locations consisted of eliminating warehouse sites with the greatest total distribution costs relative to the effect on system costs, and assigning customers to other warehouse loca-.tions. DPM was utilized to evaluate the entire array of 50 warehouse locations in terms of cost and service.

The effectiveness of alternating both the number and location of warehouses for the incentive and in-season periods was evaluated by simulating individually the demand for incentive

and in-season. Because of the dynamic changes in produce demand
and price expected through 1980, it was felt necessary to evaluate
for three different years, 1976, 1978, and 1980. The specifications for the simulation runs were as follows:

1. On a marginal cost basis, the most costly warehouses were eliminated for each demand period,
   starting with all 50 potential warehouse sites,
   until only one location was left.

2. Six demand periods were evaluated--the two yearly
   marketing periods--incentive order program and in-
   season sales--for the years 1976, 1978 and 1980.

3. Direct plant to customer shipments were not
   included, since it was determined that these
   shipments would not have an impact on the
   warehouse configuration.

Product stocking policy was examined by segregating
demand into product groups. Computer simulation runs were made
to evaluate the sensitivity to partial product line stocking on
an in-season-only and full-year basis. The results of these runs
were quite similar to full product line warehouses for comparable
marketing periods. The project team therefore decided that
further partial line stocking policies need not be investigated.

The results of all deletion runs indicated that the total
cost curve is extremely flat over a wide range of warehouse
locations. A sample of the results is presented in Figure 8.12
for the 1976 in-season and 1976 incentive order program.

Based on a review of all of the results, the project team
determined that a network of 19 field warehouses, plus the 6
in-transit locations, best satisfied the multiple needs of a
distribution system for a four-year forecast time period. The
warehouse locations selected met the objectives of providing the
highest practical level of customer service--85% of the sales within
2 days--at the lowest total cost of logistical operations, while
allowing for system flexibility to accommodate business contingencies

FOR 1976 IN-SEASON DEMAND

FOR 1976 INCENTIVE ORDER PROGRAM

DC Location[1] Deleted	Total[2] Cost Ratio	100 Miles	300 Miles	500 Miles	Number of DCs Remaining	DC Location[1] Deleted	Total[2] Cost Ratio	100 Miles	300 Miles	500 Miles
All DCs in Delete	1.00	60.9	96.7	99.8	50	All DCs in Delete	1.00	56.4	95.0	99.3
Mobile	0.98	60.8	96.7	99.8	45	New Orleans	0.98	56.4	95.0	99.2
Chattanooga	0.96	60.8	96.6	99.7	40	Chattanooga	0.95	56.2	95.0	99.2
Cincinnati	0.93	58.4	96.3	99.7	35	South Bend	0.92	53.9	94.0	99.2
Des Moines	0.90	51.9	93.6	99.7	30	Phoenix	0.89	44.7	91.6	98.5
Lubbock	0.87	44.0	88.6	97.3	25	Indianapolis	0.86	38.2	88.9	97.8
Indianapolis	0.84	41.0	86.9	95.9	20	San Francisco	0.83	31.1	84.7	96.0
Orlando	0.81	33.5	78.4	92.1	15	Orlando	0.79	25.2	76.5	95.1
Baton Rouge	0.79	26.0	69.8	89.8	10	Charlotte	0.75	6.1	67.8	86.6
Minneapolis	0.77	18.0	62.4	85.1	8	Fresno	0.74	13.7	61.9	80.1
Houston	0.78	9.3	33.1	71.0	6	Omaha	0.73	7.7	39.6	71.4
Los Angeles	0.78	5.2	23.4	63.7	4	Birmingham	0.72	6.5	34.2	68.5
Chicago	0.79	1.8	14.6	52.1	2	Chicago	0.73	3.4	24.2	56.3
Montgomery	0.81	1.0	13.8	47.0	1	Louisville	0.74	2.1	17.1	46.0

[1]The deletion or "sort down" run was performed to define the lowest cost warehouse configuration for each number of locations from 50 warehouses to 1 warehouse. Partial results are presented to illustrate the rate of change of costs and service for the change in number and configuration of warehouses.

[2]The cost components considered relevant for these computer runs included handling, transportation, and inventory. The component costs and total costs are printed as part of the standard output report formats of DPM.

Figure 8.12. Partial Results of Field Warehouse Deletion Run Utilizing DPM.

and logistical strategies. The recommended configuration of warehouses required the following changes to the current 24 field warehouse system:
>1. Closing of 8 existing warehouse locations.
>2. Addition of 3 new warehouse locations.

Utilization of LREPS: Selection of Best Logistics Systems Operation

The remaining objective consisted of determining a transition and implementation plan from the current to the proposed warehouse configuration. The operations planning was performed
utilizing LREPS. The following three operations plans were
selected for evaluation:

>Plan 1: Base set of 12 field warehouse locations
>throughout the year.

>Plan 2: The base set of 12 field warehouse locations
>of Plan 1 plus an additional set of 7 locations
>throughout the year.

>Plan 3: The base set of 12 field warehouse locations
>of Plan 1 throughout the year and the utiliza-
>tion of 7 additional locations of Plan 2 for the
>in-season demand period only.

The criteria for comparison of the three plans included,
but was not limited to: (1) the effect on distribution costs,
(2) effect of the system on service-delivery time, (3) ability of
the system to allow customer order pickups, (4) ease with which the
system can be implemented, (5) ease of maintaining the on-going
system, and (6) ability of the system to meet demand from changing
markets and new product introductions.

The simulated results for the LREPS--Operations Planning
Simulator runs for each plan, as projected for 1976 input, are
presented in Figure 8.13. The results for the three plans for the
planning horizon 1976 through 1980 indicated that the percentage

	Retain Existing	Plan 1	Plan 2	Plan 3
Sales $ (000)	483,710.4	483,710.4	483,710.4	483,710.4
Weight Sold Lb. (000)	312,547.4	312,547.4	312,547.4	312,547.4
Freight to Customer	3,801.3	4,826.4	4,413.4	4,715.2
Freight to Warehouses $ (000)	3,867.8	1,787.2	2,234.0	2,127.8
Handling Cost $ (000)	739.0	263.6	365.0	360.0
Order Cost $ (000)	555.6	555.6	555.6	555.6
Storage Cost $ (000)	1,463.0	1,227.0	1,127.6	1,259.6
Inventory Cost $ (000)	6,301.2	5,749.0	6,262.4	6,147.3
Total Cost $ (000)	16,727.9	14,408.8	15,958.0	15,165.5
% of Sales Orders Within:				
1 Day Order Cycle	30.62	15.62	21.57	16.43
2 Days Order Cycle	56.50	32.86	40.45	34.61
3 Days Order Cycle	71.14	42.86	51.78	44.94
4 Days Order Cycle	80.08	48.46	60.90	55.29
5 Days Order Cycle	84.73	56.46	70.15	64.74

Figure 8.13. Partial Results Summary of LREPS Operational Planning Simulator Runs for Year 1976.

difference in total distribution costs between the three plans would
remain relatively constant over the planning horizon.

The level of service, as measured by the proportion of
orders filled within the 5-day order cycle, was appreciably better
for Plan 2. This is accentuated when the service achieved for the
in-season demand is separated from the yearly service comparisons.
The in-season service results were as follows:

In-Season Service Time

Percent Sales Orders Within	Present System	Plan 1	Plan 2	Plan 3
1 day	43.6	10.9	36.9	33.0
2 days	61.9	26.1	56.7	50.2
3 days	71.9	27.6	73.0	63.4
4 days	78.4	47.2	82.1	74.6
5 days	83.6	59.5	86.8	78.9

This measure of order cycle time during the in-season period is
critical in achieving customer sales.

Plan 1, utilizing 12 field warehouses, has the highest
risk of customer service, the lowest risk of inappropriate placement of inventory, and the lowest potential for maintaining or
generating customer pickups. Plan 3, which incorporates a base
set of 12 field warehouses and an additional set of 7 during
in-season, has the potential to reduce inventory stock during
the incentive order priod, but in-season service is somewhat less
than Plan 2. The best in-season service and potential for customer
pickups would be provided by Plan 2, with 19 field warehouses
utilized throughout the year. An added benefit of Plan 2 is that
it provides greater geographical placement of warehouses to provide
increased service for the expected new products. These products
will account for significant volume and are expected to have broader
market coverage and more uniform demand throughout the year than
the current product line. A summary of the results, which served
as the basis for recommending Plan 2, was as follows:

System Comparison Between Plan 1, 2, and 3
and the Existing Logistics System
(000)

	Existing	Plan 1	Plan 2	Plan 3
1. Annual System Savings Potential	Not Applicable	$2,319	$770	$1,562
2. In-Season Service	Highest	Lowest	High	Moderate
3. Ability for Customer Order Pickups	High	Lowest	Highest	Moderate
4. Ability to Implement	Not Applicable	Moderate	High	Lowest
5. Ease of System Maintenance	Moderate	Highest	High	Lowest
6. System Ability to meet Changing Markets Requirements	Moderate	Lowest	Highest	High

A summary of the recommendations from the study is presented next.

Selection and Presentation of Recommendations.--The results
of the analysis of this logistical situation suggested that the
system of field warehouses be changed from the present 24 locations
to 19. The recommendation of Plan 2 calls for the elimination of
8 present public warehouses and addition of 3 new public warehouses. The 4 manufacturing plants and 6 in-transit locations
would continue to be utilized for customer delivery.   The
system of 19 field warehouses would function on a year-round basis.
Product stocking policy at all field warehouses should include all
products for which there is adequate demand. Customer order pickups,
in that they constitute a substantial portion of the present
business and are desired by many customers, appear to be cost
justified and could best be continued under the implementation of

Plan 2. This plan also achieves an annual cost savings of 0.77 million dollars.

Phase III: Implementation

The users implemented the recommendations over a period of one year and achieved the cost savings expected.

Conclusion

The utilization of two computer models is not necessary to assist in all or possibly even a majority of strategic and operations logistical planning situations.

However, there are many situations where the general approach described could be beneficial to total logistics planning. It is important to recognize that the approach could work conceptually as well or better for selected logistics situations with a mixed integer program or other optimization models utilized as the strategic planning model. In fact, the authors are currently involved in a project that will utilize a mixed integer program and LREPS to assist in developing the strategic and operations plans for an organization. Regardless of the specific models, it will become more common in the future to utilize both strategic and operations planning models as presented in the above case study.

Suggestions and Considerations

Today, increasing attention is being paid to effective logistics planning, using the best techniques and capabilities available. The following are some of the factors that indicate the growing acceptance of logistics system modeling:

- Managers are experiencing increasing pressure on decision making from:
  - dynamic business environment, including broader world market development

- stronger competition
- rapid technological change
- logistics systems increasing complexity
- Corporations are becoming better prepared to use modeling:
  - more and better trained managers and analysts
  - growing understanding of logistics
- Modeling offers stronger package:
  - total system modeling capabilities now available
  - model builders continue to evolve new, better techniques

In addition to the case studies presented in this chapter, there are many other successful applications that have demonstrated the cost/benefits of logistics system models. The successful utilization of logistics models is, however, not achieved without technical and/or management concerns.

Common Areas of Concern

A partial list of some of the more common areas of concern by project phase is presented in Figure 8.14.[1] Adherence to these concerns does not guarantee a successful project but does "stack the odds for success."

Selection of Modeling Technique

There are many factors that must be considered in selecting the most appropriate model for a particular logistics systems study. The choice depends on a balancing of such factors as:

- flexibility required as defined in Phase I to explicitly model the full range of logistics system complexity and size
- capability, if required, to explicitly model production and/or warehouse capacity limits

---

[1] O. K. Helferich and R. W. Kallock, "A Way to Achieve Effective Distribution Planning," Handling and Shipping, September 1976.

	DO	DON'T
PHASE I: Project Organization	1. Establish project importance through top management endorsement.	1. Permit a project with narrow functional support to be misrepresented as a distribution strategy study.
	2. Organize multi-department project team including: marketing, order entry, traffic, warehousing and management information.	2. Raise excessive expectations about the computer's ability to answer all questions and substitute for management experience.
	3. Select project team leader based on motivation and understanding of the Company's business	3. Assign management misfits to the project team.
	4. Consider using experienced distribution planning consultants to objectively supplement in-house staff capabilities and time.	4. Overexpose non-technical persons to compute technology and terminology too soon.
	5. Develop detailed project plan including tasks, timing and assignments.	5. Ignore short-term improvements through spin-off of sub-project teams attacking tactical concerns.
	6. Conduct formal management briefing high-lighting objectives, approach, timing and concerns.	6. Commit to timing and personnel requirements for Phase II without completing Phase I.

Figure 8.14. Stacking the Odds for Success in Computer Modeling Your Distribution Systems: Partial List of "Do's" and "Don'ts".

PHASE II Analysis & Recommendation	DO	DON'T
	1. Organize data collection effort carefully to facilitate revisions and updating.	1. Over simplify the problem and alternatives to make analysis easier. You risk losing management confidence.
	2. Monitor data collection regularly to resolve questions and insure accurate progress.	2. Attempt initially to simultaneously analyze multiple dissimilar divisions.
	3. Test validity of each set of data in reference runs made to compare alternatives.	3. Permit undisciplined data collection efforts to result in undocumented findings and disorganized files.
	4. Develop results presentation format to facilitate management understanding.	4. Allow excessive time to pass between reviews on data collection progress.
	5. Conduct working review meetings during analysis of alternative systems to insure adequate input of managerial experience.	5. Present computer output to non-team members without a clear interpretation of each item.
	6. Concisely present major findings, conclusions and recommendations to top management.	6. Give in to pressure and prematurely establish unrealistic timing and result targets.
	7. Prepare detailed implementation program including tasks, sub-tasks, personnel and timing.	7. Overlook distribution operations improvement opportunities identified during analysis.

Figure 8.14. Continued.

DO	DON'T
PHASE III Implementation	
1. Establish communication medium to facilitate progress review and problem identification	1. Participate in the initial planning process unless you are committed to implementating the recommendations.
2. Review assignment status of project team members and reassign where appropriate.	2. Permit passage of time and concentration on short term problems to undermine sound distribution strategy program implementation.
3. Establish schedule and responsibility for updating strategic plan every 2 years or sooner as appropriate.	

Figure 8.14. Continued.

- flexibility to emphasize any one or all of the various
  logistics functions such as transportation, inventory,
  warehousing, production, procurement, etc.
- provision to determine the optimum (minimum cost for
  a specified customer service level) logistics system
  design
- provision to measure the impact on customer service
  for the desired range of logistics alternatives
- capability to perform secondary computer runs to
  evaluate different sets of input assumptions and
  "What If" questions
- data collection and preparation requirements
- project team and management background experience
- estimate of elapsed time, costs, people, effort, and
  computer requirements from start to completion of model
  utilization

Future Utilization of Models

As indicated earlier, there is increasing interest and
utilization of models for logistics systems analysis for both
strategic and operations planning. This final section of the
Chapter, presents several comments regarding future utilization
of computer models.

First, utilization of analytical models has become more
practical than in the past to assist in defining improved logistics
systems. Recent developments in mixed integer linear programming
that are solved by Bender's decomposition now enable optimization of
much larger and more complex logistics systems. The capabilities
and output formats are presented in Appendix A.[1]

---

[1]A. M. Geoffrion, "A Guide to Computer-Assisted Methods
for Distribution Systems Planning," Sloan Management Review,
Winter, 1975, pp. 17-45; and A. M. Geoffrion, "Working Paper No.
219: Distribution Systems Configuration Planning: Case Study in
the Application of a New Computer-Based Method," Western Management Science Institute, Graduate School of Management,
University of California, Los Angeles, CA.

Second, the usefulness of dynamic simulation models to evaluate logistics operations cost/service tradeoffs has been demonstrated. Utilization of dynamic models will increase as more companies begin to evaluate short term operating policy tradeoffs such as inventory versus transportation. The capabilities and output of one such model, LREPS, are presented in Appendix A.

Third, static simulator models will continue to be utilized for strategic logistics design analysis because of the flexibility offered to the user.

Fourth, the advantages of both optimization and simulation will be achieved on future projects in one of several methods-- such as incorporating optimization techniques within computerized simulation models,[1] and/or by utilizing an optimization and simulation model in sequence. The use of a mixed integer linear program in conjunction with a dynamic simulation model has been selected for several logistics systems studies including the Department of Defense Materiel Distribution System. The use of a static simulator to define the best strategic logistics plan followed in sequence by the dynamic model to determine the best logistics operating plan, as illustrated in the "seasonal chemicals product" case study will also find more application in the future.

Fifth, utilization of logistics models by non-manufacturers will increase. As an example, a major southeastern utility is currently utilizing a dynamic simulation model to evaluate materiel centralization. The use of models in general will increase since the logistics manager is now just beginning to have the proper support staff, data base, and scope of responsibility to effectively utilize models.

---

[1]William Farrell, Chester H. McCall, Jr., and Edward C. Russell, "Optimization Techniques for Computerized Simulation Models," Technical Report 1200-4-75 (Los Angeles: CACI, Inc., June, 1975).

APPENDICES

352

APPENDIX A

DISTRIBUTION SYSTEM DESIGN TECHNIQUES[1]

---

[1]A presentation by Omar Keith Helferich to the Fourteenth Annual Conference of the National Council of Physical Distribution Management, October 13-15, 1976.

Three State of the Art

Model Alternatives

Model	Orientation	Static vs Dynamic	Analytic vs Simulator
MILP Mixed Integer Linear Programming	Strategic	Static	Analytic
DPM Distribution Planning Model	Strategic	Static	Simulator
LREPS Operations Planning Model	Operational	Dynamic	Simulator

MIXED INTEGER LINEAR PROGRAMMING[1]

MILP Target Issues

Cost optimization

Number, location, and annual volume of plants and distribution points

Assignment of plants to distribution points, and distribution points to customers

Allocation of plant output to distribution points/customers

Annual transportation flows

Allocation of plant and distribution point output for capacity constrained situations

MILP Normal Operating Range

20-50 product groups

2 echelons

50-200 customers and/or markets

20-50 production points and/or vendors

20-100 distribution points

Weighted average transportation rates to meet requirements of mode, interval and class

Average inventory input by distribution point

All distribution variable costs input as cost per hundred weight

All fixed costs can be input by distribution point

Customer service input through assignment of customer groups to distribution points

Capacity constraints input by distribution and/or production point

---

[1] The information presented on MILP is based on the work of A. M. Geoffrion and G. W. Graves.

MILP OUTPUT REPORT FORMAT

1. OPTIMAL SYSTEM SUMMARY

DISTRIBUTION CENTER	OPTIMAL THROUGHOUT	— FIXED COST	VARIABLE COST	INBOUND TRANSPORTATION COST	OUTBOUND TRANSPORTATION COST
1	X	X	X	X	X
.	.	.	.	.	.
.	.	.	.	.	.
.	.	.	.	.	.
. K	X	X	X	X	X
Total	X	X	X	X	X

2. DETAILED SOLUTION BY PRODUCT

(A) OPTIMAL PRODUCT 1 TRANSPORTATION FLOWS

FROM PLANT NUMBER	THROUGH DC NUMBER	TO CUSTOMER NUMBER	QUANTITY SHIPPED	TRANSPORTATION RATE	TRANSPORTATION COST
1	1	1	X	X	X
.	.	.	.	.	.
.	.	.	.	.	.
.	.	.	.	.	.
. P	K	L	X	X	X

MILP OUTPUT REPORT FORMAT

2. DETAILED SOLUTION BY PRODUCT

(A) PRODUCT 1 INBOUND SUMMARY

PRODUCING PLANT	TO DC NUMBER	QUANTITY SHIPPED	INBOUND TRANSPORTATION RATE	TRANSPORTATION COST
1	1	X	X	X
.	.	.	.	.
.	.	.	.	.
P	K	X	X	X
Total		X	X	X

(C) PRODUCT 1 DISTRIBUTION CENTER SUMMARY

DISTRIBUTION CENTER	PRODUCT 1 THROUGHPUT	VARIABLE COST	INBOUND TRANSPORTATION COST	OUTBOUND TRANSPORTATION COST
1	X	X	X	X
.	.	.	.	.
.	.	.	.	.
K	X	X	X	X
Total	X	X	X	X

MILP OUTPUT REPORT FORMAT

3. CUSTOMER OUTBOUND COST SUMMARY

CUSTOMER NUMBER	TOTAL OUTBOUND TRANSPORTATION COST
1	X
.	.
.	.
.	.
L	X
Total	X

4. OPTIMAL CUSTOMER ASSIGNMENT TO DISTRIBUTION CENTERS

	Customer			
BUNDLE	1	2	. . . . .	L
1	X	X		X
.	.			
.	.			
.	.			
B	X	X	------DC Number------	X

MILP SOLUTION FLOW

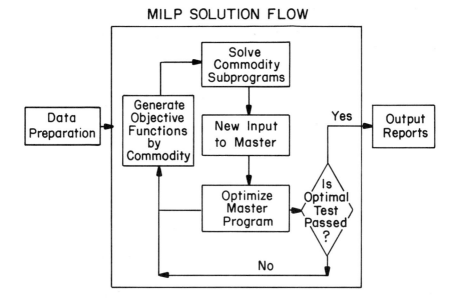

DISTRIBUTION PLANNING MODEL

DPM Target Issues

Impact of distribution policies on customer service and distribution cost

Number, location and annual volume of plants and warehouses

Assignment of plants to distribution points, and distribution points to customers

Annual transportation flows

Impact of stocking policies and stocking locations by product group and customer type

DPM Normal Operating Range

50-100 product groups

3-99 echelons

200-10,000 vendors, production points and/or distribution points

Specific point-to-point rates and/or equations by mode, class, or weight interval

Working stock or safety stock factors input by product group and distribution point

Inventory costs by product group and distribution point

All distribution variable costs input as cost per hundred weight, unit or cube

All fixed cost can be input by distribution point

Customer service measured as percent and amount shipped within 8 mileage service intervals

Five methods for assigning customers or markets to vendors, production points, or distribution points:

- Least cost
- Best service
- Least cost at a desired service level
- Fixed assignment
- Combination of all of the above

DPM OUTPUT REPORT FORMAT

1. CUSTOMER SALES

DISTRIBUTION CENTER	LEVEL	DOLLARS	WEIGHT	UNITS
1	X	X	X	X
.	.	.	.	.
.	.	.	.	.
.K	.X	.X	.X	.X
Total	-	X̲	X̲	X̲

2. DISTRIBUTION CENTER TRANSFERS

DISTRIBUTION CENTER	LEVEL	DOLLARS	WEIGHT	UNITS
1	X	X	X	X
.	.	.	.	.
.	.	.	.	.
.K	X	.X	.X	.X
Total	-	X̲	X̲	X̲

DPM OUTPUT REPORT FORMAT

3. COST REPORT A

DISTRIBUTION CENTER	LEVEL	OUTBOUND FREIGHT	TRANSFER INBOUND	WAREHOUSING COSTS	PRODUCTION COSTS
1	X	X	X	X	X
.	.	.	.	.	.
.	.	.	.	.	.
.	.	.	.	.	.
.	.	.	.	.	.
K	X	X	X	X	X
Total	-	X	X	X	X

363

DPM OUTPUT REPORT FORMAT

4. COST REPORT B

DISTRIBUTION CENTER	LEVEL	INVENTORY COSTS	COST OF DELETION	TOTAL LESS INVENTORY	TOTAL
1	X	X	X	X	X
.	.	.	.	.	.
.	.	.	.	.	.
K	X	X	X	X	X
Total	-	X	X	X	X

5. SERVICE REPORT (DOLLARS AND WEIGHT)

DISTRIBUTION CENTER	LEVEL	50 MILES	100 MILES	150 MILES · · · · · · ·	Y MILES
1	X	X	X	X	X
.	.	.	.	.	.
.	.	.	.	.	.
K	X	X	X	X	X
Total	-	X	X	X	X

DPM OUTPUT REPORT FORMAT

6. DISTRIBUTION CENTER PRODUCT REPORT

DISTRIBUTION CENTER	LEVEL	PRODUCT	SOLD TO CUSTOMER	SOURCE	INBOUND RATE	VARIABLE COST	PRODUCTION COST	TOTAL COST	INVENTORY
1	X	01	X	X	X	X	X	X	X
.	.	.	.	.	.	.	.	.	.
.	.	.	.	.	.	.	.	.	.
.	.	.	.	.	.	.	.	.	.
.	.	.	.	.	.	.	.	.	.
K	X	01	X	X	X	X	X	X	X

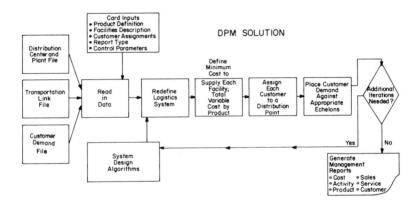

LREPS OPERATIONS PLANNING MODEL

LREPS Target Issues

Plant/warehouse size by sales dollars, weight, units and cube in terms of average and throughput level variation over time.

Impact of changes in inventory management parameters:

- . Inventory reorder policy
- . Inventory cycle, transit and safety stock
- . Stocking policy
- . Inventory turns

Impact of changes in transportation management parameters:

- . Mode utilization
- . Shipping order and reorder policy
- . Schedule distribution and pooling

Impact of changes in storage policies:

- . Break bulk or pool centers
- . Storage warehouses
- . Product group movement versus inventory
- . Partial line versus full line stocking

Impact of customer service policies:

- . Order cycle time average and consistency
- . Stockouts and back orders

Impact of changes in material sourcing policies:

- . Production cycles/schedules
- . Vendor lead times
- . Procurement sources

Impact on costs and service of changes in:

- . Customer service
- . Order size
- . Seasonal patterns

LREPS Target Issues (Cont'd)

Impact on service, costs and profit of changes in marketing strategy.

LREPS Normal Operating Range

50-500 product groups

3-99 echelons

20-10,000 customers and markets

50-300 vendors, production points, and distribution points

Specific point-to-point rates and/or equations by mode, class and weight interval

Option evaluations by distribution component (see target issues)

Sales and throughput quantified in 6 different ways:

. dollars   . units

. weight   . lines

. cube   . orders

All variable distribution costs input as a function of:

. dollars   . units

. weight   . lines

. cube   . orders

All fixed costs input by distribution point

Mean and standard deviation of customer service quantified in terms of order cycle time, and lead time

Order cycle time quantified as frequency distribution by time intervals

Stockouts and backorders measured

Customer assignment to production and distribution point by preselection or least cost algorithm

LREPS OUTPUT REPORT FORMAT

1. CUSTOMER SALES

DISTRIBUTION CENTER	DOLLARS	WEIGHT	CUBE	UNITS	LINES	ORDERS
1	X	X	X	X	X	X
.	.	.	.	.	.	.
.	.	.	.	.	.	.
.	.	.	.	.	.	.
K	X	X	X	X	X	X
Total	X	X	X	X	X	X

2. COST REPORT

DISTRIBUTION CENTER	OUTBOUND TO CUSTOMERS	OUTBOUND TO DCs	INBOUND	HANDLING	ORDER PROCESSING	FIXED	INVENTORY	TOTAL
1	X	X	X	X	X	X	X	X
.	.	.	.	.	.	.	.	.
.	.	.	.	.	.	.	.	.
.	.	.	.	.	.	.	.	.
K	X	X	X	X	X	X	X	X
Total	X	X	X	X	X	X	X	X

LREPS OUTPUT REPORT FORMAT

3. ORDER CYCLE TIME

DISTRIBUTION CENTER	TRANSIT TIME AVERAGE	STD. DEV.	NET LEAD TIME AVERAGE	STD. DEV.	BACKORDER TIME AVERAGE	STD. DEV.	TOTAL LEAD TIME AVERAGE	STD. DEV.
1	X	X	X	X	X	X	X	X
.	.	.	.	.	.	.	.	.
.	.	.	.	.	.	.	.	.
.	.	.	.	.	.	.	.	.
K	X	X	X	X	X	X	X	X

4. NORMAL ORDER CYCLE TIME DISTRIBUTION

Percent Sales Dollars/Pounds within:

DISTRIBUTION CENTER	10 DAYS	20 DAYS	30 DAYS	40 DAYS	50 DAYS
1	X	X	X	X	X
.	.	.	.	.	.
.	.	.	.	.	.
K	X	X	X	X	X

LREPS OUTPUT REPORT FORMAT

5. INVENTORY CONDITION REPORT

DISTRIBUTION CENTER	AVERAGE INVENTORY(1)	TURNS	NUMBER OF REORDERS	BEGINNING INVENTORY(2)	ENDING INVENTORY(2)	CURRENTLY ON ORDER(2)
1	X	X	X	X	X	X
.	.	.	.	.	.	.
.	.	.	.	.	.	.
.	.	.	.	.	.	.
.	.	.	.	.	.	.
K	X	X	X	X	X	X
Total	X	X	X	X	X	X

NOTES: (1) At cost of goods in dollars

(2) In units

LREPS OUTPUT REPORT FORMAT

6. SERVICE REPORT

DISTRIBUTION CENTER	NUMBER OF STOCKOUTS	UNITS STOCKED OUT NUMBER	PERCENT	STOCKOUT TIME AVERAGE	STD. DEV.	ORDERS BACKORDERED NUMBER	PERCENT	DOLLARS LOST DUE TO STOCKOUT
1	X	X	X	X	X	X	X	X
.	.	.	.	.	.	.	.	.
.	.	.	.	.	.	.	.	.
.	.	.	.	.	.	.	.	.
K	X	X	X	X	X	X	X	X
Total	X	X	X	X	X	X	X	X

7. WEIGHT SHIPPED BY FREIGHT CONDITION

Pounds shipped by freight condition

DISTRIBUTION CENTER	01	02	03	04	05	11	12	18
1	X	X	X	X	X	X	X	X
.	.	.	.	.	.	.	.	.
.	.	.	.	.	.	.	.	.
.	.	.	.	.	.	.	.	.
K	X	X	X	X	X	X	X	X

LREPS OUTPUT REPORT FORMAT

8. SHIPMENTS TO OTHER DISTRIBUTION CENTERS

DISTRIBUTION CENTER	DOLLARS	WEIGHT	CUBE	UNITS	LINES	ORDERS
1	X	X	X	X	X	X
.	.	.	.	.	.	.
.	.	.	.	.	.	.
.	.	.	.	.	.	.
K	X	X	X	X	X	X
Total	X	X	X	X	X	X

9. RECEIPTS FROM OTHER DISTRIBUTION CENTERS

DISTRIBUTION CENTER	DOLLARS	WEIGHT	CUBE	UNITS	LINES	ORDERS
1	X	X	X	X	X	X
.	.	.	.	.	.	.
.	.	.	.	.	.	.
.	.	.	.	.	.	.
K	X	X	X	X	X	X
Total	X	X	X	X	X	X

LREPS OUTPUT REPORT FORMAT

10. PRODUCT INVENTORY REPORT

DISTRIBUTION CENTER	PRODUCT	SHIPPED TO CUSTOMER	ENDING INVENTORY	AVERAGE INVENTORY	CURRENTLY ON ORDER	FORECAST
1	A	X	X	X	X	X
1	B	X	X	X	X	X
1	C	X	X	X	X	X
1	D	X	X	X	X	X
1	E	X	X	X	X	X
1	F	X	X	X	X	X
1	G	X	X	X	X	X
1	H	X	X	X	X	X
2	A	X	X	X	X	X
2	B	X	X	X	X	X
2	C	X	X	X	X	X
2	D	X	X	X	X	X
2	E	X	X	X	X	X
2	F	X	X	X	X	X
2	G	X	X	X	X	X
2	H	X	X	X	X	X

LREPS OUTPUT REPORT FORMAT

11. PRODUCT SERVICE REPORT

DISTRIBUTION CENTER	PRODUCT	BACKORDER QUANTITY		UNITS STOCKED OUT		NUMBER OF REORDERS	NUMBER OF STOCKOUTS
		CURRENT	AVERAGE	NUMBER	PERCENT		
1	A	X	X	X	X	X	X
1	B	X	X	X	X	X	X
1	C	X	X	X	X	X	X
1	D	X	X	X	X	X	X
1	E	X	X	X	X	X	X
1	F	X	X	X	X	X	X
1	G	X	X	X	X	X	X
1	H	X	X	X	X	X	X
2	A	X	X	X	X	X	X
2	B	X	X	X	X	X	X
2	C	X	X	X	X	X	X
2	D	X	X	X	X	X	X
2	E	X	X	X	X	X	X
2	F	X	X	X	X	X	X
2	G	X	X	X	X	X	X
2	H	X	X	X	X	X	X

375

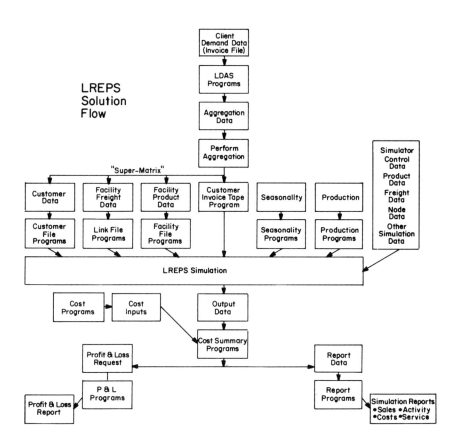

LREPS
Solution
Flow